DEDICATION

I am dedicating this book to my wonderfully supportive saint of a husband, Martin.
Martin, you inspire me to be a better version of myself.
I pinch myself for each additional day I am privileged to share with you.

ACKNOWLEDGMENTS

Stefanie Rosenberg, you are not only my sister; you are my sounding board and the first person I trusted to ever read my words. Thank you for your encouragement, edits, and unconditional love.

Jane Gangi, thank you for reading this book in very rough form. You inspired me to publish my story. I appreciate your friendship, guidance, intelligence, and your unyielding support.

Linda Haines, I dub you the Grammar Queen. My words read so much better because of you.

Caryn Golden, thank you for your friendship, love, and for the example you provide all women every day of your life.

Mom and Dad, you are wonderful parents. My pursuit of parenthood was ignited by such great models.

The entire staff at CFA, thank you all for believing in our dream. You are the gold standard in both medicine and bedside manner.

IN THE BEGINNING

PERHAPS EVERY WOMAN'S beginning is the same. The question, "So, when are you going to have a baby?" is repeatedly asked the moment you and your husband say, "I do."

Why does everyone, and by everyone I mean family members, close friends, and inappropriate strangers, perceive they have the right to ask you that particular question once a wedding band finds a home on your finger?

To say I was not focused on a timeline as to when I would start popping out babies on the day of my nuptials is an understatement. In all honesty, I had long questioned whether or not I could handle the responsibility of parenting. My reasons for my uncertainty were varied and maybe a little illogical, but they seemed perfectly legitimate to me.

Logical or not, my first reason I had for questioning whether motherhood was in my future evolved from my relationship with my friends and family. Before my friends had babies, we would chat uninterrupted for a solid 20 minutes or more. My girlfriends were always therapy for me and vice versa. As soon as they transformed from my married friends to mothers, those conversations went out the window. If something stressful happened and I needed to vent, I no longer could do so with my friends. Motherhood duties prevented the completion of any actual conversation. The same held true for my friends. If they were having trouble at work or at home or even as a mom and wanted to vent to me, their children prohibited such a conversation from occurring.

It's not as if children demanded all of their mother's time on purpose, it was just that they had needs 24 hours a day. If we went on a shopping trip, it was no longer about picking outfits for each other and leisurely shopping, it was now about finding the cutest baby ensembles. If babies or small children accompanied us on our trip, it became about squeezing friendship time together while still keeping to their child's nap schedule or finding a place in the mall that offered some sort of child friendly distraction. When my friends' focus changed, our relationships changed as well, but that alone was not the reason I waited.

If anything made me put my mommy plans on hold, it was the behavior of complete strangers' children. As I would observe parents walking around malls and grocery stores with screaming children in tow, I could not help but wonder if I would ever be able to handle such a lifestyle. Toddlers threw boxes of cereal in the aisles followed by wailings of, "*I don't want that kind.*" Arguments and deals mothers and fathers would have with their children trying to negotiate good behavior so they could finish their errands and then go get ice cream or play in the park were in plentiful supply.

The shocking lengths bribing parents would go for their children to try to make them behave frightened me. I understood the developmental needs of young children, but understanding it and living it were vastly different worlds. The worst was bearing witness to parents completely giving up and allowing their children to scream, run, and bump into people. In one instance, a little girl in a rampage knocked a shopping basket out of my hands and to the floor. The result was a bag of peaches thumping and bruising, a can of diced tomatoes rolling down the aisle, and a jar of capers that luckily did not break. It felt like I was moving in slow motion as I scrambled around picking up my future purchases as I wondered how the mother would react to her daughter's antics. Although the catatonic mother watched her child's destructive behavior, she did not make any sort of apologies on behalf of her child and seemed completely unfazed by its occurrence. Children throw tantrums. I understand that. I do not understand parents who ignore such behavior and who make no apologies to the strangers impacted by such conduct. The fact that this lack of reaction seemed more the rule than the exception in what was once a civilized society heightened my fears.

When I was a child, my parents would have never tolerated outbursts or rude behavior in public. I am eternally grateful that they modeled the importance of good manners. If they were unable to control me, there would have been apologies made to the public and serious consequences for me later at home. Manners used to be important, and these days, do not seem universally emphasized as a priority. The golden rule of treating others the way you wish to be treated seems a distant dream. I am reminded about that fact some days in my professional life since I happen to be a teacher.

To be clear, I adore my career. My students make my day-to-day life a complete joy and an unpredictable wonderland. I doubt that any teacher laughs more than I do in my classroom. However, there are moments where it is clear that some students come from households where manners are not emphasized. Whether the evidence of bad manners comes from the way students speak to others or simply from a lack of the words *please* and *thank you* in their vocabulary, the problem has seemingly gotten worse rather than better over the years.

We sometimes refer to a popular saying, which is the apple doesn't fall far from the tree. Few exceptions have been noted where students who lack manners come from parents who lack manners. As far as baby making plans were concerned, I would categorize parents asking me about my timeline as those leaning towards individuals with bad manners. There were many parents who genuinely took an interest in my life and asked about my family making plans. Those situations were acceptable because there was an honest wish for my happiness and nothing more.

However, there was that *other* category. That category was limited to parents who viewed themselves simply as my customers. This group of parents wanted to know my business for their benefit and no one else's. The majority of my students and their parents have always been delightful and supportive in every way imaginable. However, if the exception proves the rule, then those few parents who viewed themselves as my customers, and therefore perceived my private life as their business, proved the rule. Such a phenomenon, of course, demonstrates bad manners.

After being subjected to inquisitions by numerous parents in that *other* category regarding my motherhood plans, I began to guard many areas of my private life from everyone. Several separate sets of parents, whom I barely knew, asked me to divulge my baby making plans with them. Each time I was asked, a proper response was a mystery to me. Usually my retort was along the lines of, "I already have 25 children." Regardless, students' parents literally begged me to wait to get pregnant until they could be assured that my pregnancy would not impact their child's educational experience. I actually understood their position and the reasons why they did not want their child's education disrupted, but I would be lying if I did not admit how much such a request stung. And, to be truthful, there were only three sets of parents who asked me to put motherhood plans on hold, but still, there were three...

Ultimately, my students' parental desires added another layer of procreation hesitation. But, if I am to be completely honest, the issue that caused me the most anxiety was the anticipation of my future dining experiences.

Try to enjoy a meal in any family style restaurant and my point is clear. Samantha, my sister, was my first exposure into this alternate reality. Try as she might, she could never eat a fraction of her meal at a restaurant because she was always busy entertaining her children. Samantha did not entertain her children to be cute; it was a necessity to prevent them from making a scene and embarrassing her and those dining with and around her. Naturally, entertaining children meant the inability of culinary enjoyment or proper digestion. My sister's challenging dining experiences were echoed by most of my friends. When William and I joined our friends with their children at a restaurant, chaos ensued.

Even eating a meal at home seemed impossible. The home meal scenarios involved a lot of coddling and pacifying of any and all children in the vicinity of the meal. Although there was less emphasis on sparing embarrassment in the actual home, there was the cutting up of meat, making new meals if they refused to eat what everyone else was eating, and arguments about which cup or plate they found acceptable. In addition, parents had the expectation of themselves to hang on to their children's every word, which halts and interrupts any and all possible adult conversation. In my mind, the bottom line to choosing parenthood meant an acceptance that the world stopped revolving around you and began revolving around someone else.

Perhaps I seem spoiled and a little overly concerned with the dining experience, but my point is or was that I did not know how I could ever do what parents are supposed to do naturally. Attentive parents are good parents and they put their needs last all day every day. Would I ever be ready? What if I wanted to speak with my friend for five straight minutes? Maybe my hunger pangs would be so severe I would never be willing to sacrifice eating in order to entertain my children at every meal. Was I too selfish and self-absorbed to take on a parenting role?

I questioned whether or not genuine parenting skills existed somewhere inside me. Since I could not be certain I possessed these instincts, I tried to imagine them magically flooding through my body the moment a child of mine was born. I was not convinced this would happen. Regardless of my doubts and fears about parenting, I always walked around with my enigmatic plan to some day have two children. In the meantime, I put all realistic thoughts of motherhood out of my head. Instead, I focused on my wonderful relationship with my husband, the demands of my career, and faithfully swallowed the birth control pill day after day.

And then, it happened. I am not sure why or how, but out of the blue, I felt it. An intense desire to nurture came out of nowhere and smacked me upside the head. The uneventful events of that moment makes my transformation from spoiled self-absorbed brat into hopeful caretaker seem completely insane. I was sitting on my couch, grading papers, when a longing enveloped my soul and stopped me mid-correction. It was like a switch was magically flipped in my head and my heart. My breath stopped as I realized that I wanted to have a baby.

My paranoia about sacrifice magically dissipated and I knew that I was ready to become a mother. I wanted to dedicate my every waking moment to another person's life and no longer had concerns about interrupted phone calls, meals, or shopping excursions. No one was more surprised than I by the sudden development and urgency that gripped me. Perhaps it was the imminent exodus of the twenty-something age that put me over the edge, perhaps it was something else entirely. I guess I will never be certain. Regardless, I knew in my heart of hearts that I was ready to put my "It's all about me" mentality to rest because it was time to begin a family. My biological clock had officially begun to tick.

Making babies

I BROUGHT UP the topic of procreation with William, who was an easy sell. He had always dreamed of having four kids, although was willing to settle on two. William was ready to be a father, I knew, by the end of our second date. Since our second date was long ago, it took about three minutes of conversation for us to conclude that I should get off the birth control pill at the end of the packet. Although William had insisted that the timeline for baby making had always been up to me, once we reached this point in our lives, I was not really certain how to approach the process. Up until this time, our sex lives were about avoiding pregnancy at all costs, not encouraging it. Birth control was a concept well understood, but the pursuit of pregnancy was a bit of a mystery.

Pregnancy had long been a fear of mine. As a youth, my mother gave me the sex talk in her own unique way. She explained, "Sex will hurt a lot, you will bleed like crazy, and you will probably get pregnant, so wait until you are married." Those words made a long lasting impact on me; ask my poor high school boyfriends who probably took a lot of cold showers. The same questions could be asked of my college boyfriends as well. Pregnancy had been such a deep-seated fear of mine for so long, it seemed odd to finally find myself plotting to have a child. I was about to have sex for the reasons nature intended, or so I had been raised to believe. Naturally, I did what so many people do during a time of uncertainty; I consulted the Internet.

After a small amount of research regarding baby-making logistics, I discovered that there was a tiny window when the egg could be fertilized and that was it. Basically, you had to know when you were ovulating and plan intercourse around ovulation. I wondered how there were so many accidental pregnancies in the world when the chances only came a few times each month. Upon further reading, it seemed that some men possess super sperm that can live for up to a week or more in a woman's body, so that kind of explained it, or these unplanned pregnancies were happening because girls were having lots of sex all the time. Not knowing whether William had the super long living sperm, we planned our baby making activities for days 13 through 17. I had found out that since my cycle was 28 days, I most likely ovulated on day 14 or 15.

During our first planned session I remember thinking, "Oh my goodness, we could have just created a baby, at this moment." Our sex life became purposeful and magical over the days following our decision to abandon birth control methods. We were not just copulating for fun, now there was a goal. I was convinced a baby was being formed inside me immediately. From the very first day of birth control free sex, just to be safe, strenuous workouts were avoided and sit-ups were banned. I read anything and everything I could get my hands on about preparing my body for pregnancy. Sushi was no longer allowed, deli meats were out of the question, and soft cheeses, well, I had never really eaten them anyway, so that was not a big deal.

I replaced birth control pills with prenatal vitamins prescribed by my OBGYN, Dr. Simpson. Of course, when he prescribed them he asked me, "Why are you actively trying to complicate your life?" That statement was followed up with, "A life without children is very desirable, trust me." Dr. Simpson loved to tease me, but he did wish me rapid results. Sure enough, when my period was due, it did not come. I had always been very regular and was quite confident that I would get pregnant right away, but even I was a bit surprised by this rapid result. After my period was way past due, I went out and purchased my very first pregnancy test.

I'll never forget making that purchase. I teach in the same town where I live, so I was terrified that a student or parent would catch me purchasing the test kit. Although I was only one person, the school system in which I was employed had thousands of eyes in the public arena and I was nervous. Aimlessly, I picked up several bags of cotton balls, to cover the entire box. The cotton balls were followed by other unnecessary items including toothpaste, a six-pack of gum, a magazine, and a new toothbrush on various sides of the secret box to ensure that glimpses of the product could not be made by anyone in the store, no matter whom I might run into that day.

Perhaps most people have not paid much attention to the packaging, but the letters that spell out pregnancy test are in a very large font on every side of every box of every brand. Maybe I should contact the people who make pregnancy tests and alert them to this privacy issue? Regardless of my font fears, I was forced to remove the package when I approached the register. Tentatively, I looked over my shoulders in both directions, once again, to make sure that no one would bear witness to my furtive purchase. Miraculously, there were no people behind me in line, which I assure you, had never once happened previously in my experience. When the pharmacist caught a glimpse of the kit, she wished me good luck, and I smiled with confidence. I ran out of the store, kit in hand, and drove with my heart beating in my throat all the way back to my house.

In my head, I had already planned the way I would break the joyous news to my husband. A disc jockey from a New York radio station once relayed an idea that I just loved. He said his wife did not do this, but he heard this idea somewhere and would have loved it if she had surprised him this way. I would set an extra place for dinner and when my husband asked me about the extra place setting, I would simply say, we were expecting company for dinner, in about nine months. The idea seemed inspired and I couldn't wait to implement it. When my husband unraveled the clue and figured out that I was telling him I was pregnant, he would lift me up, twirl me in his arms, and we would start planning for our first child. We would purchase several boxes of saltines and ginger ale in case of morning sickness. After the first three-month hurdle, I would do my best to control what I ate to make sure my body was best prepared to give birth and make certain that I did not get ridiculously fat. Of course, I would try, but who was I kidding, I would eat whatever I wanted and get enormously fat. I am short with limited will power; there was no way around that one.

The fantasy swirled in my head as I waited for the results of the pregnancy test. When the suggested time for the pregnancy test elapsed, I glimpsed a bright pink line on the test. Oh my goodness, I thought, it is positive! Excitement filled my heart and my head, but then I caught the view of a diagram on the side of the box. Apparently, one line meant not pregnant. How could that be? What a cruel joke for the test kit makers to play on a woman in my situation. There should be either a line or not! I was stunned to be viewing a negative result. I thought that it had to have been a mistake and, truly, if I squinted, could see the very trace of the second line forming. The second line was so faint, it did not convince me and I started to panic.

After scanning the directions for the fifth time, I realized that the results might prove differently if the test were taken in the morning. Returning to the Internet, I found dozens of stories of women who had tested too early and received false negatives.

Since there were two kits in the box, I decided I would take the next test in a few days. OK, so I couldn't wait until first thing in a few days. I woke up at 3:39 a.m. on the second day and took the test then. Once again, it was negative and my heart sank. Perhaps I was not pregnant, but where was my period?

My period would not arrive again for several months. Within that time frame, I would be tested for pregnancy once by my general practitioner and twice by my OBGYN. Finally, I could not take it anymore and called my OBGYN with my concerns and he diagnosed me with amenorrhea. The diagnosis is simply defined as a missed period for no real reason, but it was common after getting off of the pill. This was confusing to me since I had previously gone off the pill and had my period return immediately. But, he was convinced that it would arrive in due time, and he was correct, it did.

Once my period had finally returned to my life on a regular basis, my husband and I purchased an ovulation test kit, actually several of them. We began to time ourselves, count days, take basal body temperatures; you name it, and we tried it. An ovulation test kit that used saliva to detect the magical fertile window was even purchased. Yes, it was as disgusting as it sounds and I could not figure out how to use it at all. It didn't matter, I was the type of person who believed if you wanted something and worked diligently, that you would eventually reach the goal of your dreams.

In the February of the following year, about a year after I had gone off the pill, my period was once again late. We had just traveled to Florida to visit my parents and I was experiencing weird cramping. I remembered my sister telling me that when she got pregnant with her first son, she had weird cramps, but no period. Realizing this I decided that I needed a pregnancy test that very minute. However, we did not have a rental car or any way to travel to a drug store without my parents. William and I debated whether we should wait to purchase the test until we got home. It really wasn't much of a debate; after waiting a year we weren't going to wait longer than necessary.

All dreams of surprising my husband with the wonderful news were beyond insignificant. Instead, we had to come up with a way to make the purchase without letting my parents know. We brainstormed items that we "left at home" and needed to purchase to create a cover story. Since my parents are huge Costco loyalists, this was not easy. They had packages of deodorant, shampoo, toothpaste, razors, and every other toiletry that one could desire. The only idea that was even remotely credible was my need for a specific type of sun block that they didn't already own. As anticipated, my mother and father tried to offer me several different types of bottles that they had in their stocked cabinets, but I stayed strong in my story and tried to convince them that only a certain brand would do for my sensitive skin.

Perhaps it does not paint a positive picture of my maintenance needs because my parents believed me. Regardless, an hour later, my father brought my husband and me to a nearby Wal-Mart. We then needed to figure out how we were going to pull off this purchase in front of my father without him catching on to our real motives. My father is extremely observant and nothing ever gets by him. Worse, he is the type of person who wants to complete errands in a flash. This meant that he escorted us over to the sun block aisle and waited for us to make our purchase. William and I continually exchanged nervous glances as I pretended to read boxes of different SPF products. William whispered that he would go find one and purchase it in secret if I could distract my father for about 10 minutes. As soon as William left the sun block area, my dad wanted to know where he was going. I made up a story about him wanting a certain type of razor. My mind started racing and my heart followed suit. Clearly, my job was to keep my father far away from the pregnancy aisle, which meant I needed to redirect him, but how? The first idea that popped in my head was to go over to the aisle that sold electronics. What could I pretend to want to shop for on vacation in the electronics department? I did not know, but then I thought about CDs. Innocently, I asked my dad where the CD aisle was and of course he escorted me over there immediately. I pretended to be looking at one CD after another until I imagined that enough time had passed for William to make the covert purchase. I decided not to purchase any CDs and luckily, when we approached the register with sensitive skin sun block in hand. William was standing to the side with a bag and a hidden smile. The fake out did the trick and our secret was still safe.

As soon as we returned to my parents' house, I took the test. The bathroom door remained locked and I stared, alone, at the test window waiting for happy news. Unfortunately, my hopes were peaked and quickly dashed when a shocking negative sign stared back. How could this be happening again? I used paper towels and tons of tissue and wrapped up the test and its cruel results and walked back into the bedroom where William was waiting with bated breath. One look at my face revealed the sad results, and I placed the wad of paper in my purse. Clearly, I could not discard the failed test in my parents' home for fear they might see the stick, so I planned to discard it in a public trash can when the opportunity presented itself. Although we were initially disappointed, we decided not to react yet and were determined that I should take another test in a few days if I still did not have my period. Although I was heartbroken, there was little else I could do. I began going to the bathroom every hour or half hour, just to see if my period had arrived. A few additional days passed, and it hadn't, so I took the second test. Once again, it was negative. What was going on with my body?

When I flew back home, I immediately called my OBGYN, Dr. Simpson, and relayed my story. He asked me to visit his office to check my status. My first stop in the office was another pregnancy test, which I found laughable. Naturally, it was negative. After some poking and prodding, Dr. Simpson invited me into his office, as he always did after an examination. His eyes met mine and it was obvious that he was about to hit me with some bad news. My head was swirling and I could actually feel the pity oozing out his pores before he uttered the words that no woman ever thinks she will hear. "I am sorry to tell you this, but I suspect that you have fertility issues."

Initially, I did not believe him. My cycle had always been regular, like clockwork. I got my period right before my 13th birthday, which was average. I was at the right weight, I worked out, and I ate somewhat healthy. How could I have a fertility problem? Fertility issues were for women who had ovarian cysts, who smoked, drank, took drugs, were morbidly obese, or who had irregular periods and horrible cramps, not for "normal" women like me. At least, that was the information I had garnered in my previous research. Seriously, fertility issues could never plague *me*. Surely my husband and I just had our timing off. Dr. Simpson asked me to make another appointment, but this time, with my husband. He insisted it was the best strategy to discuss our options. As I fought back tears, Dr. Simpson tried to calm me down by presenting worse scenarios. He pointed out that I didn't have cancer, I wasn't going to die, and there was probably a simple solution for my fertility issues. These were excellent and legitimate points, and momentary guilt plagued me for feeling sorry for myself. Dr. Simpson gave me a hug and told me to call him if I needed anything.

The moment I was in the safety and isolation of my car, I broke down in the parking lot and cried for ten minutes. The tears would do me no good, I knew that, but all the logic in the world would do nothing to prevent them from falling. Thoughts of disappointment overwhelmed me as my head encouraged me to feel ashamed that my body was not behaving in the manner in which it was expected. Immediately, terrible guilt consumed me for once upon a time doubting the fact that I would want children of my own. Perhaps my past self-absorbed thoughts and tendencies had brought this fate into my husband's and my chances at having a baby.

The other issue that raced through my mind on the ride home was William. How do you tell your husband that your dreams of having a family might be out of reach? Even though I had once been filled with doubts in my head about becoming a mother, my husband did not have a single doubt, or at least, never expressed one to me. If you were to ask anyone, people would declare that William was born for the role of dad. He had no problems acting silly, roughhousing, or playing make-believe with little boys or girls while, being nurturing, loving, and compassionate. No one was destined to be a father like my husband and I could never have anticipated not being able to provide him with such an opportunity. Clearly, I could not accept having to face him without a plan. Since I was a woman of action and one of proposing solutions, I coped with the possibility of having fertility issues the only way I could; I engaged the Internet to conduct additional research. Adoption was the key word I entered into countless search engines within minutes. If having babies the old fashioned way was impossible, I had to provide us with a plan B.

Perhaps you are wondering why I did not conduct an Internet search for in-vitro fertilization or other medical interventions. In-vitro fertilization, fertility medications, and surrogacy were three alternatives I had never considered. My thought was simply that God or fate or whatever worked in mysterious ways. If it was somehow decided that one would not be able to procreate without interference, then that was the universe's way of telling certain people that they were meant to adopt. An inability to procreate, in my mind, meant that there must be a child out there that was destined for us. Weren't there hundreds of thousands of children out there in need of good homes?

Within 30 minutes of searching it was clear that I knew absolutely nothing about adoption. Like so many other people, I was under the impression that you could adopt a child fairly easily. Were there not statistics constantly available regarding the hundreds of thousands of children needing good homes? In my research, it appeared that there were virtually zero children who were free and clear for adoption. Fostering was a possibility, but even that process took months, and often, the fostered children went back to their biological parents. Within my hazy memory, I recalled various people mentioning that the adoption process was difficult, but what did they know? Well, apparently, they knew a lot more than I did.

Searching domestic adoption (adoption within a home country) led me to quickly suspect that the process was potentially taxing and in some cases, impossible for hopeful adoptive parents. If I were to pursue adoption, there was never any doubt that I would adopt a child domestically. The first reason for this decision was that I am not an overly active traveler. In fact, I abhor traveling by plane. When it is time for a vacation or visiting family, yes, I board an airplane, but every moment is torture to me. An adoption of a child from Africa, Russia, or China, would involve a lot of travel during the process.

Beyond the simple fear of constant airplane travel, a deeper fear regarding the unknown laws and conditions deterred me from considering adopting a child from a foreign country. Clearly, I knew little about adoption in my own country, and I lived there. What rights did adoptive parents really have when they were not citizens? Could another country promise me a child, take my money for processes, and provide no services? I had read and heard about situations like that. What if the child promised to me was not really in need of a home at all? Who would choose me to parent a child in a foreign land?

In domestic situations, the birth parents usually choose the adoptive parents. There was something that seemed so cosmic and fated about this process in my mind. If someone actually selected me to parent his or her child, it was like receiving a seal of approval from the universe that I was truly meant to share and nurture another life.

I searched through the 1-800-adoption website, foster care websites, and even private adoption agency websites. My computer directed me through countless search engines, including Yahoo, Lycos, Dogpile, and Google. An insatiable need to possess as much information as quickly as possible consumed me. When William arrived home that evening, I relayed my doctor's message, but rapidly spun our infertility possibilities into the excitement of adoption possibilities. Although he humored my pitch, William was not ready to give up on having a biological child; that much was evident. He lovingly encouraged my adoption information search, but he thought we should follow up with Dr. Simpson before deciding on any next step.

My adoption information search did not begin and end with the fated day I received the bad news from my doctor. Although William had a good point about exploring all options, my adoption obsession path continued for months. The information confused me more exponentially with each click of the mouse. According to the tales of woe that I had come across on the World Wide Web, adoption was not only difficult, but it was heartbreaking in many instances. First of all, the cost alone was shocking. Adoption fees totaled an average of around $40,000. When I expanded my search to international adoption, just for comparison, those bills (including travel) for some reached into the $60,000 range.

The staggering domestic adoption costs did not always include the cost of the birth mother's medical bills, which also had to be covered by the adopting parents in many cases. Considering we have such a conservative government against abortion, I wondered how it was possible for any pregnant woman, regardless of financial circumstances, to need someone else to foot the medical bills. Of course, this thought flashed in my head before I discovered the type of medical service needed by pregnant women. As soon as I realized how many appointments and procedures were involved, I wondered how anyone in any circle of life could afford to give birth. Although I was not all that well versed in the laws of those who were uninsured, the information brought me to my first realization that nothing was easy for anyone in this situation, on any side.

An acquaintance of mine named Shelly had been through two successful domestic adoptions. Both of her adopted daughters were beautiful, kind, and seemed to adapt well to their adoptive families. The adoption was never kept a secret and I wanted to know what the process was like first hand from someone who had gone through it. Shelly, who was very open and lovely, enthusiastically relayed the story of the adoption process in a phone conversation with me. It took her two hours to go through all of the ups and downs in her adoption experiences. There were many "almost" adoptions that happened for Shelly and her husband along the way. There were underhanded and manipulative birth mothers that pulled at her heartstrings and promised her a child, only to ask for money, and then disappear. She had made international adoption attempts that ended in heartbreak as well. Shelly found herself, many times, fearing that the situation would never work out. Even when her first child was placed in her arms, it was stressful. She explained that the adoption laws at that time (she was unsure if this was still the case) prohibited her from entering the hospital. For this reason, the baby was given to her in a parking lot. She said she felt like she was doing something illegal like buying drugs or in this case, baby stealing.

Shelly and her husband fell in love with their child immediately, but were plagued with worry. The state from which their daughter was adopted allowed the birth mother one calendar year to change her mind. Fear of losing her child kept her up at night. She admitted that every time the phone or doorbell rang, her heart dropped to her stomach in anticipation that the birth mother had second thoughts. Every night she would dream that her daughter's birth mother would demand her child back, which would leave Shelly childless and heartbroken.

At the end of our conversation, I found myself questioning whether or not adoption was something I could handle. Clearly, you had to be prepared for heartbreak, major debt, and unbelievable faith that eventually it would work out. I did not think I was strong enough to handle all of these factors. This woman relayed only one story; clearly there were thousands of others out there that might have been different and less painful. I went back to searching for happier, easier, and better adoption stories on the Internet.

The Internet rapidly put me over the edge. I explored blogs of hopeful adoptive parents, private adoption agency websites, public agency adoption websites, and any website in which Google would find the word adoption somewhere in the title or content. It would be an exaggeration to claim I read all of them, but I read many. I read story after story of hopeful parents suffering from the heartbreaking loss of adoption difficulties. Some of those difficulties included the financial strain, marital strain, and adoptions gone terribly wrong. How wrong? Several stories on the web shared accounts of almost adopted children returning to birth mothers who had a change in heart or change in lifestyle and were now able to care for the child they once thought they could not. Of course, there were a few stories of hope, but by the time Google brought me those stories, fear and doubt were the official victors and the adoption process was dropped from my realm of possibilities.

If adoption was too much to bear, then fertility treatments were suddenly less taboo. This meant that it was officially time to make the dreaded appointment with Dr. Simpson to discuss fertility options. There was just one issue standing in the way; William's sperm had to be evaluated. For any men out there, my sympathies are with you. To say that the sperm analysis was not an easy task is an understatement. William put it off day after day, week after week. Eventually, I made a big deal over the fact that it was a painless, almost pleasurable experience and that he should just do it.

Although it was not my best moment, William was as desperate as I was to get to the bottom of our issues, so eventually he listened and produced a specimen. Unfortunately, the results were not good. His sperm count was low. Apparently, 20 million is the cut off for low sperm count and his count was 12 million. Still, this did not make the process seem impossible. It was not as if he had a count of zero, which gave me the courage to schedule our appointment.

It was strange entering the doctor's office with William. He had accompanied me on trips to my regular doctor and even to the emergency room, but never to my OBGYN. Who wants their husband tagging along when your feet will end up in stirrups? However, I needn't have worried at this point because the stirrups were not a factor in this visit. We had entered the medical office to have a conversation that neither of us wanted to have.

Dr. Simpson scanned my husband's results and within seconds offered up the name of a fertility specialist. After he gave us the name of this doctor, he began to explain a procedure called ICSI in-vitro fertilization. He said, "Basically, we will pump you up with a lot of hormones. The hormones will come in the form of injections and pills. These hormones will cause your ovaries to produce many, many eggs that might be fertilization-worthy. Once the ovaries are ready, which will be monitored by frequent blood tests and internal ultrasounds, daily towards the end, you will have your eggs extracted. Once the eggs are extracted, your husband's sperm will be carefully injected into the egg in the hopes that embryos will form. Once the embryos form and grow over a few days, a few will be transferred to your uterus, and you will be tested for pregnancy after two weeks. You will have to endure painful shots during this time in your bottom, and if you do become pregnant, you will likely have to continue the injections for eight to ten weeks. The success rate for someone your age in this procedure is around 50%."

Being deathly afraid of needles, I think I stopped processing his words after the phrase "pump you full of hormones" was uttered. In my head, I was listening, but in my heart, I was done. It sounded awful, just awful. We left the doctor's office and William turned to me and declared that he did not want me to go through such an invasive procedure. He reminded me how lucky we were to have found each other and how happy we would always make each other, even if children were not a part of the package. It was true. William and I met at a prestigious university where we were both employed. He noticed me during my interview and thought, "Wow, she is cute, I hope they hire her." Although I did not notice him as quickly as he noticed me, when I finally did, it was not long before I was completely smitten.

He was the manager of several co-workers stationed near my desk. Every day, as I would overhear their conversations, I marveled at his kindness towards his employees. He was incredibly patient and friendly every single day. At that point, he was sharing a cubicle with another man and I thought his name was Jim. One fated day, my manager asked me to find William and let him know that a specific meeting had started. I walked straight over to William and asked him, "Hi Jim, Do you know where William is because I have to let him know the meeting already started and my manager is waiting for him." William kindly explained that I was in fact speaking with William and that Jim was the guy that also sat in the cubicle. Although I cannot pinpoint the exact moment I realized I wanted to marry William, it was probably during the time I thought his name was Jim. From the time the first greetings were exchanged, I knew this was a man who would make me infinitely happy.

William continued to make me happy every single day. This meant, of course, there was a selfish part of me that wanted to shut down the entire idea of in vitro fertilization along with him, but I could not let silly fears about a procedure and shots in the bottom prevent my husband from becoming a father or me from becoming a mother, which I now wanted more than anything else in the world. So instead, I reassured William that it would not hurt us to visit the fertility specialist and hear what he had to say.

DR. GOD COMPLEX

B EFORE I COULD change my mind, I made an appointment with the recommended fertility specialist, Dr. Reginald. We walked into the office and were greeted by posters of Brooke Shields and various parenting magazines. Brooke Shields' image was everywhere in the office because her experience with in vitro fertilization was ultimately successful. I stared at the table full of parenting magazines and pregnancy magazines and thought it a bit presumptuous. As we tried to find a place to sit, we felt unsettled. The room was packed with women, all who seemed much older than I, and I felt out of place. After a half hour wait, Dr. Reginald appeared and called me through the big glass door.

He was a very handsome man. Although numerous male doctors had examined me in my life, I could not recall thinking that any of them were remotely good looking. Dr. Reginald was extremely nice on the eyes. He was shy of the 6 ft mark, but he had a physique like a soccer player. His head of hair was full, but short, neat, and preppy, just the way I like it. I remember analyzing his features and wondering if he was a designer baby. Seriously, he was that good looking.

Obviously, attractiveness was not a requirement of fertility doctors, but it clearly made an impression on me. Before I could soak in his good looks completely and barely after exchanging curt greetings, Dr. Reginald asked me to undress from the waist down. Suddenly, the spell was broken and I thought, what is this about, weren't we just supposed to chat? There was no initial explanation forthcoming. He barked the orders and told William and me that he would meet us in the exam room when we were ready. Within three minutes of meeting a strange, albeit, attractive man, my pants were off and tissue paper covered me from the waist down. When he reemerged without much more of an explanation, he quickly revealed that he wanted to look at my ovaries up close. An ovarian ultrasound requires a wand placed in a woman's most private area. This meant that within five minutes of meeting this new doctor, a wand was inserted in a place that very few men have explored in my life. This made me extremely uncomfortable, but I felt more comfortable when Dr. Reginald commented that I had excellent ovaries and a lot of eggs. He also added that he was used to seeing older ovaries. William and I exchanged glances and tried to thwart off giggling over this strange topic of conversation. After all, I guess he was trying to give my ovaries a compliment, and at this stage of the game, I would take any words of encouragement. He let me get dressed and then called us into his office.

In a five-minute period of time, I had met a new doctor, stripped down, and had my ovaries explored. During this five-minute period, Dr. Reginald probably conversed with us for about 45 seconds. It was not that he was a man of few words; it was that he was full of himself. He did not seem to feel the need to provide long explanations nor did he ask us if we had any questions. His manner was beyond brusque. If I were to apply appropriate adjectives to describe Dr. Reginald carefully, it would not be difficult to find the perfect words. The first adjective that pops into my head is pompous, the second is arrogant, and the third is best left to one's imagination.

To say that he had no bedside manner is a huge understatement. Considering the field he was in, I found this personality flaw alarming. We were just another hopeless couple; nothing set us apart from his 1:00 or his 3:00 appointments. Although on a large scale I can almost understand his attitude, as a feeling human being, I really could not understand his persona. My first impression was of his physical presence and I was very impressed. My second impression was of his emotional being and I discovered that I was far from impressed. Regardless, this was the doctor my OBGYN recommended and I trusted Dr. Simpson emphatically. Besides, if Dr. Reginald made it possible for us to have a baby, who cared about his pompous nature?

When we reentered his office after viewing my ovaries and follicles, he brusquely suggested we pursue insemination instead of in vitro fertilization. I did not know the difference, but I liked hearing that in vitro was not his first choice. All insemination entailed was a few blood tests and ultrasounds. There might be one shot in the stomach needed to begin the ovulation process, but other than that, no drugs. Already I loved this idea and his self-important attitude suddenly held no significance.

He explained that William would deposit sperm, which would then be washed and spun. The "sperm washing" would remove bad sperm and isolate the strongest specimen to send through the cervix. An hour or so later, William's washed sperm would be inserted into me and carefully guided into my uterus through a flexible catheter. I would lie down for about 10 minutes after the procedure, which would not really hurt, then be on my merry way. This sounded like a grand idea! We were all for it! We had to go through some genetic screening first, but after that was all said and done, we could get started. They did the blood test on William right there and then, but they would not do mine. Basically, the nurses on call that day took one glance at my pathetic and tiny veins and suggested I go straight to a lab. That appointment was made for the upcoming weekend.

If you ever hear about genetic testing, know that it calls for about 12 vials of blood. I had no idea that this was the case when I entered the lab, but when the phlebotomist began piling up vials and labeling all of them with my name, I started to panic. Now, I have had to go through many blood tests in my life. Allow me to provide you with an accurate description of each experience. It goes something like this: "Wow, your veins are so tiny, did you drink or eat anything before you came here today?" By the way, my answer was always yes. Having been through many blood tests in my life I was well aware that it was best to drink at least one glass of water before going to a lab. The amount of times that information has been passed on to me is a count I lost many years ago.

The consumption of water never seems to help anyone find my vein, but I faithfully drink water before each test. Supposedly, it helps with the blood flow once the vein is located, or so I have been told. Following the comments made about my tiny veins, the phlebotomist then proceeds to secure a tourniquet around my right arm. He looks at what does not pop out, asks me to make a fist (which, by the way, I do automatically), starts whacking my veins, sighs, and then takes off the tourniquet. Next, he places the tourniquet on the left arm and watches nothing pop out, and the right arm experience is repeated. Additional sighing follows this procedure, and then serious poking begins. After a poke is made, which is usually not a direct hit; the needle is moved around, which hurts like crazy. The phlebotomist moves the needle around hoping against hope that he will hit that tiny vein. If he does, I then get to hear about how slowly my blood comes out and once again I am asked if I drank a glass of water before I arrived. Because of this slow blood flow, the tourniquet must stay on for the entire duration of the blood test.

Normally, the above scenario is a nuisance, but when 10 or more vials of blood are required, it moves out of the nuisance zone and lands in the realm of torture. The genetic testing resulted in my arm shaking wildly and I was positive I was going to throw up all over the phlebotomist. When it was all over, I was left with an enormous bruise that made me look like a drug user, but the objective was achieved and I was relieved. Personally, I was just glad to report that there was no vomit on anyone at the end of the test.

No genetic problems were detected in either my husband's blood or in mine, so we were all set. We were told to call the fertility clinic on the first day of my period. Great! Only a few weeks from now I would be preparing to get pregnant. It was such an exciting time for us. But, it was not as easy as one might imagine. The first problem that I ran into was detecting the first day of my period, because when you are told to notify someone of the first day of your period, it does not mean the first day of spotting. I always thought the first day of spotting was the first day of a period, but apparently, it was the first day of flow. So, how do you truly know when you are flowing? I suspected, but I had no way of knowing. It didn't really matter that much to them, as long as you did not start coming in too late. You see, as soon as the first day of your period arrived, you would call them and they would have you come in about 10 days after to start monitoring your ovulation cycle. So, for someone who calls too early, it just means a few extra blood tests and ultrasounds. Which again, for normal people with normal veins, extra tests are not a big deal. But for someone with tiny veins that are basically invisible to the naked eye, it becomes a problem.

When it was time to go in, of course, my blood results had shown that I had come in too early. I was asked to come back day after day for additional blood tests, but by day 14, there was still no sign of something called the lutenizing hormone. Also known as the LH surge, the lutenizing hormone is detected in women who are about to ovulate, or drop their egg. Since no LH surge was detected, the fertility group of doctors decided that I needed an ovulation trigger. I not only had to undergo blood tests, but internal ultrasounds, which revealed that my follicles were a great size. The problem was that my follicle size and my blood results had not quite matched, so a subcutaneous injection (which can be done in the stomach, the arms, or the thighs) was prescribed. William was initially instructed to administer the shot that evening, but a nurse ended up giving me the injection during my exam.

It hurt, but only for a second. All that was left for us to do was wait. After the ovulation trigger was administered, the doctors asked me to return exactly 36 hours later for the insemination process. While we were waiting for the doctor to perform the procedure, William and I talked about whether or not we wanted a boy or a girl. But it didn't matter, we just wanted a baby. We were giddy with anticipation! When the doctor entered, he told us that William's washed sperm count was only eight million and he likes to have at least 10 million, but they would still try using the sample. William was devastated, but I was still hopeful, because in reality it only takes one magic sperm.

I have been asked by a lot of people to describe what insemination feels like. It is touted as a painless procedure, but that is not completely accurate. Granted, it was not horrifically painful, but as the catheter was inserted, I felt strange cramping that I cannot compare to anything I previously experienced. Then, when the sperm was injected, additional cramping followed. There was an extra problem because the doctors couldn't figure out the best catheter to use in my small body. It eerily reminded me of blood tests because three different sized catheters were inserted until the doctors decided that they had found the best tool for the job. Beyond the small hiccups, the procedure was quite simple. In fact, it was similar to a pap smear, which is uncomfortable and icky, but not overly traumatic.

In the days following the insemination, I constantly imagined feeling something growing inside of me. Every cramp, even for a second, was a sign that a baby was on the way. A twinge here, a twinge there made my heart jump for joy. There were plenty of websites devoted to early signs of pregnancy. Most of the signs would not appear until after it was time for a pregnancy test. It did not matter, I eagerly searched my body for any pregnancy signs and grabbed on to the hope that I was experiencing some kind of hint that everything would be changing.

Change was not to come because a few weeks later, my period arrived like an unwelcome guest. Regardless of our devastation over the failed insemination attempt, the fertility doctors were not discouraged. The first point that they made was that there is roughly an 18% chance of insemination success. That was not an encouraging statistic. Beyond that, the doctors explained that sperm count fluctuation was very common and nobody knew the reason why. Since they had hope for our success, we tried to as well. William began taking vitamins and herbal supplements to attempt to maximize his sperm count. Although there is really no proven way to increase sperm count, we figured any assistance was a good idea. When we went back the next month to repeat the process, it was determined that I did not need the ovulation trigger. This was already a good sign. This time, when the doctor entered the room to complete the procedure, he was elated that the washed sperm count had increased to 15 million. Hooray! Now we were in business. This time we knew it would work.

The two weeks after the insemination were torture, but nothing compared with getting my period, again, and again, and again. Each time we tried insemination the washed sperm count dropped lower and lower; at its lowest it was three million. What was going on? William's urologist retested him and his sperm count was well above 40 million. He was convinced that the fertility clinic had messed something up, but really, what could we do?

After four failed insemination attempts, we felt despair. We could have tried it again but the doctors confessed that after four failed attempts, they usually move to a more aggressive procedure. William and I had already gone this far, so we decided that it was time to pursue in vitro fertilization. Before I would be permitted to attempt this process, I would have to receive a histosonogram. Basically, a catheter would be sent up my private area and a balloon filled with ink would be sprayed. The ink would show whether or not there was a clear or blocked path from my fallopian tubes to my uterus. To me, the description of the procedure sounded horrible, but it was far worse than I anticipated. In a nutshell, I found the process to be an excruciating 10 minutes.

The reason my experience was so terrible, was likely due to the fact that one of my tubes appeared blocked. I say appeared because the technicians couldn't confirm that it was blocked. Apparently, I was a mystery to them because the ink suddenly stopped traveling, but did not build up as though it were behind a blockage. They made me turn on my side to see if the ink would travel. I screamed in agony. Since the ink did not move any further with my body twisting and turning at the technician's request, the team was officially perplexed. Although they had seen blocked tubes before, mine did not fit into the blocked tube explanation. The technicians advised me to speak to my doctor after he interpreted the results.

When I went to my follow up appointment with Dr. Reginald, he confessed that he also did not understand what had happened. He explained that if my tubes were really blocked, the ink would gather and expand near the blockage. Since that did not happen, there was likely something like a bowel (gross I know) or some sharp turn in the way. The only method to learn the absolute truth about the status of my tubes would be achieved by subjecting me to the test a second time. My response to such a proposal was, "No thanks."

Dr. Reginald did not concern himself with having me repeat the test since we were using the in vitro fertilization process. He clarified that tubal blockage was not a concern for patients using in vitro because the doctors would place the embryos right inside my uterus. So, why did they make me do it in the first place? I still have no idea. With the in vitro process, apparently the need of both of my fallopian tubes would be bypassed anyway, so he excused me from the additional torture. The nurse, Lydia, excitedly escorted us to a conference room to give us all the in vitro details. She looked me in the eye and pledged, "I just know this is going to give you a baby." I knew it, too.

I entered the fertility office's conference room and was soon joined by William. Lydia removed a spongy item and several different types of syringes and fertility medications that would soon invade my body. She started demonstrating the proper way to administer the fertility medication and my heart became fluttery. I felt eager to start because I knew that this was the route that would bring us a family. Lydia delivered several subcutaneous injections on a model and these did not bother me that much. After all, I had withstood several injections to jump start ovulation during the insemination attempts; I knew I could handle those shots. But then, she brought out the big needles, which would be used for progesterone injections.

After the transfer was completed, progesterone injections would be required nightly. The needles used to inject the progesterone were enormous. Unfortunately, long and thick needles are necessary to administer an intramuscular injection. An intramuscular injection is a fancy way to say that an injection must be given via the hip/gluteus maximus area, otherwise known as the butt cheeks. The needle was two inches long and the medication was a goopy, syrupy consistency. She told us that this medication needed to get injected slowly and warned William about the potential of hitting a vein and checking the syringe each time for blood. The initial fluttery feeling was replaced by dread as I envisioned this goopy consistency entering my system day after day for (if we were lucky and the procedure worked) anywhere from eight to ten weeks. I tried to put the syrupy medication and long needle out of my mind and focus on the big picture of the miracle of birth.

As I tried to imagine the joy of becoming a mother, Lydia woke me out of my reverie to instruct us that ice packs should be used to numb the area before the injection because it would hurt a lot. She made a point to let us know that William should alternate the injections every night from one butt cheek to the other, to prevent scarring. Lydia then suggested that we use the ice packs after the injection, to try to keep the bruising to a minimum. Was she serious about butt bruising? The imaginary baby I had briefly envisioned in my daydream popped out of my head. Instead, I started to imagine my black and blue bottom. How would I drive my car, sit in a chair, or even use the toilet with bruised butt cheeks?

While still worrying about my bottom, Lydia escorted us back into Dr. Reginald's office to view pictures of ovaries. First, he held up a snapshot of an 'average' ovary during a monthly cycle. Next to the average ovary, he placed a picture of a "super-ovulation" ovary, where 10 huge follicles all competed for space. He was trying to be clear about the purpose the fertility medication was serving. The medication was meant to increase my follicle count. Extra follicles produced extra eggs, which would lead to increased chances of fertilization and hence, pregnancy. The average woman has a single dominant follicle every month. If the woman's follicle produces an egg, sperm have a small window to mix with the egg, fertilize it, which leads to conception. However, if multiple follicles are nurtured that also release eggs, the sperm has multiple chances to successfully fertilize an egg. Although there were a lot of ifs in the scenario, it was genius.

The brilliance of the process bypassed my husband because he was more concerned with the side effects that I would have to endure. Dr. Reginald explained that I would feel very bloated and would probably need to wear bigger or loose pants for about a month. That did not sound terrible, so I was starting to feel pretty good about the process. After our mini education on in vitro fertilization, we were given the complete run down of our process.

Basically, I would be put on the birth control pill for 14 days to control my cycle. My only real job was to phone the fertility clinic on the first day of my period. At that time, I would fill a prescription for the birth control pill, which I would begin on the second or third day of flow. Fourteen days later, I would need to visit the office for blood work to make sure I was ready to go. If all blood test results came back the way they were supposed to, I would begin the injections and some oral medications as well. Accompanying this were blood tests and vaginal ultrasounds approximately every other day at the beginning, and then every day at the end.

This information made William and me grateful that we were timing the IVF procedure carefully to coincide with my summer break. Daily visits to a doctor would not work well with the inflexible schedule of a schoolteacher. The daily visits were necessary in order for the doctors to be certain that the egg extraction was performed on the perfect day. Once the results showed that my body was ready for the egg extraction, I would come in for a 10-minute procedure designed to carefully remove all of my eggs. Anesthesia would be administered for this procedure, so there was no pain to worry about during the extraction process. Once the eggs were extracted, the doctors would tell me how many eggs they successfully retrieved, and then call me later with more details. The eggs would be mixed with William's sperm and embryo formation would then occur. After several days, embryos would be transferred back to my uterus and if any embryos attached, would form a baby.

With each piece of information that was shared, I could not comprehend how the in vitro fertilization process was developed. I know there are many scientists out there who dedicate their lives to research, but this seemed improbable and amazing. To think that people hatched this procedure, no pun intended, was astounding. Instead of fear, I felt unbelievably fortunate that brilliant minds had focused all of their energy on fertility when I was so desperate to achieve a pregnancy. Now I just had to wait for my period.

When you want something to happen, the time span spent waiting feels like forever. Of course, my period eventually came and I immediately placed the phone call to the fertility clinic. Lydia, the fantastic nurse, advised me that on day two or three, I should begin a week's worth of birth control pills so that my cycle would be controlled. After the final birth control pill, I would need to return to the office for an ultrasound and blood test, and move on from there. I was a pro at taking birth control pills, so that was not a big deal. However, they prescribed pills that I had never taken before, and I felt the need to read the directions.

Normally, such a task would not have been met with challenges. However, my friend who was visiting caught me in the act. She asked why I was taking birth control when I had previously confided in her that I wanted to get pregnant. She caught me off guard.

What was I thinking? How could I be so stupid to read the instructions when she was in the next room? I tried to come up with a quick cover story and looked at my husband who was no help at all. Instead of a cover up I blurted, "We are doing in vitro and they make you start with birth control pills."

The truth was revealed and it did not feel like a weight had been lifted. Instead, William and I felt increasingly vulnerable. We had not decided whether to tell people or not, but now the decision was made for us. The problem with telling people that you are enduring fertility treatments is that the topic becomes the elephant in the room with every future conversation. From that moment on, each time I spoke with my friend, an inevitable question about my pregnancy status would be hovering above us, even if neither of us articulated the topic. Since I was not quick enough on my feet to divert the conversation, our private lives were about to become public.

After telling my friend, William and I decided we should probably let certain people in on our secret. We told my parents, my sister, a close aunt, and three of my friends. William's parents were not told because he did not want them to know. They rarely called the house. His reasoning for inviting certain people in on the information was based strictly on who was likely to call the house before, during, and after the process, and whether or not we could keep the information from those people. We thought that if certain people knew about our fertility issues, it would make our situation easier. This was our first error in judgment.

After the timing was deemed right via blood tests and internal ultrasounds, the doctors instructed me to begin the plethora of medication to over stimulate my ovaries into super production. Doesn't that sound fantastic? Someone actually coined the phrase "Super production!" The first night was one of the scariest because William had to administer the first injection and he was uneasy. He had to give me a drug called Follistim and another called Gonal F. There were a few steps to makes sure that he was administering the right amount of each injectable drug. The longer it took him to figure out whether or not the correct amount of medication was being given, the more nervous I became, and so did he. The first injection had to go in the stomach area, and that just seemed like a ghastly place to have an injection. Of course, I had received one there before, but it was not administered by my husband.

William swabbed my entire stomach with alcohol to make sure that the area was sterile, I closed my eyes and waited for the inevitable prick, but before he was able to do it, he started breathing in and out loudly for mental preparation. His loud breathing did not do anything to reduce my anxiety level, but I understood he was trying to gather the courage to stick his wife with a needle in her stomach, so I continued to brace myself and said nothing. He tried to be gentle, but the needle would not go in with a gentle press, so he had to try again with more effort. He finally broke through my skin and submerged the needle. Once the needle was appropriately embedded, he began counting to five to make sure all of the medicine was indeed deposited into my system.

It was a very long five seconds, but I think it was longer for William than it was for me. When it was over, there was still another injection to get through and the same events basically repeated themselves. After both medications were in me and out of the syringes, we just stared at each other. We were both terrified of the entire process and although neither of us verbalized our feelings, it was clear that we were both thinking the same exact thought, which was, "What are we doing?" Whatever reservations we had regarding the process were largely diminished by our desire to have a family, so we held our thoughts inside and remained quiet.

Night after night at exactly 10:00, William gave me the injections, which made me less than thrilled around bedtime. There were oral medications to take as well, and they were numerous: Estrogen tablets, steroids, antibiotics, and for some reason, baby aspirin were all required each day. Keeping all the medication straight became a juggling act. I went to a local pharmacy to procure a pill organizer to be certain that I was doing exactly what I needed. After a few days, I had to go back to the fertility doctors to get my blood drawn and to receive internal ultrasounds to have levels checked. Each day the nurses called with the blood results and told me that I should increase the medication, add a new one, or stay the course. This went on for nine days, several of which included having my parents staying at our house. My father even drove me for one of my blood tests and scan days. He looked nervous and petrified sitting in the waiting room for me; my heart broke when I glanced at the expression on his face.

After the ninth day of the in vitro procedures, I received a disturbing phone call from Dr. Reginald. He told me my estrogen/progesterone numbers, which of course, I did not understand, were not good and that he did not like what he was seeing. Contrary to Dr. Reginald's words, the rest of the doctors in the office that morning had told me that everything looked great. They had instructed William and me to expect to give the final stimulation medication at a specific time the following day. This would mean that the extraction would be completed the following Tuesday. That was the original plan, but Dr. Reginald did not agree with it.

His message was confusing to me. Apparently, there was something with my hormone levels found in my blood test that caused him pause. However, Dr. Reginald was talking in doctor speak and I had no idea what he was saying. What I did understand was that he came across as obnoxious and rude.

Belligerently, he told me that he did not like my numbers and had not yet decided what he would do with me. Although I heard his words, I could not comprehend the message. He seemed angry with me over the results. It was as if he was accusing me of having an evil master plan to throw his protocol off with my blood levels. He continued to talk in circles as if he had no use for my presence on the other end of the telephone. At one point in his rambling he told me that I might need to come in for the extraction on Monday instead.

Since I assumed he was informing me to see if I had any questions, I asked him if my coming in on Monday for an extraction would change the timing of any of my medications. He snapped at me, chastising me with; "I would have told you if it had to be changed," and I remained silent. My outside voice was restrained, but my head was swimming with many comments, all of which politely remained in my head as the seconds of uncomfortable silence ticked by. Dr. Reginald must have sensed that he had crossed a line, although perhaps that is giving him too much credit, but he half-heartedly apologized and explained that he was having a bad day.

When I am having a bad day, it is not acceptable for me to snap at my students or their parents. I can understand getting irritated with someone who is rude to you, but I would never call a parent and be rude for no reason. I, the patient, had asked him a very simple question, one that deserved a calm answer. My voice had not been raised, I had not shed a tear, I just asked a question and he reacted in a very unprofessional and unprovoked manner. When he hung up the phone, my heart and head filled with resentment. After crying and fuming for a few minutes, I called William and relayed my conversation with Dr. Reginald to him in one breath. I didn't know what happened or what I should do; all I knew was that the fertility clinic wanted to see me back in the office the following day. He reassured me that all would be okay and promised to escort me back to the office the next day.

The following day, I returned to the office feeling trepidation. The other doctors were kind and comforting, assuring me that Dr. Reginald tended to overreact and all was fine with my blood work and scans, which would make Tuesday the day of the extraction. Good news, but it all seemed odd that one doctor thought one way and everyone else thought another. William and I put it out of our minds and prepared for Tuesday. Instructions were very specific; there was a medication called Pregnyl that acted as a trigger for ovulation. Pregnyl actually contained the hCG hormone, which is the same hormone pregnancy tests look for to determine whether or not a woman is pregnant. It had to be given at an exact time, so we were watching the clocks like hawks. Pregnyl consisted of a powder and a liquid that have to be mixed a certain way; it was all quite complicated, which of course did nothing to calm our nerves. We got through it okay and it was back to the doctor's the next day to check my hCG blood levels to make sure the medication did in fact get into the blood stream. If the hCG was properly detected, the extraction would take place the following day.

William had done a great job because my hCG levels were plentiful in my blood-stream. Meanwhile, I was not feeling well. My abdomen was so enlarged that I felt like there were several babies growing there already. This apparently was the stimulation medication on overload and would reduce with the extraction, or so I was told. The day before the extraction was nerve racking beyond tolerance. William and I did not know what to do with ourselves, so we went to see a mindless comedy to try to take our minds off everything. I could barely concentrate on the non-story line of the movie because I was so focused on the extraction. I had positive thoughts, but I was scared since I didn't really know what to expect. Hours dragged on as we were both at a loss for words throughout most of the day.

The next morning, we were the first appointment of the day at the clinic, and we were early. The team took me in quickly and an anesthesiologist introduced himself. He had a very difficult time finding my vein (I know, shocking) but eventually found it and gave me something to calm me down. I was shaking violently with fear, nerves, and anxiety, but when he gave me the medication, I stopped shaking. Of course, as time ticked by, I began shaking again, which the doctor commented was a sign that he did not give me enough medication.

Eventually, the staff led me to a bed and asked me to place my legs in stirrups. More medication was eventually administered in my I.V., and the next thing I knew,

William was there and the procedure was over. The doctor came by and happily rejoiced, "There were 19 eggs!" William and I could not believe that there were 19 eggs. The doctors told us at most there were usually 12 eggs. How did we get so lucky to make 19?

We were on cloud nine during the 30-minute drive home. Nineteen eggs! At least half of them should be viable, we thought. We would be able to freeze embryos and have our family without going through all of this again. William and I felt pure joy; our dreams were going to come true! When we got home, I went to bed, exhausted from the anesthesia, and William fielded phone calls and made some of his own to share our great news with everyone.

A few hours later, Dr. Reginald phoned. I was reading a book and William came in with a pained expression on his face. I could not imagine what was wrong, but he explained that Dr. Reginald reported that of the 19 eggs that were extracted, only one was mature; the rest were premature. They were going to watch the one egg, but it did not look good. With the other 18, they would attempt something referred to as a day one rescue. It was possible that some of the immature eggs could mature and they could transfer them into my uterus, although statistically speaking, such a procedure usually did not result in a pregnancy. He relayed that a situation as ours had never happened before. In addition, he confessed that he had never even read about a similar outcome. We felt berated by his final statement, "I do not like the results at all and am very unhappy."

He was unhappy? Once again, I was flooded with a boatload of resentment toward Dr. Reginald. I resented his attitude, his snide bedside manner, and his practice. He acknowledged what had really happened was that the fertility team extracted the eggs too soon. Since the eggs were all immature, a few more days, or maybe even one more day would have increased the probability of maturation. Somehow, an entire team misinterpreted the blood and ultrasound tests. How could this have happened? My heart shattered into a million pieces and I was beside myself. 19 eggs, 19 and only one received the label of mature. After all of our visits to the clinic and all of those medications administered, we were left with nothing.

After placing all of the happy calls, William had to immediately follow them up with the "terrible news" call. Everyone he told was dumbstruck. No one knew what to say, but who would? The worst part of this problem was breaking the news to my mother. She cried hysterically on the phone, which is opposite how the situation should have developed. I bestowed words of encouragement to her to try to get her to stop crying. This was not her direct loss; this was William's and mine. But, she kept it up, and I had to be brave and tell her that everything was going to be okay. She hurt for me and I understood, but I did not want to deal with anyone else's pain.

I knew then that William and I should never have told my parents and I regretted confiding in them. My mother sobbed, "It's not fair, you and William would make the best parents; I am so sad for you. You are not going to give up are you? You are going to try again?" Her comments were the antithesis of what I needed to hear at that moment. Again, I understood she wanted me to become a mother and that she was devastated for me, but it was not the time for such a discussion. The last thought in my mind at that point was to consider repeating the process again.

The process was not officially over. To add insult to the emotional and physical injury, in the off chance that one of the eggs would be ready for transfer in a few days, I had to begin the progesterone injections that very night. I did not want to even bother, being so distraught with the bad news. But, in case the embryo developed, I knew I had to go through with it. The problem was that I had to lie on my stomach and it was so swollen I could not imagine how I would safely do so. This was the strangest part of all. I was told that relief would come with the extraction, but strangely, my stomach became even more bloated and pain traveled throughout my body. When William shared his concern with the nurse, she asked me how swollen my stomach was, but I could not articulate the swelling description clearly. Swollen stomach or not, the injection had to be given in the upper thigh (a.k.a. buttocks) and since lying on the stomach was out of the question, I had to lean against a wall.

How can I sum up the experience of the injection? It hurt...a lot. William accidentally hit a nerve and the pain emanated everywhere in my body. My screams frightened us both. It felt like battery acid was searing up and down my spine, but it couldn't be helped until the injection was over. Later, we remembered being told that the injection would hurt more if given too quickly, which, obviously, it was. Of course that was probably because I tearfully screamed, "Hurry up" as the injection was being administered. Poor William, he was so traumatized by my reaction he never wanted to give me another injection again. He really was brave and strong, but I didn't have the ability or wherewithal to thank him at that moment. Honestly, I think the reason the injection really hurt was because I suspected there would be no need for the medication in the likely event that there were no embryos to transfer.

The next day, William called the fertility clinic and revealed that there was absolutely no way he would ever be giving me a progesterone injection again. The nurse was very sympathetic to the situation and suggested that we use an alternative vaginal medication. Of course we would try anything that did not involve painful serum zipping through my system, so he picked up the medication from the pharmacy. This medication needed to be given four times a day and was rather disgusting, but I did not care.

Disgusting was a much easier issue to handle than pain. He brought the medication home and I administered it at once. It was grotesque and reminded me of yeast infection treatments, but it was a huge relief in comparison to the experience the previous evening with the progesterone injection. We found out a few hours later that it was a good thing we continued with the medication, but not because of the one mature egg. The one mature egg stopped growing, or died, but two of the premature eggs turned mature and would possibly be ready for transfer the following day. Hope was granted once again and our spirits rose. We were instructed to arrive for the transfer at a specific time and I was to come in with a full bladder, which meant 36 ounces of liquid consumed one hour before the procedure.

The amount of liquid that needed to be consumed was a tough one for me. Generally speaking, I do not drink a lot at once. Since I am in a profession that prevents me from taking lavatory breaks whenever necessary, I limit my intake in one sitting. Instead, I spread beverage consumption throughout the day. As a result of this habit, being forced to drink a huge quantity at once was a problem. I know, it sounds like a bizarre issue that most people would be fine with, but the prospect of consuming all of that liquid and not being allowed to go to the bathroom almost frightened me more than the thought of another progesterone injection.

Nevertheless, I did as instructed. Instead of drinking all the water and then driving in a bumpy car with a full bladder, I brought it to the office and drank it before the appointment. William and I sat in the car in front of the office while he encouraged me to drink every last drop and then we walked into the clinic full of hope.

Our hopes were immediately dashed. They kept us waiting well past the time we were supposed to be taken, which meant my bladder was screaming at me. Dr.

Reginald came down and announced that he would be performing the transfer, which did not do anything to raise our faith after his rude and pessimistic attitude of the past week. To his defense, he tried to be nice to us, but it was extremely obvious that he was trying. Nice was clearly not his natural state. He asked me if there was anything that I was worried about and I told him that I had been in a great deal of discomfort since the extraction. It was more than discomfort; it was out and out pain. It hurt to breathe in too deeply and I couldn't lie on my side without wincing in pain. My abdomen popped out more than before the extraction, and he told me that I would get relief from the bloating after the extraction.

With that, he sent an internal ultrasound into my region and proclaimed that I was suffering from OHSS, what is known as Over Hyper Stimulation Syndrome. All of the medication stimulated my ovaries so much that my ovaries began leaking the built-up fluid into the rest of my abdomen and other surrounding areas. He said there was definitely more fluid in me than the average patient, but it wasn't a life or death-threatening case. The doctor then quoted me a statistic that only around two percent of all in vitro patients suffered life threatening OHSS and that I should be fine.

Regardless, there was a lot of liquid in places that there should not have been which did explain the pain. If I wanted to, he said he could take a needle and insert it into my stomach to drain the fluid. After my stomach shots, this sounded like an overly invasive procedure, so I asked him what would happen if I decided against that idea. He said that it would go away on its own since it was not a dangerous amount. Then he commented that performing the fluid extraction was not something he would recommend to me because it might decrease the chances of the embryos sticking. The best medicine was probably complete bed rest. My choice was obvious. After all of the events over the past few days, there was no way in the world I was going to jeopardize the embryos from sticking and forming, and the prospect of a huge needle entering my abdomen was less than enticing, so I decided against the procedure.

After we decided against the fluid extraction, it was time for the transfer procedure. Before he began he told us that three eggs had matured and he would transfer all three of them into my uterus at once. This prospect terrified me. What if they all took? My sister's friend went through something similar, and all three took, but then two died and the third was born extremely early. I relayed my concerns, but Dr. Reginald explained that the embryos were not great quality and I should approve the implantation of all three to increase my chances. Our hopes were diminishing, but we decided to give it all we had. The transfer itself was uncomfortable, but in the scheme of the in vitro fertilization process, probably the easiest part. The only difficulty was in waiting the 30 minutes after the transfer to go to the bathroom.

Over the next few days, every cramp, once again, brought joy to my heart. We would have to wait two weeks to take a pregnancy test, but I had high hopes. William kept talking to the embryos and instructed them to grow. I talked to them too, but usually not out loud. I had to walk around with this huge mystery and silently willed them to turn into a baby or babies. We went to the movies and shopping. We just looked at each other and talked about anything and everything that could distract us. I tried not to convince myself of a positive outcome, but it was impossible not to believe in my embryos developing into at least one baby.

After the two weeks had passed, it was time for the blood test. I had never in my life been so happy to have my blood drawn. When we arrived to the clinic, it was under construction and we were asked to wait downstairs in the same area where we waited for the transfer procedure. After a long wait, a nurse came out for me, experienced the usual trouble finding my vein, but finally had success. We were ensured a call soon, so I went home and waited by the phone while William went to work.

It was the typical situation when one is waiting for an important phone call. The phone rang a thousand times, but it was not the one call I was waiting for. Every time the phone rang I jumped out of my skin. My mother called, my sister called, my aunt called, my best friend called, and William called, but the fertility clinic did not call. William and I had decided against telling anyone that a transfer had occurred. We thought it best not to get everyone's hopes up again, not to mention the fact that I couldn't bear the thought of dealing with my mother's emotional instability over this matter. Therefore the only people who knew were William and me and the burden of the secret did nothing to ease the anticipation.

William called me again around 5:00 and I told him I still had not heard and guessed we would not be hearing. Since the nurses left by 4:00, and they were the ones to make the phone calls, it was probably bad news. Either that or they were so busy that they didn't even notice that my results came back in from the blood work and completely forgot to call me. Still, it was nice that I could hope for another day. While we were talking about the possible reasons, call waiting interrupted and I knew, and William knew, that this was probably the phone call, but we didn't articulate our collective thought. I got off the phone with William and sure enough, it was the nurse from the clinic, not the nurse we knew and loved because she was on vacation, but another nurse who was not warm and fuzzy. She apologized for not getting back to me earlier but explained that they had so many patients and not enough staff to accommodate them all. Clearly, this was less than encouraging information. She then apologized because my test results yielded a negative. I was not pregnant. She instructed me to get off all medication and come back in for blood work in a week. At the end, she asked me if I was okay. I managed to squeak out, "I've been better, but I didn't think that it worked." I thanked her for calling and got off the phone as quickly as possible. It was official. My heart was broken.

The next few days that followed were difficult. I remained swollen and in pain from the OHSS and wanted the physical reminders of the procedure to go away. William was as positive as could be because he is just that wonderful, but he was heart-broken as well. We eventually were asked to go back into the fertility clinic together and Dr. Reginald spoke with us. He tried to get us to commit to another round of in vitro immediately, but as the summer was coming to an end and I was heading back to school, such a prospect was impossible. I could not make all of the morning lab visits necessary and still make it to my classroom on time, especially during the opening of a school year. There were so many unknown variables and raw emotions that we decided we could not consider repeating the process until next summer.

The decision was mostly an emotional one because we were drained. We did not want to reenter the process for several reasons. One of the many reasons is that insurance only covered the procedure for a maximum of two in vitro processes. We already used up one and failed miserably. More than that, since it was obvious that they extracted too early, we did not feel confident in putting our last fertility chances into the hands of this clinic. In addition, Dr. Reginald was an ass. It was not actual hate that I felt for the man; I just never had a desire to see him again. He was an unsympathetic, brusque, arrogant jerk who clearly had a God-complex and nothing to back it. We decided to put our family plans on hold once again.

After our failed attempt, we regretted telling people because inevitably, we heard, "Well, you're going to try again, aren't you?" Other words of wisdom included, "You couldn't expect that it would work the first time," and "God will give you your baby when you aren't trying." Of course my favorite line came from women who conceived and delivered babies without any issues, "If I were you, I would keep trying in vitro until it worked." This suggestion staggered me. I would like to think that if I had not gone through the procedure myself, that I would never have had the audacity to tell someone who had gone through the emotionally and physically draining procedure that if I were them I would do it again.

The point is many people are not good at putting themselves successfully in other people's places. Empathy is perhaps not a learned behavior, but an instinctual one, and the weeks and months that followed our failed attempt reminded me of this over and over again. When someone I considered a good friend would say to me, "Don't give up hope, it will happen for you," I wanted to scream. When others offered the inevitable slew of stories of people that they knew who had given up and suddenly found themselves pregnant, I wanted to roll my eyes. Those anecdotes bothered me more than anything else in the world. Yes, I knew my friends and supporters were trying to be positive, but really, I just wanted to smack them all upside the head. What I needed at that time was for people to simply admit that the situation was terrible, end of story. Things sometimes just suck.

Not only did my friends give me a complex about the situation, the media was worse. When news broke about any celebrity pregnancy, I kept thinking, "Stop reminding me of what I can't have, okay?" Obviously, there was no conspiracy against me, but it felt that way. Eventually one week turned into another, which turned into a month, and, the passage of time enabled me to move forward.

In Vitro – Part 2

ANOTHER SCHOOL YEAR began and for the most part I was able to focus my energy on my class instead of my empty uterus. I had an amazing classroom full of kids that year, so it made it easy to focus on other aspects of life. The stars were aligned when the class lists were made because mine was filled with curious, kind, energetic, and enthusiastic students. For the first time in my classroom, every student participating in hands on activities took pride in cleaning them up. In addition, good manners were prevalent and phrases like, "Excuse me, thank you, please, and you're welcome were plentiful. Literacy and math conversations were reflective and engaging. Every day was a joy. To look at the big picture, I was extremely lucky. I had a wonderful husband, a job that I loved, a house (granted, it was kind of a dump, but how lucky were we to have our own house?), and a loving family. I could not focus all of my energy on the negativity of our fertility issues.

Eventually, even with the wonderful life we already had, the desire for a baby overwhelmed us. The desire propelled William and me to explore other fertility clinics. One of my friends knew someone who had achieved success through a clinic near my husband's office, so she sent us a link on success rates on fertility clinics in our state. This clinic, it turned out, had a much greater success rate than the other fertility clinic that we had used, so we decided to go in and take a look. It boasted the best success rates of fertility clinics in the state. It was not in a convenient location for the daily trips needed, but, clearly, that had not helped us before and was an idiotic reason to select a doctor, which I had learned the hard way. Since it was literally down the street from my husband's office, I took an afternoon off from work and met him at his office so that we could travel to the clinic together.

We met a doctor that reminded us of the actor who played Bill Cosby's father on the Cosby Show. His physique and speech patterns were similar. I know this is

completely an aside and an unimportant detail, but, regardless, we liked him immediately. He was sympathetic to our past experience with in vitro fertilization and was
as convinced as we were that a different course of action was necessary. Although this
doctor would likely deny his responses to us in a court of law, he outright accused the
other clinic of negligence.

Before we were to pursue a course of treatment with this new clinic, which promised non-negligence, they required some tests. So once again, blood tests galore, a
historosonogram, and all of the previous fun poking and prodding from the first cycle
of in-vitro were repeated. I know what you're thinking because I thought it too. I just
had these tests, why do I need to go through them again? Simply, it had been more
than a year since the previous tests had been performed and it was policy. So that was
that. Who can argue with policy? Once again, I found my veins poked and my uterus
prodded daily.

In conjunction with my second IVF cycle, I decided to try to increase my odds
by receiving NAET treatments. NAET is an acronym for Nambudripad's Allergy
Elimination Technique. It all began with a doctor named Devi S. Nambudripad who
suffered terribly from various allergies. In summary, she had been given acupuncture
treatments and had fallen asleep holding a carrot immediately afterwards, which had
previously been causing her allergic reactions. When she woke up, she was no longer
having allergies to carrots. It sounds insane, but a great many people believed in the
technique, so I thought I would try it. Initially, when I sought out NAET treatments, I
did so for food allergies. My digestive system seemed to hate every type of food and it
made day to day eating increasingly difficult. Not that I want to paint a disgusting picture, but I am a teacher. If I need to use the bathroom for any reason, I am not permitted to do so. A teacher does not have the luxury of suffering from any digestive issues.

A treatment is easy to explain, but strange to believe. The practitioner picks a
treatment for you, as you are only permitted one treatment per visit. With each treatment, the patient holds a small vial, smaller than the size of an AAA battery. While one
hand is holding the vial, which represents your allergen, such as chicken, the NAET
specialist presses down on your arm muscles to analyze your reaction. If you have a
poor reaction to a specific allergen and need to be treated for it, it works as follows.

The patient keeps the vial in her hand and grasps her fingers over it as she lays
down face down on a table. The practitioner will then hit acupressure points as the

patient remains still. After the initial acupressure points are activated, the patient remains holding the vial and resting for about 20 minutes. When the time has passed, the practitioner will test the patient to determine whether or not she has overcome the allergy by (while still holding the vial) pressing down on her other arm to see if she is able to resist. If the patient overcomes the allergy, the NAET specialist will then press a few more acupressure points to end the session. At the end of the session, the patient is directed to avoid whatever the allergen is for the next 25 hours. The 25-hour period is the time it takes the allergen to move through all of the meridians in a person's body. At the end of the 25-hour period, the allergy to whichever treatment a patient has received has been cured. Believe me, I know the whole procedure sounds insane, but I was convinced there was an improvement in my own health. I am aware the improvement could have been a coincidence. But you know the old adage; desperate times call for desperate measures and a leap of faith.

While I was visiting the NAET practitioners for various food allergy treatments, I discovered that it might be able to increase my fertility chances. Naturally, I decided to receive treatments for my fertility. Besides the cost, what did I have to lose? Each treatment was around $65, and I had received over a thousand dollars worth of treatments, and no, it was not covered by insurance. Amazingly enough, there were vials representing the ovaries, reproductive eggs, fallopian tubes, uterus, estrogen, progesterone, testosterone, and every other hormone and body part that was related to having a baby.

Besides receiving treatments for each part of the body, NAET boasted it could do more. Although my practitioner did not have vials for all of the various medications I was prescribed during the in vitro procedure, I was told I could bring in the medication and could receive an NAET treatment for each one. All that was needed was for me to hold the medicine in my hand, the way I normally held the vials. The treatments were identical otherwise. In total, I received about 20 treatments of NAET targeted at increasing my fertility. At the end of my treatments, it was time to begin the stimulation phase of the process.

The stimulation cycle was similar to the previous one with one great exception; we decided to get started while I was still in school. This made the process simultaneously easier and far more difficult, if that makes any sense. Work was a great distraction and prevented me from focusing all of my energies on the process, but it was also a burden because of the morning blood monitoring/ultrasound stress. We decided not to tell anyone at first, but after the first few days of almost being late to school, I knew I had to come clean with my principal and my team members. My principal wondered why I did not wait until the end of the school year to put myself through this. Her response felt like a slap across the face. We had always been friends and she was asking me why I did not want to wait.

My retort was impulsive, cold, and direct, "If I were to have considered waiting, I would have never shared this private issue with you. My husband and I have been working on having a family for three years; we don't want to wait another minute to try to begin the process again."

She explained it was not that she was concerned about me possibly being late in the morning and needing 10 minutes of class coverage, but she knew me and thought the stress might put me over the edge.

I was so busted.

Of course she had a valid point, but my mind had been made up and besides, we had already started the treatments. I also told a few of my teaching team members and they were very understanding. Besides my sister, that was it. We decided that no one else needed to know. And once again, the cycle began. I knew I would be out for a few days due to the extraction and probably about a week to rest after the transfer, so I made up two weeks worth of substitute plans, just in case. I had never been out of school more than two days in a row before, so this made me feel selfish and guilty. Perhaps my principal had been correct; I should have waited until the summer again. But, I didn't, so it was too late.

The medication cycle was pretty much the same with a few different name brands here and there. Instead of Gonal F we used Follistim; instead of Pregnyl we used Novarel. Apparently, they all performed the same job, so the names mattered little. The blood tests were worse because the technicians at this clinic were not able to find my veins on any given morning. Each morning consisted of an inevitable parade of technicians appearing and disappearing and my arms were filled with the splotchy evidence of their attempts. But, whatever, I was honestly immune to it at this point, most of the time anyway.

The toughest part for us was making sure that we arrived first at the clinic each morning. The policy for this group was first come first served. If we were the first people in the office and the first to sign in, I was the first to have my blood drawn and to have an ultrasound scan. This was a lot of pressure. I knew I had to be first because otherwise, there was little chance I would arrive to my classroom on time each day. Although I did have people lined up to cover my room if such circumstances resulted, I did not want it to come to such a result each day. We would get up at 4:30 in the morning and were never in the car later than 5:30, just to be safe.

Most days, we were not only the first patients in the building, but we were the first people in the parking lot. After adding all of the time together, William and I spent hours sitting in our car waiting for any fertility clinic employee to show up and let us in to the office. There was no chance we would allow anyone to beat us as the first patient. Only once were we not first and that was due to an accident on the highway. By the time I was ready for the extraction procedure, I only needed five minutes of coverage in my classroom on one of the blood tests/ultrasound days.

After all of the stress of squeezing in daily blood tests and ultrasounds was over and it was finally time for the extraction, William and I were uneasy that it was going to be a repeat of the previous experience. As we waited in the waiting room before I was called in, we communicated by silent and frequent hand squeezes. By the time they called us in, we were more than ready.

Just like the first time, I was given an I.V. and the anesthesiologist had a very difficult time placing it. Since I had already experienced an egg extraction, I was a lot less anxious this time around for the procedure. The unknown outcome was a great source of stress, but the procedure was a walk in the park. Once again, the medicine was administered, and when I woke up, it was all over. After waiting about a half an hour, good news came that 11 eggs had been extracted, five of which looked very promising. My heart sunk to hear that I had gone from 19 eggs in the first round to only 11 this time. But, trying to focus on the positive, I reminded myself that with the 19, none of the eggs ended up with much promise. I would rather have 5 out of 11 eggs be of good quality than 0 out of 19. Who could ask for more than almost 50%? We went home and later received the phone call that four still looked good and that they would call us again with an update.

Four embryos were not five and that bothered me. Would we receive a phone call the next day telling us that only two looked good or that they were wrong and none did? I was nervous, but in addition to my wild nerves, I found myself in a great deal of discomfort. It was reminiscent of the first night after my first extraction, but more brutal. If I turned on my side I couldn't breathe at all and felt immense pain. Walking was a problem; just a trip to the bathroom was difficult. I found if I remained lying on my back, I did not feel much pain, so that is what I did. My stomach was puffy and I knew that I had once again suffered from OHSS. Only this time, it was much more severe. I had the brilliant idea that I could go back to work for one day before the transfer and I did, but it was difficult. At one point, a team member stopped into my room and reminded me that we had to pick the kids up from recess. During that walk around the building I honestly thought, "I might need an ambulance." Not to sound like a drama queen, but I seriously felt like I was going to keel over. To anyone considering the in vitro process, please take my advice and stay home throughout the entire process.

I somehow made it through the rest of the day, but barely. The drive home was excruciating and I cried in pain throughout the entire commute. When William called to check on me, I was still crying and told him that I felt horrible and that I feared something was terribly wrong. He promised to come home as soon as possible. Although he did, it did not alleviate my discomfort or fears. I felt progressively worse with each passing moment. William was confident that the doctors would have some great advice for me during the transfer, which was scheduled for the following morning.

When it was time to go in for the transfer the following morning, the walk from the parking garage to the doctor's office was exceedingly difficult for me. I felt really dizzy, out of breath, and just plain sick. Afraid to complain or discuss my physical issues, I planned to say nothing, but when the doctor looked at me and asked if I was okay, I replied "Not really." He started pressing different areas of my stomach and acknowledged that it was swollen, but did not think it looked too terrible or dangerous. He cited that there were visible signs of OHSS, but nothing life threatening, just like the first go round. He asked me whether or not I felt comfortable doing the transfer that day.

Of course I was doing the transfer; nothing was going to stop me. After all, I had taken the week off from school. Additionally, he told me that success was more likely if the transfer was done with fresh embryos. The alternative option was freezing the embryos; then thawing them out at a different time in the future. The problem, we were told, was that many embryos that were frozen did not survive the thawing process.

Our chances of success were greater if we transferred the embryos now, so obviously, we did the transfer. Three embryos, which were excellent quality embryos according to the staff, were transferred into my uterus. There were two other embryos that they decided to cryopreserve for our future family, although after hearing about the reduced chances of it working, I wondered if we should even bother. As with the first transfer, the procedure itself was not a big deal, but I still felt a great deal of discomfort. After the procedure, the nurse asked, "How do you feel?" And I replied honestly, "Awful." She countered my response and reminded me that I should feel great because my chances were wonderful. So of course, I was excited, but I dreaded the ride back home.

When I arrived back home, I walked up the stairs very slowly and began heading towards the bathroom when I suddenly could not breathe or take another step. The room started to spin and close in around me. I screamed William's name and he came to me in the hallway and I collapsed. Although terrified, William calmly carried me into the bedroom and I was somewhat cognizant. My heart beat wildly and my pulse raced uncontrollably. Clearly, there was something very wrong. My pain level was off the charts and now it was affecting my ability to stand, sit up, and walk at all. Once I was on my back on the bed and able to speak, William placed a frantic call to the fertility office.

Due to his insistence, William was eventually given the ear of the other doctor on staff at the fertility clinic. The very kind doctor (whom we had never met) gave William his cell phone number and was then instructed to call back in a few hours, if no change had occurred. The situation became progressively worse, so of course, the doctor received a follow-up phone call. It felt like there was a 50-pound weight on my chest, on my lungs, and every other major organ in my body. I couldn't move or turn in any direction at all; if I did, I couldn't breathe and coughed incessantly. I couldn't do anything without wincing in pain or feeling like my body would give out from under me. William tried to explain as best he could, and the doctor requested that I return to the office at 6 a.m. the following morning.

Waiting until the next morning meant we had the entire night to contend with. In the middle of the night, I had to go to the bathroom and William escorted me. I caught a glimpse of myself in the mirror and thought, "Oh my God, I look like I am about to die." My eyes were black and sunken; I had never looked so sickly than at that particular moment. My own reflection actually frightened me.

Since William was staring at me, he too was frightened. He checked on me every five minutes to make sure I was still breathing throughout the rest of the night. When it was 4:30 am, he carried me to the car, and slowly drove back to the fertility offices. I had ice packs all over my stomach to try to feel some relief from the pain. I moaned and cried the entire duration of the ride. When we arrived a little before 6 a.m., William left me in the car to run upstairs and inform the staff that I could not walk. As I sat in the car I wondered if my baby had any chance at all. I did not want to imagine that we once again experienced all of the ups and downs of fertility treatments without a resulting baby. It was just too cruel to envision.

My thought process was interrupted when William returned to the car. He was out of breath from running and felt terribly that he even had to leave me alone for a second. William picked up my hand, told me how much he loved me, and waited with me in the car for a nurse to come down with a wheel chair. We both cried during those moments, but the nurse arrived soon after with the wheel chair. Getting me to sit up in the wheel chair was an ordeal, but eventually, it happened. I continued to moan, not caring who heard me. Self-control was completely relinquished and without much awareness, I heard strange noises escaping my throat. Anyone unlucky enough to be in the waiting room witnessed a crazy version of me as the nurse guided me through the doctor's office.

Within seconds, the doctor came in to examine me, took one look at my face and whispered, "Oh God." Yes, he said, "Oh God." He used an ultrasound to examine my fluid level and concluded, "You have a dangerous amount of fluid trapped in your body. Because you are such a petite person, it didn't appear that way from the outside, but the ultrasound shows how severe your condition is. We have to drain you immediately, and I mean right now. Is that okay?"

I didn't care what the draining involved, although in the back of my mind I remembered something about a giant needle possibly being involved and somehow entering my stomach. It did not matter; I just wanted relief from the pain and anguish of the past 24 hours. The team immediately rolled me into the Operating Room (O.R.) and escorted William downstairs. They did not want him near the O.R. Although the reasons were never confirmed, I believe that the level of my screaming would have prompted him or any husband to break down the doors.

The procedure was absolutely, without question, one of the most painful experiences in my life. No drugs were permitted during the procedure because of the fragile status of the embryos. Since the embryos had only been implanted the previous day in my uterus, no one wanted to take any chances. Without any drug-induced assistance during the procedure, I felt everything. Instead of going through my stomach, this staff performed fluid drainage through my womanly parts. The draining procedure in this clinic involved a catheter with a needle attached. Does that paint a picture or what?

This staff used ultrasound technology to pinpoint, in their words, the most optimum place to poke me with the needle. Once the poke was deemed successful, they followed up with suction to basically vacuum the fluid out of my body. Every organ or region where the suction came into contact with me felt like intense stabbing, which just encouraged a lack of self-control where my emotions were concerned. This propelled me to continuously scream and cry. Somehow, I lost control of my entire sense of reality. I just let it all out.

Dr. Reginald had previously quoted me a statistic that severe and life-threatening OHSS only happened in two percent of all in-vitro cases. Naturally, I had somehow become a member of that percentage. The point is, since my case was such a rare one, the room was packed full of nurses, technicians, and doctors, all wanting a chance to witness the procedure. Oh yes, one of my better moments. As I screamed with each movement of the suction, the doctors told me I had to stop reacting because it might cause more damage. I don't know what else to say about that except, I am sorry for anyone who is in pain and prohibited from crying or screaming. It was beyond my description. I understood, but that might have been the most difficult issue of all. Then the doctor uttered, "We never have to do this, but we are going to have to insert the needle into another area to be able to suction out the fluid from the rest of your body."

Great, once again, I was the rare exception. Before going back in with the needle, the doctor reiterated a warning that I could not scream, cry, or flinch. One of the nurses grabbed my hand, looked me in the eyes and told me how sorry she was, and then told me to squeeze all of my anguish out on her hand. Perhaps this doesn't really work, but it was nice to have someone tell me that it was okay to be scared at that point, so in a weird way, it did work. Isn't it amazing how one gesture of kindness can turn you around in an instant? I have never forgotten that moment or that nurse.

I silently wished (some would say prayed) that the fragile embryos in my uterus would hang on. I promised them if any of them lived, this would be nothing more than a testament to their survival skills and all would be well. I pledged to work morning and night to be the best mother possible. When the procedure was finally over, it was reported that approximately 400 cc's of fluid were removed, which, in a small person like myself was quite impressive. Personally, I was unimpressed.

The issue that was the most concerning was that I was told I would feel immediate relief once the fluid had been drained. I didn't. I was in just as much pain after the procedure as I had been before the procedure began and this confused everyone on the medical team. For the umpteenth time I heard, "Everyone who has ever suffered from a severe case of OHSS always felt much better after the procedure." Hooray, I was the rare exception again. I wondered how many times that could happen to me in one day? Then the doctor reported, "Your pulse and heart rhythms are dangerously high and erratic. If they go much higher, you will go into cardiac arrest. I think we may have to send you to the hospital for additional tests. We are worried that it could be very serious and life threatening."

Life threatening is doctor speak for you could die. Now what? What do you do when a doctor tells you that he is worried your condition could put you in mortal danger? Ironically, for as serious as my condition might have been, my doctor barely came to check on me. Nurses guarded my bed the entire day, but I barely saw my doctor. The nurses would ask me a million questions, for which I had no answers, but no improvement was detected as the hours continued to pass. William remained vigilant at my bedside, and all I wanted to do was tell everyone that I was fine so they would leave me alone. I remained in the recovery room well into the evening when one of the doctors proposed that my heart rate and pulse rate problem might be from dehydration.

To confirm their suspicions, the doctors needed to draw blood to run some sort of test that would determine whether or not I was dehydrated. Once again, a blood draw was a complete and total nightmare. Eight attempts and three nurses later, someone was finally able to find a vein. The results from the test showed that the doctor's hypothesis was correct because I was severely dehydrated. Considering I had nothing to eat or drink for approximately two days, this should not have been such a surprise, but it took virtually all day for my doctor to figure out the reason behind my erratic pulse and heart rate. After the dreaded issues of finding a dehydrated vein for the blood test, they now had the issue of finding a vein in which to administer an I.V. This only took three different nurses and five attempts, which meant that they were getting better. Minutes after the I.V. was administered, my heart rate and pulse rate became stable. Perhaps it seems ironic that someone who had originally had a life-threatening amount of fluid in her body was in danger of cardiac arrest from dehydration. Regardless, with my issues resolved, the team of doctors and nurses finally let me go home.

Although I was still in discomfort for several weeks, I felt immensely better and well enough to go back to work. Because of my OHSS, the doctors decided I needed some sort of injection in my buttocks region a few times a week. Since William was not volunteering for that job, I asked our school nurse. I would enter her room after school, she would lock the door, and I would drop my pants. During a professional development day, when she was not required to be at school, she had me travel to her house to make sure I received the medication. When I needed an injection over the weekend, she actually came to my house to help us out. She is another person who constantly reminds me that people are inherently good. If a baby were to actually form, it truly would have taken a village just to bring him or her into the world.

As hope began to rise in my brain, the injections continued. After two extremely slow weeks went by, I went in for the pregnancy blood test before school. I felt quite confident that I was pregnant. Strange cramps and tingling sensations in my uterus convinced me that a baby was finally on board. Because I was so positive and impatient, I asked the fertility staff to call me at work with the results to prevent me from waiting until I got home for the news. What I had forgotten was that on the day of the blood test, I had a professional development day at another building. Although I was in school in the morning, the call was placed in the afternoon and I missed it. Luckily, one of our secretaries instructed me on how to check my voice mail from home, so I would not have to wait until the following day. As the boring professional development day dragged on at a snail's pace, I stared at the clock and the phone in the room with nervous anxiety and intense yearning to find out once and for all.

After I arrived home and played with the dogs outside for a half an hour (amazing self control, don't you think?), I dialed the number to connect to my voice mail. The message was a bit difficult to hear, but I will never forget the words uttered by the nurse. "Hi, I really hope you are getting this message because you are in fact pregnant.

Your numbers are fantastic and you will have to go in again next week to make sure they are going up correctly. But, I think you have every reason to be positive because the numbers are excellent. Once again, yes, you are pregnant, congratulations!"

I screamed and cried and thanked God or fate or anyone and anything that made my pregnancy possible a million times. I rubbed my belly gently and told the future boy or girl that I would do everything I could to make sure that he or she would be happy to have me as his or her mom. Although I wanted to tell William in person, he was late at work and I couldn't resist calling him. He was ecstatic. All of that worry and the near death experience were all for something because I was pregnant. Suddenly, it was all worth it, every last detail. Maybe there were even twins!

When I returned to work, I shared the news with the two teachers who knew about the process. They were thrilled to pieces for me, but other than that, it was just a normal week at work. It was normal, until a horrible storm came through destroying power lines and shutting down the town for two days. So, here I was pregnant, without power, and without water (we have well water) and I was not happy. It was very hot and humid and it made me worry that the conditions would endanger the baby. I didn't feel as much twisting and turning in my uterus and started to get concerned that the baby stopped growing, but then I would feel something again and feel better.

My next blood test appointment occurred the following week and I thought, okay, if my numbers were still good, this pregnancy would be okay. Since the clinic had orders to call me at school, I stayed late at school waiting to hear but no one called me. I called the doctor's office but the staff had already left, so I figured that they must have forgotten about me. Finally, I went home and looked at my answering machine, but again, there were no messages. Happily, I played with my dogs outside figuring that no news was certainly good news and prepared dinner for my husband.

When he walked in, I had a huge smile on my face. He looked stone faced, walked over to me and hugged me tightly and said that he was so sorry. I had no idea what he was talking about until he said, "The nurses called me at work and told me that your numbers did not increase."

Stunned, I asked, "You mean I am not pregnant any more?"

He said, "No, you are still pregnant, but you will be miscarrying, they think by the end of the week."

I sobbed and screamed and repeated the inevitable "Why?" and "How could this happen?" phrases. I tried to wrap my mind around all of the tests along the way, the needles, and the dangerous over hyper stimulation, all of it and for what? It was all for nothing, again. I was going to lose the baby, and there was nothing I could do to change the outcome. There was nothing to do but cry, so we both did for the rest of the evening until we could not cry any longer.

In my opinion, one of the worst parts about receiving devastating news is that the information gets repeated in those first few moments as you wake up in the morning. You open your eyes and initially, even if it is for a millisecond, think everything is fine, and then the bad news, whatever it may be, shoots through your head to remind you of a deep and enduring sadness. I felt my heart break all over again the next morning, and cried before I even stepped onto the floor.

Although I debated whether or not to go back to work that day, I realized that staying home would make me focus on the inevitable miscarriage, so I went. The first thing I knew I had to do was inform the two teachers who had known I was pregnant that I wasn't. When I told them they exchanged nervous glances with one other and asked if I wanted to go home. I said, no, it would be better for me to have the kids as a distraction, and off I went. It had been selfish of me to put my team members in such a sensitive situation. I cursed myself for sharing the news with anyone. What was I thinking? It was necessary to let them know about the procedure, but why did I have to tell them I was pregnant? Twelve weeks is the magic number, everyone knows that, you're not supposed to tell anyone until you are at least 12 weeks along.

However, 12 weeks was not in the realm of possibility for my pregnancy, and I had a doctor's appointment scheduled the next day to remind me of that very fact. My hCG levels did not drop, and this confused the staff completely. They decided to give me an ultrasound to see if something was there. When I heard that an ultrasound was needed, hope rose in the back of my mind. Perhaps the results had been inaccurate, we would see the baby forming, and we could call it a blessing or a miracle. As I quietly fantasized and wished for the impossible, William and I waited for the doctor to enter the examination room. With one image on the screen, my hopes were short lived as no image was detected. Following the scan, I was instructed to keep coming in every day to have my levels checked.

After what seemed to be my millionth blood test, it was found that the miscarriage was not happening naturally as the doctors had hoped. This meant that after two weeks of daily doctor's visits and blood tests to determine whether my hCG levels were going down, which they clearly were not, additional intervention would be necessary. I was asked to return to the office to allow a nurse to administer a shot of methotrexate. This was a drug that is used in cancer patients, but also a drug that would bring on a miscarriage. As if an injection could be less welcome, we found out that it was one that would be given in the buttocks region.

William and I shared tears and embraces while waiting for the nurse to come in with the injection. I could not believe that I would be accepting a drug to help rid me of a pregnancy after going through so much to achieve a pregnancy. It seemed so very wrong, but the doctors told me it was necessary, especially if I ever wanted the chance to carry another child. As always, we did as instructed and followed our doctor's advice. In addition to the emotional pain, the shot really hurt going in, and my butt was sore for about three days following.

Eventually, the physical pain subsided and after another three weeks of blood tests, my pregnancy levels were back to zero. The only good news in this was that a level of zero meant my doctor's visits were no longer necessary. It was time to try to move on with our lives.

Moving on is extremely difficult when the universe sends you reminders of what you cannot have. While I was still reeling from the miscarriage, my best friend Julia called me to tell me she was pregnant with her third child. It was terribly difficult for her to tell me and my heart hurt for the anguish I could hear in her voice as she broke the news. I loved her and was thrilled for her, but yes, it was an experience I wished I could share with her. Another friend unexpectedly became pregnant with her third child and cried to me because she didn't want a third child at that time in her life. I will admit that her confession stung a lot. A few months later both Julia's sister and brother's wife announced they were expecting babies. Besides my best friend, a staff member announced she was going to have a baby in December. Since I was in charge of the social committee at school, I was going to have to throw her baby shower.

The point is, when you cannot have children, every person around you seems to get pregnant. After a while, it stops feeling like a personal vendetta and more like a fact of life, but at first, the vendetta seems real. You initially feel happy for everyone with the life changing and wonderful news, but then you become absorbed in your own loss and focus on the fact that everyone else can have what you cannot. I don't have advice for these feelings because I honestly think they are quite natural. Staring at my friends' expanding tummies was extremely torturous for me at times. The truth is, once the babies are born to your friends and you meet them, it is different. You truly feel bliss for them and your personal sadness subsides and is replaced with joy for their joy. I am not saying you never feel sorry for yourself, but it does get easier over time, just like everything else.

What did not get easier with time were the questions from everyone around me. Eventually, I reiterated the second in vitro story to my parents and once again, my mother cried and cried. People urged me to go through another cycle since I actually had been able to get pregnant, but after the life-threatening situation brought on by my reaction to the fertility drugs; William and I decided that we were done with in vitro fertilization. No one could understand how we could give up. Again, everyone who had never gone through anything remotely close to the in vitro process gave me unsolicited advice.

Some friends told me I should wait a few years because science was always coming up with wonderful advancements. In a few years there would probably be alternative drugs and procedures that might be perfect for me, according to all those "self-styled experts." My sister and mother both offered to carry a baby for my husband and me. I did consider both offers initially, although my mother's doctor advised her against it. My sister persisted and often joked that her uterus was for rent. Although selfless and wonderful, I turned her down. My firsthand experience with in vitro fertilization prevented me from accepting her offer. I could not allow my sister to put her body through such an invasive procedure for my benefit.

Of course, many others advised me to adopt.

ADOPTION REQUIREMENTS

THE TRUTH WAS, as soon as the miscarriage had been detected, William and I had immediately resumed our research of adoption options. We decided to keep the decision private, at least initially. After being too open with our situation and fielding too many pieces of unwanted advice, we knew whatever decision we made would have to remain between the two of us.

Although we had settled on private domestic adoption, we knew little about the overall process. Eventually, we stumbled on a private agency on the other side of the state that specialized in private international and domestic adoption. After contacting them for additional information, one of the ladies who worked there called me and explained that they gave monthly informational sessions to interested adoptive hopefuls. We were unable to attend the evening it was offered, so she invited us down a different evening for a private informational session.

The woman's name was Katya Perry. Katya asked us about how we came to pursue adoption and once again, we relayed our fertility struggles out loud. She asked us if we were certain that we were done trying to conceive a child on our own and we assured her, absolutely, yes. She let us know that she had to ask us because a lot of women seek adoption immediately after a miscarriage, but a few months later, realize they want to try again. We assured her we had no intentions of ever going through the in vitro process in our lifetime.

With our assurance, she asked us what type of baby we wanted. We looked at each other wondering who would be equipped to answer that question without feeling like self-absorbed jerks. It seemed like a supermarket question to me. Okay, you are going to buy a chicken, would you like dark meat or white meat? Would you prefer original Oreos or Double Stuff? It was a very uncomfortable question and answer session. We were asked if we would accept a child with severe handicaps and special needs. Would we accept a child whose paternity was unknown because the mother had multiple sex partners and was unsure of the child's biological father? Might we consider twins, or six year olds, or crack babies? Did we want to go overseas to China, Russia, or Korea? Katya advised against international adoption for many of the reasons that had made me lean towards domestic adoption in my earlier searches, so by the end of our session, Katya, William and I were in complete agreement with the adoptive terms we hoped for.

On and on the questions droned. What we wanted is what every parent initially hopes for, a healthy child. Although she cheered us on, Katya let us know that healthy was a very tall order. Regardless, it had happened several times in the past few years with her guidance. From one extreme to the other she went as her next statement was, "If you are approved by your state for adoption, you could get a call in a day, three months, three years, or never." Never, unfortunately, was a distinct possibility for hopeful (private) adoptive parents. The reason for this is because birth parents actually have to choose you. Since no one is obligated to ever choose you, even if you have been waiting longer than any other couple, signing up with a private adoption agency offered no guarantees. In addition, we were reminded that healthy parents usually do not give up their babies for adoption, which made our hopes and dreams seem next to impossible.

As difficult as the experience may sound, it felt like a walk in the park compared to the in vitro process. Although the meeting was a bit of a wake up call and definitely gave us trepidations, we recognized that adoption was our only remaining option. All of my previous research was surrendered as adoption facts were dispensed upon us. There was one other adoption agency closer to our house, so we decided to attend one of their informational sessions. We heard virtually the same information as we had with the first agency and decided to pick one of the two. There were not many other private agencies in our state, and we really liked the first agency, which made the decision easy. Of course, there was the matter of financing. Although I had found financial statistics on the web in my earlier searches, the cost varies from state to state in accordance with the adoption laws. According to Katya, adoption was minimally $25,000. When put into those terms, it felt a little like buying a baby because, let's face it, no matter how you analyze it, that is what you end up doing. No private adoption agency is going to just hand you over a child because you might make a good parent. That is not how it works.

Although private adoption agencies will not hand you a child without a great deal of money, state departments are more forgiving in that respect. State adoptions are not costly like private adoptions, but you have little input in a state adoption. According to the social workers I spoke with from the Department of Children and Family Services, our hopes for a child were ridiculous. I was told that I would most likely have to forego a desire of an infant and forego the desire for a mentally and/or physically healthy child if I pursued public adoption. The exact comments were, "Healthy, happy kids do not need to be publicly adopted by the state. You are thinking about beautiful, sweet children in movies that fall into that category. Children who land in the system do so because their parents were abusive. The children in the system need rescuing and therapy. Anyone pursuing public adoption must have the deep-seated desire to rescue and rehabilitate."

Perhaps I did not want to rescue and rehabilitate a mentally challenged child because I often did a bit of that as a teacher. Perhaps it was because I did not want to knowingly take on such a role, period. William and I wanted to raise a healthy child and try to work hard to ensure that he or she was happy. Was that truly selfish? Many people seemed to think it was according to books, Internet, and magazine articles. I recognized that my desires were selfish, but what can I say? It was not my first selfish moment in life nor would it be my last.

Selfish or not, William and I, like so many others, felt most qualified to raise a healthy child. Our dreams had been broken by biology already. If adoption was our only choice, there was no doubt that a private and domestic option was the correct path for us. The dream of someone magically selecting William and me to parent her child danced around my head once again. This decision meant, of course, that we needed to be prepared to break into our very modest savings account immediately. Private adoption agencies require a down payment, like when purchasing a car. I wish I could describe the process in a different and more romantic or ethical way, but that is the reality. Although the agencies tell you the $5000 fee is used to pay for the home study, I have my doubts.

The home study process is not really all that horrible, but it is taxing on one's patience. The state requires knowledge about your medical, financial, and mental state, and the requirements are extraordinary. We both had to receive meticulous physicals, including blood work, followed by a formal written evaluation by our doctors.

In one of the informational sessions, we were told that if there were any history of anti-depressant usage or therapy, we would likely be considered as ineligible adoptive parents. The state demanded all tax documents, copies of our mortgage agreement; a certified copy of a deed on the house, and on and on the list of requirements went. We also were required to have our fingerprints monitored by the state and federal government. I had already been fingerprinted multiple times as it is a teaching prerequisite, but my fingerprints on record were not adequate for this process and I had to repeat the process. I could not help wondering why hopeful adoptive parents had to take all these steps when normal people with normal reproductive systems could parent without any prerequisites.

In addition to all of the formal requirements, we were expected to scribe our autobiographies. This was an egotistical and daunting process. Obviously, we were expected to state how wonderful we were in every facet of life. What parts of a life are worthy of being written about? That was the challenge for William and me in the weeks we spent writing and rewriting our life stories. Would anyone out there be remotely interested in anything about either one of us? What if birthparents viewed our lives as boring or unimpressive?

Beyond our personal written work, we needed to procure five different letters of reference. Of the five letters, only two were permitted to be from family members. Selecting references was a very difficult decision for us because who do you choose to write a letter on your behalf for such an event? We were also not permitted to view the letters that our five references wrote. I have no explanation for that rule. In the end, we chose the people who we hoped understood our history the most. Our friends were wonderful and all wrote the letters immediately, but it was intimidating nonetheless.

Hands down, the single most menacing part of the process was the physical home visits by the social workers from the adoptive agency. What if they did not approve of our home? Perhaps they would not find it large enough. Maybe a visitor would not like the fact that we basically lived in the woods. Would a person actually open our cabinets and search the contents we purchased? The answer to that question is no, but we were nervous. Overall, the process may not sound like a huge undertaking, but it really is and it quickly became a frustrating process. Mind you, I completely understand why it is necessary, but that does not undermine the irritation. Each required hurdle inevitably delayed our even being considered for parenthood. What if the perfect child for our family was being born while we were filling out paperwork? That was a recurring nightmare for me.

Eventually, the interviews, the home visit, the autobiographies, the paperwork, and all the required educational classes were completed. Oh, did I not mention the classes? William and I had to attend many hours of parenting classes. The classes were about an hour away from our home and required travel during rush hour to get there. The commute to the classes was just one more piece of stress on an already giant pile. We met other adoptive hopefuls in these classes and we couldn't help but think, hmmm, that is our competition. I am certain they were thinking the exact same thoughts, though no one in the room verbalized it.

In one of the classes we attended, a social worker named Trudy explained that she was not only a social worker, but also an adoptive parent herself. This meant that she had already endured all of the steps that we were subjected to on our adoption paths. She shared with us the worst possible scenario, one that she endured. Trudy, who ended up being our assigned social worker, was selected to adopt a beautiful child and brought the child home. After falling in love with the child, the birth parents came back and decided that they wanted to parent the child after all. This was a familiar story to me via the Internet, but hearing it firsthand made it all the more terrifying. Trudy lamented, "No one thinks that it will happen to them. You try to warn yourself not to fall in love with the child in your care, but it is impossible to protect your heart for more than 30 seconds."

That scenario was my worst nightmare. I am certain it was everyone's worst nightmare in the room. To overcome all the obstacles and to take possession of the child, only to have the child ripped away from you was unthinkable. I wondered how birth parents could do that to other people. In my mind, anyone who decided to put her child up for adoption should automatically forfeit parental rights. If you even have a thought that you are not capable of parenting; I imagine that you are truly not the best person for the job. Perhaps that is a harsh outlook, but I had very little sympathy for someone who was blessed with biology when I had been cursed.

Unfortunately, the laws do not support this mentality. In fact, the laws are very biased towards the biological parents. In the state of Connecticut, biological parents are afforded heaps of time to change their mind about their parenting role. Such a stance basically takes the hopes and dreams of adoptive parents and throws them in the garbage, but apparently, in the society in which we all live, that is acceptable. Public adoption was worse than private in this regard because children in the system were placed there for extreme reasons.

As the DCF social worker had explained, children were available for adoption via the public only if they were neglected or abused and eventually removed from their birth parents' home. That meant that birth parents took on the job of parenting and failed miserably in a shocking and horrific manner. Instead of mental and physical abuse preventing such people from ever parenting again, in most cases, from what we were told, they were afforded multiple chances to remain in their children's lives and to eventually return to their role as their parents. At least if biological parents in a private adoption situation changed their mind, one might not worry about abuse being a factor. Regardless, the rights of the birth parents seemed wrong to adoptive hopefuls. When one couple expressed this opinion and everyone in the room nodded in agreement, the social workers told us that it was a law that was impossible to change. I wondered about that. Once again, we had to jump through hoops to be approved for adoption, but what did these biological parents have to do?

After the classes, home visits, interviews, and required paperwork were completed, William and I were finally approved for adoption. But, even though we were approved, there was one additional step. We had to create an adoption portfolio. This portfolio, we were told, was everything. Birth parents used the portfolios like a catalogue of potential adoptive parents for their baby. If our portfolio was unappealing and did not catch the eye of a birth parent, then we would not get chosen as parents. My perfectionist tendencies engaged and propelled me forward.

The portfolio design was a lot of pressure. I traveled to several different craft stores in an attempt to find beautiful background paper. I wanted the background paper to somehow be a symbolic representation of William and me. The background paper was one detail that was probably considered insignificant to most; it was the pictures that carried the most weight. I searched through my house for the perfect photographs. Unfortunately for us, the photographs were a major problem because both of us were mediocre photographers. We are more often the type to soak in a moment than take a snapshot of one, so suddenly our lifestyle was an obstacle to overcome.

We began to take our cameras everywhere, and even then, we often did not find an opportunity to snap a picture, but oh did we try! After securing enough pictures, I purchased a tool to cut pictures into fun shapes and a special glue stick to make everything just right. I did not stop there. What could be more powerful than pictures? Captions, I realized, could really communicate our voices to strangers. I chose words as carefully as I could and typed captions in a variety of fonts. The different fonts were printed out and spread on a table to ensure that I selected the perfect accents for each snapshot. After weeks of taking this picture out, putting this picture in, moving this caption to that side, and rearranging our portfolio 500 myriad ways, we finally completed the task.

Now that one copy was done, the agency required five copies, which turned into a hassle. William took our very carefully crafted portfolio to Kinkos and asked for five colored copies. At first, we were going to have Kinkos bind the portfolios as well as copy them because they told us it would cost about $180 and we figured it was a worthwhile investment. However, Kinkos called William a few days later and told him they misquoted him their price and it would actually cost $550. Considering we would be spending all of our money on the actual adoption process, we knew we could find an alternative way to get this done, so he cancelled the binding order and stuck with straight colored copies instead.

When he picked up the colored copies, he noticed that the quality was substandard; it looked as if they were low on toner, but he had to get back to work and did not say anything. When I saw the copies, I was disappointed at how poor the quality was because this was for a very important, life-changing event. The pictures were all washed out and the captions were unreadable. We needed to bring in our "A" game and Kinkos was presenting us with our "H" game. The copies went back to Kinkos, William appealed to the manager's conscience, and they redid the colored copies. We are not the type of people to bring anything back under normal circumstances, but this was our future. At the end, William and I had five good quality copies of our portfolio. After searching for a binding method (thank you Staples for a great selection), we were all set. And then, we waited.

The waiting was torture. I had heard stories about how difficult the waiting process could be but you cannot truly appreciate it unless you are in the thick of it. Every time the phone rang, I thought, is that about our future child? A blinking answering machine instilled ridiculous amounts of hope, followed quickly by disappointment. Months passed by and we still found ourselves waiting. This was around the time the movie *Juno* came out. I constantly pictured someone like Ellen Paige looking at my pictures and deciding whether or not she would pass over my pictures because I was not edgy enough or pretty enough, or into swimming or whatever. Should I learn some new skills and take up new hobbies to attract a birth mother towards my portfolio? I questioned this every day. As all this was going on, something astonishing happened, I missed my period.

I'M WHAT?

I HAD BEEN regular since all of the in vitro procedures had ended, but I really did not consider that I might actually be pregnant. Well, I should not say that; I immediately thought it was a possibility, and then scolded my brain for its optimism. I went to my calendar and counted the days that had passed since my last menstrual cycle. Sure enough, I was a few days late and had no symptoms of an impending period. Since we had an old pregnancy test in the closet from our trying days, I dug it out, took it, and waited.

After the three-minute time period passed, I looked at the test and saw one line, which meant not pregnant. Oh gee, I thought, how could I let myself get such an idea? But then I noticed that there was a very faint second line. This particular pregnancy test would either present a minus sign or a plus sign, and I really thought that I might be looking at a plus sign. So, I skimmed the instructions and sure enough, it told me that even if the second line was faint, I was probably pregnant. I still didn't believe it, but I had something I had thought I had lost: hope.

A few days later, and still without a period, the hope increased. I decided it was time to purchase a second pregnancy test. I was on my way to meet my friend to help her with wedding details, so I decided to stop at a grocery store near her to purchase the test. Since she did not live in my hometown, the town I taught in, I did not think I would have the issue of running into any of my students while buying a pregnancy test. I literally walked into the store and I heard, "Mrs. Porter!" One of my former students was shopping with her mother. I could not believe it. I walked slowly and carefully around the store to see if they were leaving, but it looked like it would be a while. I thought, well, maybe I could sneak the purchase, so I went over to the aisle where the pregnancy tests were located. Someone was having fun with me that day, because I walked over there and an employee was busy pricing the tests. Maybe it is my own thought process, but I think buying a pregnancy test is a very personal product to purchase. I did not want to make my selection with a stranger's pair of eyes on me. I decided to leave the store and find another destination to make my purchase.

Luckily, in my friend's city, there are pharmacies everywhere, and there was one right across the street from the grocery store. Hesitant this time, I tentatively walked in and looked around carefully. The store was virtually empty. Eventually, after wandering around searching for the correct aisle, I located the pregnancy tests and started reading the boxes, all the while feeling tense and as if all eyes were on me. Of course no one was concerned with my shopping habits, but that didn't stop my paranoia. Did you know that there are pregnancy tests that actually display the word, "pregnant" or the words "not pregnant?" There are kits that display plus signs and others resulting in one or two lines. Some tests claim to be accurate days before a missed period and some make very few claims at all.

After quickly skimming the prices and the features of sticks that would ultimately simultaneously interpret my urine and future, I finally made my selection and went over to the register. There was no one there. Feeling my face turn red, I began willing a clerk to come to the register and rescue me. I am not one to make a big stink over waiting in line, and the fact that I had a pregnancy test kit in my hand made me even less inclined to flag someone over. After a five minute wait that seemed like an eternity, a man walked over and asked me if I was being helped.

Off topic, but I always laugh when someone clearly sees you are not being helped at all and inquires as to whether or not you are in fact being helped. Clearly, I wasn't which made me smile and respond, "Not yet." He then asked me why I had not tracked someone down to ring me up. Sure, that is what a rational person would have done, but even so, is it my job to track clerks down? If that was an understood practice, then shouldn't there have been some sort of bell I could ring to capture someone's attention? All of these questions were bubbling in my head, but my nervous mouth just said, "I don't know, but I haven't been waiting long." Feel free to criticize and judge me harshly for that one.

I ran out of the store and threw the fortune-telling bag in my trunk, in case my friend and I used my car to run the wedding errands. I covered the bag with my earth friendly tote bags from the local grocery stores and went to meet her. Every three minutes or so, I wondered if I was in fact with child. I tried not to obsess, but old habits die hard. When we looked at her dress I thought, oh, she is the most beautiful bride and then I immediately thought, will I be pregnant at her wedding? Our day together was a test of stamina. But strangely enough, when I arrived back home that evening; I did not take the test. Even stranger, I did not take the test the day after that, or even the day after that. I loved the hope that I felt and I was afraid of having to let go of it, but after the third day, I could not bear to wait any longer and tested myself in the middle of the night.

There was no mistaking the positive results this time. The plus sign appeared almost immediately and I just smiled and silently screamed (so as not to wake my husband) and wrapped it up and threw it in the garbage. I did not want to tell William, not until I went to the doctor. The thought of disappointing him again was too much for me to bear, but the oddest thing happened. He had awakened when I had made my trip to the bathroom. I am hardly exaggerating when I say that he never does that. I get up in the middle of the night all the time and he never stirs, never. He asked me if I was okay and I knew I had to tell him, so after stammering and trying to think of something clever to say, I just blurted out that I was in fact pregnant. His response shocked me because he screamed, "I knew it!" Don't ask me how he knew it, but he did and then he joyously added, "Something I did worked!" Up to that point in my life, that had been the best moment ever.

William was elated, but also reserved. We both knew I needed to see a doctor to find out if all was okay, so we practiced cautious optimism. Of course, I can claim that we practiced caution, but in reality, I was filled up inside with joy. I knew that the good Lord would never have presented me with the miracle of a natural pregnancy after all this time just to torture me to take away this new life growing inside of me. This of course meant that I began to plan. I did the math and figured out that my baby was due in March. I thought about what it would be like to teach while my body changed and grew. I thought about the delivery, epidurals, contractions, and even names. Long term planning is my specialty, but of course I thought in terms of the short term and feared morning sickness, holding the information in for three months, and getting through an impending visit by my parents only a few weeks away.

Yes, that's right, my parents were planning a trip to visit me and stay with me for five long days. I knew I had to see the doctor before I saw them, so the Monday following the second positive pregnancy test, I called the doctor's office to make an appointment. The message given to me was that there was no need to rush over to see them, which is why they scheduled an appointment for me two weeks later. Yes, two weeks. I couldn't believe it. Every pregnancy test on the market advises to call a physician right away if there is a positive result. I did, but my doctors were not interested in even looking at me for two whole weeks. When William called me later in the day to check up on me, I reported the appointment status.

He was as anxious as I and decided to call the doctor's office to see if I could get in sooner. That is the beauty of having a husband like William. He is willing to make those phone calls and ready to beg when I do not have the stamina or courage to do so, which is most of the time. I know, it is a terrible personality flaw, and it is one I am working on improving. William phoned the office and spoke with a nurse, explaining our fertility-challenged history and our anxiety. Luckily, the nurse understood and fit me in a few days later.

A few days might as well have been a few years. No one tells you how very tough the waiting is, so please allow me. Each day of pregnancy feels like a month when you are anxious about getting to that magical 12th week. I would literally count the days left on the 12-week countdown multiple times a day, and this started before my very first doctor's appointment. When I went in to see my doctor, Dr. Simpson, who is a lovely man by the way, if I haven't mentioned it, he walked in and asked, "Well, how did this happen?"

He was thrilled to pieces that I was finally pregnant, and without any assistance. What a miracle! He examined me and immediately afterward called my husband and me into his office. After congratulating William, he told us was that we needed to rely on a different doctor within the practice throughout the pregnancy because he did not deliver babies any longer. I was surprised to hear this news, but okay with anything. Seriously, someone could have told me that I would have to deliver my baby on live television and I wouldn't have cared. So, he asked me if I knew any of the other doctors in the practice. I really didn't, but I had encountered one of them after my miscarriage and liked him, which was enough to make him my new doctor. Dr. Simpson escorted us over to the new doctor's office, that of Dr. Robinson. Dr. Simpson kissed me on the cheek and left me with Dr. Robinson.

I found myself relaying all of my fears and anxieties to Dr. Robinson. He said the first big hurdle is to get to six weeks, where he could visually detect a heartbeat on the ultrasound, and then the next big hurdle was to get to eight weeks. At eight weeks, he should be able to hear a heartbeat. This of course made me obsessed with the eight-week mark. Each time I saw my body, I studied it to detect changes. Changes began earlier than I anticipated in my breasts. They looked different around the nipple area. I stared at them every time I showered and smiled because their different appearance reminded me that I was pregnant.

In the mean time, I had to attend my friend's wedding out of town. The last thing I wanted to do was sit in a car for five plus hours with my new need to run to the bathroom every five minutes due to the world's smallest bladder, but of course I would not miss her day for the world. Which brings me to the "just get past that event" phase of the pregnancy. Every event during my pregnancy was about getting through an event without spilling the beans or throwing up. The very first event was my friend's wedding.

It's amazing how much of a problem it is to be secretly pregnant when one does not remain in one's own home. The bed and breakfast we stayed in boasted a hot tub (off limits), wine (off limits), coffee (off limits), and omelets made with soft cheese (again, off limits). Now, if I had already bypassed the first three months of pregnancy, I could explain, "No, I am pregnant, so I can't use that, eat that or drink that." However, being secretly pregnant prevents any explanation, which probably translates into rude refusals with seemingly no reason to those people offering you those off limit items.

Although I was ridiculously tired, I could not sleep in this strange place. This left me exhausted, nauseous, and still, secretly pregnant. A triple threat of a bad destination wedding experience loomed over my head. My biggest goal was to not leave during the ceremony to go to the lavatory or to throw up, which is a small, but meaningful goal for a secretly pregnant gal. The ceremony started late, as they all do, but luckily, I was stable. There was a small need to use the lavatory but not much of a need to throw up. Everyone at my table kept asking me why I wasn't having anything to drink and, I really do not enjoy alcohol in any circumstance, so I simply stated the fact that I don't like alcohol. The first course arrived, and it happened to be a salad with feta cheese. William laughed and whispered, "You can't eat that, so I'll eat yours too." And so it went. All in all, it was a lovely wedding, but I wanted to go home and hide in my house until I surpassed the 12th week of pregnancy.

William likes to say, "Murphy lives on our street." It is a spin on the, everything that can go wrong will go wrong, Murphy's Law. Since Murphy is a famous and constant pest in our existence, there was no hiding in the house for the next eight weeks. Anybody and everybody wanted to see me. Every time I met anyone, I felt like I was going to throw up the whole time. Every food and every smell turned my stomach, especially, for whatever reason, peanuts. Even the sight of peanuts on television made my stomach lurch. I kept checking the calendar to see if I was close to 12 weeks, but I wasn't.

Twelve weeks no, six weeks, yes. I reached my first ultra sound appointment. It was unbelievably nerve wracking to wonder whether or not we would get to see a heartbeat on the monitor. When I saw the flicker on the screen, I knew everything was going to be okay. It was amazing, and we even received a picture of the baby, who was apparently as big as a grain of rice. It was the most beautiful grain of rice I had ever seen, but we could not enjoy the moment long as my parents were arriving in two days time. Dr. Robinson exclaimed that William and I had created a beautiful and perfect baby. He handed us the ultrasound pictures and told us to post it for all to see. Since my parents were on their way, in reality, we had to hide the ultrasound pictures in a secure location.

We returned to the house and warned each other not to tell either my mother or father by accident or on purpose that we would be having a baby. We knew it would be difficult, but we also knew it was necessary to keep the news a secret based on past events. When my parents arrived, I wanted them to leave my house immediately. Luckily, I was not showing at all, so there were no physical signs of a pregnancy. Well, physical in one sense. Physically, I felt the most ill when my parents were visiting. Whether or not it was stress induced or a terrible coincidence, I couldn't say, but it was rough.

My father wanted to go to New York City and harped on this fact throughout his stay. The week my parents were visiting me was hot. It was 90 degrees and 80% humidity. My dad did not want to see a show, he wanted to walk along the streets and eat at Katz's Deli. Obviously, I did not even think I could handle a train ride or a car ride, never mind walking around in the debilitating heat. I used the heat as an excuse not to go because my entire family knows how much I dislike hot weather. It worked, but naturally, they still needed to be entertained. We took them out to restaurants, movies, even a comedy show at the local theater. Every moment was a test of stamina for both William and me, but we made it.

The following week, I had my eight-week appointment to hear the baby's heart beat. The ride to the doctor's office was riddled with anxiety. I was nervous that there would not be a heartbeat and tried to prepare myself for potential bad news. For whatever reason, all of the doctors at the practice I attend run late, and this day held no exceptions. Each minute felt like a lifetime, but eventually, I was called in for my appointment. Although I was kept waiting, Dr. Robinson had zero intentions of keeping everyone else waiting and rushed through my appointment. He pulled out a Doppler wand and placed it on my stomach.

Within seconds, he found the baby's heartbeat. My own heartbeat was skipping several beats as I listened in on the greatest miracle that ever appeared in my own life. The baby's heartbeat was quick and difficult for me to hear, but it was there and the doctor said it was strong. Dr. Robinson stayed with me for about two additional seconds, asked me if I had any questions, but was halfway out the door when asking me that question. He told me on his way out that he was going to schedule (when it was time) a really cool ultrasound where I could see a 3-D image of the baby and make sure that the baby did not have Down Syndrome or anything else that was too difficult to think about. I went to the receptionist and she informed me that my next appointment would be at 12 weeks. I couldn't believe it. I asked her if she was sure that it was okay to wait a month between visits and she laughed and responded that of course it was okay.

My next appointment would be held at 12 weeks, but in the meantime, I had to prepare myself for a math certification test I had decided to take in order to become highly qualified to teach middle school mathematics. It was coming up in a week. The test was in Bridgeport, CT. It was 87 degrees and there was no air conditioning in the testing room or in any room in the school. There was a fan, but I was not permitted to sit next to it as the proctor arranged us by testing subjects. I was the second row away from the window. This meant, no breeze (there was no breeze to be felt that day anyway), hot sun, and no fan for 2 ½ hours.

I was nervous that I would have to go to the bathroom or throw up or something, but there was nothing I could do. William decided to enter the classroom and spoke quietly with the proctor. I begged him not to because I could speak for myself but he did not trust me to speak up. So, with my face turning red and remaining in the hallway, he explained to the proctor that his wife was two months pregnant and nervous that she would have to go to the bathroom. She let him know that I was allowed to leave for the bathroom, but I could not make the time up that I lost. She also let him know that the bathroom was a distance away from the room.

Of course it was.

Miraculously, as nauseous as I felt, and as enhanced as my nausea was by the extreme heat and humidity, I made it through the test without incident and felt as though I passed. The best moment to be had was when I was leaving the room and the proctor winked at me and said, "Congratulations." She was the first person outside the doctors' office to know anything about my pregnancy. It felt really wonderful to let someone else in on our secret. I could not wait until I could share the news with the world, just a few weeks and it would be time!

After the math test, I had only one hurdle left before my long time summer commitments were over, and that was my book club. Every few months, my book club met to discuss books that I would honestly never pick out on my own. I considered not going, but knew that would be wrong. Besides, I needed all the distractions available to get me through the final four nerve-wracking weeks of the first trimester. The book that I had to read this time was called *Loving Frank*, and it was brutal. Here I was trying to think positively, and the book was not helping me out in that department. Many of my book club members found the book enjoyable; I happened to find it extremely boring, frustrating, and in some parts, revolting. I made myself read it as my stomach churned and disagreed with my pastime. Clearly, the baby did not enjoy it either, but I managed to read it in time for our meeting.

Our book club outings usually begin with an early dinner at a local restaurant, which, feeling as sick as I felt, provided food that was nearly impossible to choke down. I was caught wearing my sea bands and had to lie and tell everyone that my homeopathic doctor recommended that I wear them when eating. The truth is, I possessed the sea bands long before I was pregnant as my digestive system was never quite sound, so this was not a complete lie. Regardless, the meals around me made my stomach heave and I wanted to go home and climb into bed. Instead, I smiled and nodded and counted down each moment that passed as a victory.

When the club moved to the hostess's home, my pregnancy enemy, the peanut, was out in many bowls. The people around me were munching on them and the smell nearly put me over the edge. I kept running to the bathroom, patting my now very slightly swollen belly and telling the baby everything was okay, it was just a few hours and then that was that. When the evening was over and I returned home, a weight lifted off of me, as I knew the rest of the trimester was commitment free. I would pamper my body and my baby for the rest of the summer.

As it turned out, I woke up on Monday and felt terrific, really great. The nausea was gone and my breasts didn't even hurt anymore. At first, I was ecstatic; but my glee was immediately replaced with panic. I had read a thousand websites that warned of a lack of symptoms as a sign of an impending miscarriage. I prayed and willed my uterus or baby or any womanly part to move around to let me know that everything was okay, but I didn't really feel anything for two days. I shared my concerns with William and he airily brushed them off to my face, but called the doctor without telling me. The home phone rang the next day and a kind nurse was on the other end of the phone who called at William's insistence.

I had planned on waiting until my 12th week appointment to find out if all was okay. It was only a week away, but William knew me well enough to know that the stress might kill me before then. I explained the sudden lack of symptoms and the nurse laughed and reassured me that it was extremely common for the symptoms to disappear, especially for someone who was past ten weeks. Funny enough, right before she called I had started to feel some movement in my uterine area and had felt encouraged, but I asked her if I could come in and have the heartbeat checked, just to be sure.

I honestly am unsure of how I got the doctor's office. I know I drove myself there, but I can't remember feeling anything. Fear is a strange phenomenon that way; it moves you forward without your knowledge. I waited in the doctor's office and was surrounded by pregnant woman. Yes, I was pregnant too, but these women were quite far along. I looked at one and thought, "I will never know what that is like." Then I reminded myself that everything would be fine because fate could not be this cruel. Soon afterwards, my name was called. After I was hustled in to an examination room, I waited for the doctor for twenty minutes.

I was seeing a doctor I had never met before. The two doctors I actually knew and loved in that office were both on vacation. Yes, Murphy strikes again. Regardless, when the new doctor finally came in, I relayed my concerns and she nodded in complete understanding, or maybe she just nodded, I am not sure. I crossed my fingers and prayed silently as she moved the fetal heartbeat wand around my belly. She could not locate the heartbeat, but said, "You know, it might still be too early to find it this way."

I informed her that the other doctor found it easily a few weeks prior, so she tried again. Still no luck so she said, "You know, I think I might have heard it, but I am not sure, and I can tell you're concerned, so I am going to send you down to have an ultrasound, just to be sure that everything is fine."

She brought me over to the reception desk and asked them if I could be squeezed in for an ultrasound, and there was availability in a half an hour. I did the only thing I could do; I called William to tell him what was going on. I couldn't reach him, so I left a message and told him it didn't look good. Seriously, why would she send me to get an ultrasound if she truly thought that everything was fine? Downstairs in the reception room, I looked around at all of the lucky pregnant women again and thought, 'Why is this happening to me again?' Then I shook my head and reminded myself that the doctor thought that all was probably fine, and I had hope. When I walked into the ultrasound room, the technician knew exactly why I was there and handed me tissues before asking me to lie down on the examination table. My heart sank when she handed me tissues, but I still had resolve.

As she silently took pictures and measurements through the ultrasound tool, I watched the little image on the screen. Was the heart still beating? I could not tell because she kept moving the wand around. Then, I thought I saw a flutter and started to relax when it looked like it was moving. I found myself thanking everyone in the universe that I would still be a mother and almost leapt up with joy. The technician interrupted my self-reflection and whispered, "I am sorry." I was confused, did she feel like she had hurt me, what was she apologizing for? Naturally, as soon as that thought finished processing in my head I heard her add, "I can't locate a heartbeat either." To go from fear, to hope, to deep fear, to relief, to mourning within a matter of minutes is a horrific progression of emotions. I knew at that moment that my pregnancy was over. In that room, in that moment, I did not know how I would ever recover. The technician gave me a minute to compose myself and then sent me upstairs to the doctor I had only met 40 minutes prior.

I knew crying would not be easy for the doctor, so I permitted myself about two minutes of tears and then pulled myself together before walking back upstairs. The doctor started telling me about my choices, which included a Dilation and curettage procedure (D&C), pills, or to just wait it out. Since I would be teaching again in less than a week, I did not want to have a ticking time bomb inside of me wondering when it was going to go off, so I opted for the D&C, which was her recommendation. She scheduled me for the next day, well, she tried to but since it was so late in the afternoon, nearly 5:00, she said I would have to wait for a morning phone call, which would let me know when my procedure would begin.

I returned to my car and turned my phone back on, which of course was beeping loudly from voice mail messages. Naturally, they were all from William. I did not want to tell him over the phone, but realized he had the right to know as soon as I did. It would be unfair for him to be filled with hope for the rest of the day. My hands shook like crazy as I dialed the phone. He picked up before the first ringing was completed and I told him it was over. William was in disbelief; he did not understand how this could have happened, and neither did I. I questioned my shaky faith again and kept asking why I was ever pregnant again to begin with. What was the purpose in having this experience? Of course, there was no explanation, and even if there had been, at that moment, it would have hardly made a difference. As I realized the time, I knew I had to drive home and accepted the fact that someone in my condition could not drive and talk at the same time, so I got off the phone with William and assured him I would be careful on the way home.

My car turned on and the song "Baby Love," by Diana Ross was blaring. It was an ironic and sad coincidence. Diana Ross is hardly ever on the radio stations that I listen to, and the words baby love poured more salt in my giant wounded heart. Nodding my head as if I got the universe's message, I slowly pulled out of the parking lot, and drove for about a block. The tears began spilling uncontrollably out of my eyes, so I pulled over to a side street and sobbed for about 10 minutes. It was an ugly cry, which I think I have heard Oprah refer to. An ugly cry is the kind of emotional break down that is so guttural, you can only hope no one ever witnesses another's experience. I could have probably cried for hours at that point, but knew I had a procedure in the morning and had to return home.

As I walked around my house, I found myself in familiar emotional territory. I had been on top of the world and overjoyed for just about 11 weeks, and now, I was the antithesis of overjoyed. It wasn't simply emotional devastation, it was something far worse, but adequately describing the pain in my heart was and still is an impossible feat. I have had breakups with boys I loved; it kind of reminded me of that, only much more extreme. With the breakups, I always knew there would be another chance at love, and a better chance at that, but now, I doubted highly that there would be other chances at pregnancy. This was a loss so much greater than one baby. This was a loss representing all reproductive future hopes. This was a loss of motherhood for me and of fatherhood for William. This was a loss of family and future. This was a deep loss that no matter how I describe, no one, unless one unfortunate to have lived through a similar situation, could ever quite comprehend. It is a loss that no one should have to endure.

The necessary D&C compounded the loss. The D&C procedure, like everything else, proved that Murphy's Law continued to reside in our lives. I found myself scheduled for 12:00 p.m., but was not physically escorted to the operating room until 3:00 p.m. William waited with me in the pre-op room for the hours leading up to the procedure. I decided that I needed to be strong for both of us and tried to sound positive and hopeful for the future. There are a lot of people whose pregnancies have surpassed the 12-week mark and who have miscarried. Millions of women have given birth to stillborn babies and I knew I should be grateful that I was spared that kind of pain. Those are the types of statements I repeated over and over to William in the hours leading up the D&C.

The nurse came in and asked me a million questions. I told her about my tricky veins and that I needed the best person to insert the I.V. She replied that she would be inserting the I.V. herself and that I had nothing to worry about. William laughed and responded, "That's what she thinks."

When it was finally time to enter the Operating Room and time for them to administer the I.V., I don't even need to tell you this story because by now, you can guess what happened. She could not locate my vein. In fact, this technician could not locate my vein and apparently did not care. She jabbed at my hand several times as I watched in familiar horror. My hand turned blue and began to shake. After enduring many minutes of this mild torture, another technician came over and verbally scolded her and advised, "You have to take the tourniquet off her, do you see what you are doing to her hand? Step aside."

He looked up at me with kind eyes, comforted me, and told me how sorry he was for my loss. That man was the first medical professional to tell me that since the ultra sound technician had whispered that she was sorry. The doctor never even offered sympathy for my loss. Perhaps doctors cannot become emotionally invested in such a situation. If that were something experienced daily or even weekly, it would be tough to forget about work at home. Holding back sympathy and emotion must be emotional insurance for the well being for many doctors. Regardless, I thanked this technician, who had been willing to feel for a patient. His actions restored my faith as his kindness made me believe that there was an angel in my hospital room. He looked at my veins and joked, "Is this your vein? Why, it is huge, it's like a freeway." And with one stick, he found the lucky spot.

That angel was followed by another phlebotomist, who had been able to locate my vein in one shot, looked at me and uttered, "God Bless You." I said this before, but it is worth repeating. It is amazing how much a little bit of kindness can restore your heart, even if only for a moment. Immediately before the procedure was about to begin the doctor asked me if I wanted to try to have the fetus examined to find out what went wrong. She followed that question up with, "It is not covered by insurance and usually costs between three to four thousand dollars."

What made me crazy about this question, at this particular time, was that it was the first time the subject had been brought up. My husband had been sitting with me for three hours before the procedure. Three hours where we could have weighed the pros and cons and discussed whether or not to go through with such a procedure. The doctor would not permit me to speak with my husband and demanded that I reach a decision. When I had asked if I could ask my husband what he thought she said there was no time because she was needed upstairs to deliver a baby. This information rubbed salt in the wound.

Emotionally wrought, instead of pushing, which, in retrospect, I should have done, I asked the doctor to offer her opinion. She discouraged the procedure because of my young age and the cost. She also admitted that they often cannot find a cause and it ends up breaking a patient's heart even further. My heart was already in so many pieces, the thought of additional damage seemed beyond cruel, and so I decided against it. As I was lying on the table and the drugs were being inserted into the I.V. to put me under, I could not control my emotions any longer. I had been very strong all day and for whom, I am not sure, but silently, as they injected my I.V., I felt hot tears running down my face. The nurse squeezed my hand and said, "I am so sorry."

The next thing I knew, a nurse was asking me if I knew a certain man, and that man was my husband. Trying to keep my humor in tact I commented, "Well, I hope so because I married him." The nurse and William laughed at my pathetic little joke and then we remained in the recovery area. I was in a great deal of pain and did not expect it. I had heard that a D&C was not a big deal. The nurse asked me if I was in pain and my face answered that question for her, so she brought in some Ibuprofen, which probably cost about $150, since it was given to me in a hospital. But, it did make the pain subside. Ten minutes later, the nurse returned with one last insult to my injury, an injection.

I happen to have a negative blood type. If you have a negative blood type, then you possess the Rh factor. This means that you need to be given an injection after the birth of a baby, or in this case, a miscarriage of a baby whose heart had once beat inside you, otherwise future pregnancies could literally kill you or your future baby. It is complicated, but basically, if your baby's father has a positive blood type, then your baby has a fifty-fifty chance of also having a positive blood type. If this crosses with your blood during delivery, it is fatal. So, the injection is a preemptive strike to prevent future problems.

It was not as if I did not know that this injection was coming. In fact, I had requested that the injection be given to me when I was still under anesthesia. One of the first pieces of good news, okay the only piece of good news I was given at the hospital, was that they had received my request from the scheduling nurse to have the injection under anesthesia and my wish would be granted. However, when I checked with the doctor in the O.R., she had not known anything about this, and the one piece of good news was rescinded. In fact, the hospital had a policy stating that blood types had to be checked in the hospital and that they could not receive the information from an outside lab. So, even though I have known my blood type since I was a child, even though Quest Diagnostics had sent over paperwork stating my actual blood type (something that, let me say for the record, had been tested four times over the course of the past two years), the hospital wanted to perform its own test. Yes, I understood why this was the policy, but it did not mean I had to like it.

Because the blood test had to be completed in the hospital, the doctor had to wait for the lab results. Since the test takes about 40 minutes or so, the results of the blood type test would not be ready until after my procedure. That is why I had to have the shot after waking up, so I could feel more pain before leaving the hospital. In all honesty, I have had to endure several shots in my buttocks region. As you may recall from earlier accounts of fertility treatments, and during my first miscarriage, I am not a fan. Still, this shot only hurt a little. Believe me, I would tell you if it was terrible. The shot was not terrible, the miscarriage was terrible. The shot was a nuisance. The injection was the last reason the hospital needed me to stay in the recovery room. Therefore, about five minutes after the shot had been administered, it was time for me to get dressed and return to my home.

After the procedure was through and I found myself back home, I gently patted my belly and felt my empty uterus. I had developed the habit of touching my belly and feeling the joy of fluttering or movement or whatever you feel at early points in a pregnancy. Back at home, I just felt empty. My uterus was empty and so was my soul. I went into my bedroom and cried as silently as I could for the loss of my baby, and cried a little more for my childless future. For the life of me, I did not know how to get back to life, but I knew I had to pretend to do just that. Therefore, I forced myself to get back into a routine as soon as possible.

In fact, I tried to propel myself back into normal life. The next day after the D&C procedure, I traveled to my classroom with William in tow to prepare for the opening day of school. Work helped to get me through my first miscarriage and surely, it could do it again. Then my brain would start pondering how difficult it would be to fake smiles all day with a brand new class full of children. How was I going to get through this? My empty uterus was a constant reminder of my loss, and my brain could not focus on anything else.

Since throwing myself back into work did little to distract my brain, I thought talking to my friends and a few family members might help me recover. Surprisingly, as I began to confide in others, I realized that keeping the pregnancy a secret was no easier than sharing my first pregnancy and the resulting miscarriage. Because I had kept the pregnancy a secret, everybody had to receive two pieces of shocking news instead of one, which was absolutely devastating. The reaction from some of my friends was naturally, "Well this might be good news, and maybe this means you can get pregnant again."

I wanted the people who responded in such a way to keep their opinions to themselves. I understood that they were trying to put a positive spin on the situation, but when you find yourself living such a reality, the last piece of advice you want to hear is someone (who has never experienced anything close to a miscarriage) tell you that it might be a sign that you should keep trying. It is not as if the thought had not occurred in my own head, but the millions of thoughts that accompanied that first thought had everything to do with repeated disappointments, and possibly, additional miscarriages. Perhaps if I had just told people about the pregnancy, they would not have shared their opinions at such a time because such sentiment felt like little knives stabbing my heart. If anything, being secretly pregnant made every part of the resulting situation more devastating.

After the D&C, I was back at work within a few days, which made the secret pregnancy affect my every move. At work, I found myself needing to explain my depression or tears, which were constant, and did not know how to do so. With most of my colleagues, I pretended that all was fine and that there was dust in my eyes. A few of them learned the truth because they walked into my classroom while I was not so secretly balling my eyes out. I did tell some of them straight out because I needed for them to know. Of all the lessons I learned during my very short pregnancies, I learned for certain that there is no right way to handle one's self during any pregnancy. I always read books and heard from others that keeping everything hush, hush was the best strategy. Well, having tried both approaches, I do not feel overly confident that I have any deep wisdom to share. So, perhaps, my advice to others is to trust those who are trustworthy, and keep the news a secret from everyone else who will make the situation more about them than about you.

The situation did not become easier with the students entering the daily picture, but I did find myself able to control my emotions in front of them. Teachers must return to work before their students in order to set up their classrooms and attend professional development days. The first few days back without students were brutal; the first few days back with them were nearly impossible.

Survival mode kicks in when you are a teacher. Teachers know that students do not need nor should they have to worry about a sad teacher. A new school year is nerve racking enough; a teacher's job is to make the transition as smooth as possible for her students. Therefore, all of my energy went into being the happiest teacher in the world. Of course, when my students were at lunch, my happiness faded away and tears often emerged. I went through hundreds of tissues and even more Visine in those first few weeks of school than can be described. When the last student loaded up on the bus at the end of the day, the tears returned. The rides home from school were especially heart wrenching, but I took each day one minute at a time, and somehow I physically got through it.

With all that William and I had been through with the fertility world, after a month of recovery from the last miscarriage, I decided that I wanted to try to get pregnant again. I was now completely baby obsessed. After the second failed in vitro attempt, I had resigned myself to the thought that William and I would either adopt, or we would remain childless, but madly in love. I was completely okay with the unknown, until I got pregnant. The surprise pregnancy turned my hopes for the future upside down. Although I recognize that other people tried to encourage me to try again when news broke of my surprise pregnancy and subsequent miscarriage, their words did not convince me. What I can say however, is that it was not their place to make such statements. I realize this reasoning makes me sound crazy, but if you have found yourself in a similar situation, and I dearly hope you haven't, then you can relate. If you have not found yourself in a similar situation, then you're going to have to trust me.

Any time I have experienced a tragedy in my life, I always tried to find the underlying reason in the big picture. Even though I could not think of one legitimate reason for the surprise pregnancy and miscarriage, the stupid optimist in me couldn't help thinking that my overbearing friends might have been correct and the pregnancy was a sign that I should press forward and try again. Seriously, was the pregnancy experience designed to simply torture me? I was afraid that the answer was yes, but hoped that the real reason was that it was supposed to serve as a wake up call to try again. Of course, the thought of possibly conceiving and following up with a third miscarriage terrified me beyond words, but I knew I just had to make an effort. If I did not continue to try, I knew I would always regret that decision. So, I decided to ask my doctor during my follow up for the D&C appointment about my chances.

The follow up appointment was about as much fun as one would imagine. Once again, I found myself in the office surrounded by pregnant women and thought, 'Here we go again.' When it was finally my turn and my doctor saw me he gave me his sad eyes and expressed his deepest sympathy. Now, what you may not realize is that even though a D&C procedure had been completed, my body still had hormones raging through it as though it were pregnant. For those of you who are unfamiliar with this phenomenon, pregnancy hormones remain in your body for at least six weeks after a miscarriage. This of course meant that I was an emotional wreck from a combination of the miscarriage experience and the raging hormones. This was a brutal amalgamation and a ticking time bomb. Anything and everything set off my tears. Naturally, when the doctor expressed sympathy, I lost it.

What made me lose it even more was when he asked me if I might consider going back to a fertility specialist. This was not something I wanted to consider at this point in my life. My immediate thought process was that he really did not know me or had never read my files. Surely, anyone reading my files would understand that a fertility clinic was the last place I wanted to return. I then commented, "Even if I was somehow lucky enough to get pregnant again, I have now miscarried twice. What if I am one of those women who cannot carry a child to term and will always miscarry?"

I was hoping his response would be, "That is ridiculous, how could you think such a thought?" But instead, he replied, "That is a distinct possibility with your history."

Stunned by his too honest answer, I asked him if William and I were allowed to have sex again and he said yes. He even told me I could start trying again that evening, if I so desired. Talk about mixed messages. He had just confirmed that I may likely be a candidate for repetitive miscarriage, and then, in the next breath, told me I could begin to try for a baby again.

When William returned home that evening, I relayed the information given to me from the doctor. He did not believe for one minute that I would constantly miscarry and said that we should keep trying and hope for the best. A few days later, I felt what I thought to be ovulation pains, so we went for it. The days following I continued to feel weird pains in my uterine area and tried to remember what I had felt at the very beginning of my pregnancy. My excitement level rose and a visit to my regular doctor for a physical confirmed my excitement. She asked me if my period had returned since the D&C. When I told her "no" she asked if I might be pregnant again. I tried to sound casual and said, "I doubt it." But, after she pressed on and asked if I had in fact engaged in unprotected sex since the D&C, I confirmed yes, I had. Her response was not the support I was looking for because she told me that my body really needed six months of recovery from a miscarriage before being adequately ready to carry another baby.

Now, this opinion varies, and I know it does because I looked it up on the Internet. Plus, my OBGYN told me I could try immediately, so I can't explain the varying opinions. What I can explain is the confusing argument I had with my own brain. I thought about a few friends of mine who had miscarried very early, and then found themselves pregnant the next month. Their babies were fine and so were their pregnancies. I decided to ignore my Internist and listen to my heart. Since I had a leftover pregnancy test from the box I stealthily bought at the drugstore the day I was meeting my friend, I decided to go home and take it.

I took the test, and then brought my dogs outside to play. When I returned, I looked at the result and it read, "Pregnant." I jumped for joy and smiled and laughed and cried. Until I remembered something important: Pregnancy hormones remain in your body for a long time after a miscarriage; what if the pregnancy test was reading the hormones from my last pregnancy and not a new one? I figured I would test again in a few days and see, but I didn't have any pregnancy tests left, so I ordered four boxes of them on line. Yes, four, with two tests each, in total, eight tests.

A few days later, the tests came and I eagerly ripped off the paper to test again. Fully expecting a positive, I prepared myself for a joyous celebration, so when a negative sign showed up I was floored. Of course, after staring at the negative sign for 10 extra minutes willing it to turn positive, I had to accept the fact that the last pregnancy test was representative of my old pregnancy, the failed pregnancy. I was not pregnant.

Just to prove the point of how pregnant I wasn't, a few days later, my period returned. I decided that this was a good thing. After all, everything I had read had suggested that it is best to wait until your cycle returns before trying again. So, once again, when I felt ovulation, William and I had specifically planned and timed relations. My cycle has always been between 28 and 30 days, so on day 31, when I still did not have any signs of having my period; I ripped open a new pregnancy test with glee. Boy was I happy I had bought four boxes! My heart was beating in my throat and my hands shook as I waited. When time was up, I peered into the result and sure enough, there was another negative. My period arrived the following day, but my efforts would not be thwarted. I would find a way to get pregnant! What I needed, was extra assistance from fertility medications. Still unwilling to visit another fertility specialist, since I had heard that Clomid was a wonder drug, I thought perhaps Dr. Simpson would write a prescription for me and let me try it out.

By the time I finally had my appointment with Dr. Simpson, my cycle was midway, so it was too late for Clomid for this particular cycle. I cursed myself for not considering interference sooner, but there was little I could do. When my appointment arrived, I went in first and spoke to my doctor about my concerns and wishes. One of the first questions he asked me was what information was discovered when the doctors examined the fetus. Surprised that this topic was brought up I explained to him the rushed circumstances of having to make a decision without William. Dr. Simpson wished out loud that we had asked for the procedure because it could have shone some light on why I miscarried. I kicked myself for listening to the doctor in the O.R. that day. I should have paid the three or four thousand dollars for any potential information. What was I thinking? Dr. Simpson could read my face and told me that what was done was done and that there were other tests that could be performed to see whether or not I would have repetitive miscarriages. One test was actually given to target progesterone levels. Apparently, if progesterone levels are too low, a woman cannot sustain a pregnancy or ovulate correctly. Dr. Simpson explained that Clomid was often prescribed for women with progesterone level problems.

He handed me a script for a progesterone test on the 21st day of my cycle to determine whether or not I was a candidate for Clomid. Since the time of my visit had been at day 16, it was perfect timing to have the test in five days. I was so happy I did not have to wait a full cycle for that test. In the meantime, my doctor told William and me to "have relations" for the rest of the weekend.

Of course, we followed the doctor's instructions. In retrospect, it is tough to believe we were subjecting ourselves to carefully planned intercourse and ovulation-timed relations again. I thought we were done with that nonsense years ago, and yet, we found ourselves back to square one. Clearly, we were not done with any nonsense because we planned every moment of intimacy based on ovulation suspicions. When my period was due, I started to feel that fluttery feeling again and thought, wouldn't it be wonderful if I was pregnant again and didn't even need Clomid? However, before the due date of my period, Dr. Simpson called with the results of my test and told me that my progesterone numbers were a little lower than he would have liked. He told me that the goal was at least 12 and that mine was at an 8.4. As previously explained by Dr. Simpson, if a woman's progesterone numbers are low and she still gets pregnant, it can be a determining factor of miscarriage. I wondered if that was why I had miscarried. Perhaps my progesterone levels had simply been too low.

I found myself torn. On one hand, I had really been hoping to find myself pregnant in a few days. On the other hand, a positive pregnancy test would bring worry of a low-progesterone level induced third miscarriage. It turned out not to be a realistic concern because my period arrived on day 32, just as it had the previous month. My cycle had changed after pregnancy. Now, there were 32 days between cycles. This tortured my soul. 32 days, when compared with 28, meant four extra days of waiting a month. This made me less than happy.

However, a prescription of Clomid made me blissfully giddy. I was positive that this was the magic pill to turn my dream into a reality. I eagerly followed the instructions and swallowed the pill for the five days required. Not to be gross, but the pill has some side effects that many (including me at the time) do not know about. I found myself with a yeast infection, which is something I previously had only once in my life. When diagnosed with the infection, the doctor told me that a yeast infection was a potential side effect of Clomid.

In addition to the joy of a yeast infection, I found myself extremely weepy. I cried all the time and felt as though I was experiencing the loss of my baby all over again every day. And, my favorite side effect was the hot flash. Oh yes, Clomid often causes women to experience hot flashes. I had heard about hot flashes from my colleagues and my mother, but the experience of one is absolutely indescribable. Well, not really indescribable. You feel your whole body burning up, followed by the subsequent desire to rip all your clothes off your body, quickly. Then you feel beads of sweat on the back of your neck and other places, and just as quickly, the sweat is replaced with the chills. Oh, it is interesting. I kept reassuring myself that if there were a baby at the end of the experience, it would be a funny anecdote and worth every second of discomfort.

At this point, I had invested in a daily ovulation kit. For the past two months, I had surged on day 19, and this month brought the exact same results. Day 19 arrived, and William and I got busy. Day 21 arrived, and I received my progesterone blood test. I was certain my numbers would go up on Clomid, so you can imagine my dismay when I received the news that my numbers had actually dropped slightly to 7.8. The doctor told me he would increase the dosage the following month to 100 milligrams, and we would see what happened.

I did not accept those numbers at face value and began to investigate. After researching the beloved Internet, I found an article from a doctor explaining that the day 21 test only works for the "normal and traditional" patient who ovulates on day 14 or 15. Apparently, the test is supposed to be conducted approximately seven days past actual ovulation. On day 21, it might have only been 1 day after my actual ovulation. The test was being performed too early! I called the nurse and relayed this information and she told me would pass it on to my doctor. Since my doctor did not know I was ovulating so late, he would certainly not know that the test was being performed too early.

Apparently, my doctor was not interested in my actual ovulation date and told me that I would take the Clomid once again and test on day 21. I repeated my question to the nurse and the information about my ovulation timing. She replied that the doctor was given the message, but still wanted to test me on day 21. I could not believe it. Of course, it was possible that the Internet was wrong, but it made so much sense. I knew I needed another opinion, so I decided to search for a new fertility specialist.

THIRD DOCTOR'S A CHARM

No ONE IS more surprised than me that I found myself searching for another fertility doctor. William and I had decided after the second attempt to never travel down this avenue again, and yet, circumstances changed our minds. And yes, I see the irony in this fact and also considering Dr. Robinson advised me to seek out another fertility specialist. But, there I was again.

I knew I had to be bossier this time around, so when the receptionist asked me which doctor I wanted to see, I told her that I wanted to see the kindest and most compassionate doctor on staff. She asked me about my history, and then agreed that I needed a doctor with the best bedside manner and results. She had an opening in a few weeks, and I eagerly accepted the appointment. Coincidentally, my OBGYN wanted me to go to him that day for an ultrasound of my ovaries. This meant that my womanly parts would be on display for two different sets of doctors and nurses that day. Such a prospect did not excite me.

As unappealing as it was to see two different hooch doctors on the same day, I was thrilled to see the new fertility specialist named Dr. Foster. The first words out of his mouth after introducing himself and shaking my head were, "I just read your history, and it is so sad. I am really sorry that you keep finding yourself in this situation." I almost cried on the spot because his response made me feel as though he cared and understood. I loved this man, and so did William.

One of the first questions asked was whether or not the fetus had been examined upon the D&C procedure after my recent miscarriage. I relayed the circumstances surrounding that decision, and he scoffed at the suggestion that insurance would not have covered it. Dr. Foster was certain that such a procedure was covered by insurance. He explained that it was unfortunate that we did not have the chance to learn anything from the fetus, but since there was nothing to be done about it; we needed to move forward optimistically.

I was all for moving forward, but once again irritated that the procedure had actually been significant and something that I should have insisted upon. If only I had known! Regardless, he was right. It was not like we could go back, not that I ever wanted to. Instead of focusing on new disappointments over past decisions, I began to ask questions about miscarrying odds and other tests out there. I also inquired about insemination and drugs other than Clomid and progesterone levels. Dr. Foster did concur that if I ovulated on day 19, then a test on day 21 would be invalid. He confirmed my suspicions and supported the fact that I was not crazy! The Internet did not make me crazy! I was thrilled to be vindicated. However, he then said, "If your eggs are ready to drop on day 15 and are dropping on day 21 that could explain your problem. By day 21, a woman's eggs are too old to drop. If they are somehow fertilized at all this way, they would probably not be viable for a nine-month pregnancy."

Now, this was a hypothesis that I had never heard. When he said this issue was simple to overcome and could be easily managed with a trigger shot, I was thrilled. He decided he wanted to look at my ovaries right there and then to determine if this theory held merit. I nearly dropped my pants on the spot with anticipation, but held it together. Sure enough, (this was day 12; by the way), my follicles were in great shape. We all went back into his office and he was confident that if I did not surge on my own on day 14, then we had all just discovered a vital piece of information. He asked me to test for the LH surge on day 14 and day 15, and if it did not appear, he would call in a prescription for the trigger shot.

As you can guess, since this is me, the lutenizing hormone did not surge naturally. As a result, we called the doctor and he called in the prescription for the trigger shot. Much to my dismay, the injection was not covered by insurance, so $100+ dollars was rendered to our local pharmacy to make my follicles drop the egg on time. William and I had intercourse five times in three days. Morning, night, morning, night, morning and boy were we excited. On the 21st day, I went for my blood work again and knew everything would be fine. The numbers were outstanding, over 112 actually. This meant that the trigger shot caused me to ovulate at the right time and that my body did produce enough (plus extra due to the Clomid) progesterone to sustain a pregnancy. This was great news.

However, I did not feel pregnant. I stared at my breasts every time I showered and willed them to look like pregnancy breasts. Once again, whenever I felt a twinge of any kind, I had flashes of hope. Doing period math, I decided that I would likely receive my period on the 28th day of my cycle. The past few months, my period arrived exactly 12 days after ovulation. Since I had previously ovulated on day 20, the arrival of my period would be expected on day 32. This past month, I had ovulated on day 16, with the help of the trigger shot, which meant 12 additional days, brought me to day 28.

Each day inched on at a snail's pace. I obsessed about being pregnant every waking moment. I even dreamed about being pregnant. I imagined my due date in October and thought it would be lovely to have a baby in the fall and have beautiful changing leaves every birthday in the life of my child. By the time day 28 came, my patience level was gone. I literally checked to see if my period arrived at least 15 times that day. If more than a half hour went by and I realized it, I checked again. No period!

I still had pregnancy tests but told myself not to take one until day 32. All day, that is what I told myself. The hope was like a drug, it made everything seem possible. I smiled all day long as I felt a flutter here and there in my uterine area. A few times the pessimist in me thought that I was feeling exactly the same way I had felt the past few cycles before my period, but since my period had not arrived, I brushed the pessimism away and wondered how I would make it through the first trimester in school.

Day 29 came and there was still no sign of any period. After going to the bathroom 34 times that day to check for my period, I realized that I had to take a pregnancy test because I was making myself crazy. I had to know, but I did not want to get William's hopes up, so I waited for him to take the dogs out for their nightly stroll. The minute he closed the door, I ran into my bedroom and dug out the opened box from the previous month. I aimed for the stick, covered it up and left the bathroom to prevent myself from staring at it. After the suggested two minutes had elapsed, I ran into the bathroom to see that beautiful plus sign.

Unfortunately, there were no traces of a plus sign on the stick, and believe me; I squinted to try to detect one. A big fat negative line mocked me and my heart was crushed to a pulp. I wrapped the stick in a paper towel and buried it in the garbage. I could not let William know what I had just done. Before he returned to the house, and this is extremely embarrassing, I actually went into the garbage to give it one last glance to make sure that a positive sign had not shown up after the fact. Of course there was no plus sign because I was not pregnant.

My period arrived the next morning. Every time I walked towards the bathroom, my heart sank lower and lower. Life suddenly seemed meaningless and hopeless again, and I found myself incredibly depressed. It seemed as if there were no real reasons to smile. I knew I could not continue on this path.

However, as much as I understood that my energies needed to be focused on something besides motherhood, my planning and obsessive nature were equally difficult to release. Pro-activity was my new motto, and as I was not willing to give up on having a baby, I listened to the fertility specialist and went in for additional blood tests. The tests were administered to find out if my body would automatically reject a pregnancy. A few days earlier, William returned to the urologist for yet another sample of his sperm. A different type of waiting was then sending us into insanity. There were various possible outcomes. The first possible outcome would be a sperm count that was in some way or form less than stellar. The number of sperm might be fine, but motility and formation needed to be fine too. If any of these sperm factors were less than desirable, then William would be dealing with guilt over his body's failure. If my tests showed that my body was not a good host for a pregnancy, a completely different set of circumstances would lead to me dealing (again) with guilt over my body's failure. If the tests were both fine, then we were back to the diagnosis of "unexplained infertility." It's the unexplained that caused me grief more than anything else. How could a type-A person like me deal with the unexplained?

As far as the miscarriage test was concerned, well, that was another mini disaster. I went to the lab, certain there would be roughly 10 vials of blood drawn, based on the prescription. I must admit I do not actually know how to interpret a blood script. Regardless, there were so many words listed, I was certain numerous vials were coming my way. The phlebotomist took out four vials and started to prep me. My mouth got ahead of my brain and I asked, "Are those all the vials you need?" He assured me that four were all that was needed, but then grabbed another vial, just to be sure.

The fact that he grabbed an extra vial was a bit alarming, but having five rather than 10 vials drawn was a thrilling victory. Although this was small, it felt like it might be the first sign that obstacles might get smaller for William and me. The results were important in finding out whether or not obstacles were decreasing in size. These specific blood tests were so important to me; I couldn't help but beg the phlebotomist to make sure that the test results got to their proper destination. He laughed and assured me that they would.

While I was waiting for the test results, which I was guaranteed would take no longer than two weeks, William and I decided to try insemination again. When I went for my day-12 blood test and ovarian ultrasound, a different doctor named Dr. Warren was waiting in the examination room. Like Dr. Foster, he was extremely kind. I found it refreshing that there was no sense of arrogance in either doctor at this fertility clinic. When he examined my uterus, he commented that the lining was thin. The previous month, my lining had been nice and thick; I know this because Dr. Foster said, "Your lining is nice and thick." Now it was thin. Dr. Warren hypothesized that it might have something to do with the fact that I had been taking Clomid for three months.

Apparently, repeated use of Clomid thins the lining of some women's uteri. Naturally, I had to fall into that percentage. I asked him what it meant and he said probably nothing. Then he moved the ultrasound wand to my ovaries and showed me that I had four nice sized follicles. That made me happy. With my husband's iffy sperm and my egg issues, we had been told that we needed multiple eggs to have the slightest chance of one actually being fertilized. Now I had four chances this month. But that thin lining bothered me. I asked him if it might be a good idea to skip our insemination attempt this month. He said no, citing studies that had neither proved nor disproved success. I hesitantly agreed to go through with the insemination, but the thin lining gnawed at my optimism.

On our way out, the nurse explained that she would call my husband at work with further instructions. She mentioned that I would be returning to the office on Sunday for the insemination procedure, and then I was on my way.

The first action I took when I returned home that evening was to search the term "thin uterus lining" on Google. Hundreds of links appeared before me and I obsessively clicked on them all. According to the different bits of information I could actually decipher, it seemed that a thin lining could be a miscarriage red flag. It also meant that the chances of conceiving at all were reduced. I had asked the doctor if I should skip this month and he said no. Did he say no because he truly believed that a thin lining was not a guaranteed failure?

I voiced my fears to William, who encouraged me to trust the doctor. He obviously had the right attitude and I wished I could raise my optimism to reach his level. Poor William, I have no idea how he put up with my insanity. I think the husband gets the short end of the stick in the fertility process because he feels so helpless. Time after time William lamented how difficult it was for him to sit back and watch me go through test after test while he waited in the background. Often he wished he could go through the processes on my behalf, and truthfully, I would not have minded if that were biologically possible. Regardless of his anxieties, he remained a rock and my greatest cheerleader every step of the way. He inspired me to keep trying.

William's persistence was just one of his inspiring qualities. He took on the job of calling the clinic for detailed instructions since I had trouble making personal phone calls during my work day. Although William was as good as his word and called the clinic, no one returned a phone call to him. He remained persistent and placed additional phone calls. When those calls were not initially returned, he then checked his messages obsessively all day. In the evening, while we were at home, he checked his work voice mail multiple times and discovered that someone from the clinic had finally called him. The nurse who left the message instructed William to administer the trigger shot to me on Saturday. She also informed him that we needed to come to the office on Sunday for the insemination procedure.

When William relayed this information to me on Friday evening, I asked him what time we were supposed to administer the shot and what time were we expected at the clinic on Sunday. Apparently, those small details were not left on his voice mail, so on Saturday, we phoned the clinic again. A nurse named Marie told us that she would have someone call us back by 11:00. I thought I remembered Dr. Warren saying something about the shot being administered Saturday morning, so I had William inject me before I left the house because unfortunately, I had a hair cut appointment scheduled for 10:30 in the morning. As vain as it may sound, I didn't want to skip my appointment because my bangs were blocking a good portion of my vision. William agreed to sit by the phone and wait for the news while my hairdresser gave me the gift of unobstructed sight. Although he held up his end of the bargain, the clinic did not hold up theirs. We did not receive a phone call, so we called again around 12:00. At that time, everyone had left for the day.

Perfect.

Now we were in a pickle. We knew we had to go in for our first insemination attempt on Sunday, but we did not know what time. As Sunday morning arrived at 8:00, we phoned the clinic. We spoke to a phone service. We relayed our story to them but they told us they had no idea how to help us. Of course they didn't, they were a phone service. This was way out of their jurisdiction. They thought the clinic opened up at 9:00, so we called again at 9:00. The phone service was still picking up the calls. This time, we spoke to another person and they thought the clinic opened up at 10:00 and closed at 12:00.

Considering the clinic was an hour away from the house, I was not willing to wait until 10:00 to call again. Instead, we drove there ready for the issues to fly all over the place.

When we arrived and announced our presence, the entire staff was confused. No one had any idea what we were doing there. William and I began to explain the series of misinformation and they finally understood. The receptionist chastised us for showing up without an appointment, but we stood strong and reminded her that no one returned any of our calls. Since this was our first attempt at insemination at this clinic, we did not know what we were supposed to do. The rest of the staff at the clinic understood that their failure to provide us with detailed instructions caused us to show up without an appointment. Therefore, they found a way to squeeze us in.

It took an hour to prepare William's sperm. When it was ready, I was called into the procedure room. It had been several years since I had been inseminated. I did not remember it being that big of a deal. I thought there might be a bit of cramping for 20 seconds, but nothing overly taxing. Dr. Warren was once again the man on duty, so in he walked with a tiny little vial of washed sperm. He reported that the motility and numbers were not overly fantastic at 7 million, but then assured me that as long as the count was over 5 million, we had nothing to worry about.

After the sperm were sent up to the proper area, I was instructed to lie down for 10 minutes before dressing and leaving. My watch battery had died several weeks before and there was no clock in the room. Since there was music playing, I figured that after three songs had passed, my 10 minutes would be over. Just to be certain that a full 10 minutes went by, I waited until the end of the fourth song to get up. I then met William and a wonderful nurse on staff outside the exam room. The nurse cheerfully said, "Okay, we'll see you both back here tomorrow."

The reason we had to repeat our visit is because this fertility clinic tried insemination on two consecutive days. This was a different protocol than the first clinic I had visited, which encouraged me to have positive thoughts. I had written sub plans for the morning only and called in a half-day medical appointment. Our appointment was for 10:00. According to my calculations, 10:30 would mark 48 hours since the trigger shot had been administered. Everything I had read urged couples to have intercourse during the 48 hours that the egg was dropping. If they took me on time, I figured the sperm could hit the egg as it made its final descent, assuming another sperm had not hit it already in the previous day's attempt.

William was instructed to deposit his sperm at 8:30 a.m. This gave me an hour and a half to wait around the doctor's office. I figured, since I was there, I might as well ask about my miscarriage test results. A nurse told me she would look into them but assured me if we had not heard anything, everything was probably fine. That sentiment provided me with little comfort, but there was nothing more I could do. Once again, I read boring magazines and waited for the insemination process. After 10:00 had come and gone, I started to panic.

A nurse had come out periodically and assured me that it would not be long, and then she came out and said five more minutes, around 11:00, we were finally given the green light to enter the procedure room. William and I were convinced that something terrible had occurred. Perhaps they dropped the sample or worse, perhaps the numbers were so low they did not want to waste our time.

Our concern was misguided because they were merely running late. The numbers actually doubled from the previous days and Dr. Warren was very hopeful. At the end of the procedure, he instructed me to take progesterone for 12 days and by then I would know whether or not I was pregnant. William and I exchanged glances and inquired, "Progesterone?" Dr. Warren confirmed the need for progesterone and offered to call in a script for me. He instructed me to start taking it on Wednesday morning.

My initial reaction was, 'Ugh, more medication.' But then, I focused on the implications of something else he had said. I would know if the insemination procedure worked after 12 days. If my period did not arrive in 12 days, I could assume I was pregnant. Instantly, I calculated period math in my head and realized that 12 days would be two Saturdays following the insemination attempt. It was going to be a long 12 days.

In the mean time, I was still waiting for my miscarriage test results. After an additional week and a half had passed, we received a cryptic message on our home phone. The message we heard was, "Hi, this is Sarah from your doctor's office. I wanted to talk to you about your blood test results. We are going to have to redraw your blood. If you want to call me back to discuss this matter, I will be in the office until 3:30."

Since I did not return to my house until 6:00, I missed my opportunity by a mile to return a call. Redraw the blood? What, did they not draw enough blood? And after I made a big stink about how few vials there were and how it was such a nice surprise? I knew it, I am not a medical professional, but I knew it! My blood started to boil. Of course, soon more of it would be removed from my system anyway, which is probably why it started to bubble in the first place.

As soon as William entered the house that evening, he barely had time to greet me before I whined about the blood test trauma. I don't know how he managed to put up with my tirades, but he lovingly looked at me and then gave me a bear hug. "Murphy continues to live on our street," was his immediate and appropriate reply. William offered to call the doctor's office on my behalf and find out what happened. I mentioned earlier that he had been in charge of these types of phone calls. Fortunately for me, William was willing to take on the role of my personal phone secretary during the school year.

When you work in the educational profession, calling a doctor's office is nearly impossible. I can make a phone call approximately two times a day. One of those times is during my lunch break, but my lunch break coincides with doctors' lunch breaks. I have tried to call many doctors during my lunch to hear a recording explaining that the office was at lunch and would be back in an hour. The hour was over, of course, when I was back in class. The only other time for me to make phone calls was when my students were at their specials, such as art, physical education, music, or library. I have approximately 30 minutes to do this.

Within that 30 minutes, however, I also have to go upstairs to the office and retrieve my mail, make copies, prepare for the next lesson, and go to the bathroom, so really, I have about 10 minutes where I might be able to make a phone call. These available 10 minutes can only be utilized on the phone if another teacher does not need to meet with me during this time. Now, 10 minutes might seem like enough time to make a phone call, but that doesn't take into account the hold time you often experience when calling a doctor's office. Even if I am not placed on hold, I spend the 10 minutes staring at the clock instead of focusing on the conversation. If teachers are late picking up their students from their special, then another grade level is thrown off schedule and disaster ensues. Teachers must be on time to the minute. Early is okay, but late is a no-no. This is why I don't like to make phone calls during school and why William has become my personal phone secretary.

Since William agreed to make the call the next day, all I could do was wait it out. I e-mailed him from work a few times to find out if he had heard anything, but he was at meetings all morning and had not yet had time to make the call. When I met him at home later that evening, he told me that the woman who had called the previous day named Sarah had the day off.

Of course she did.

Although he interrogated another employee at the office to find out what the deal was, he could not learn much. Since William was persistent, another nurse, named Ann, searched through Sarah's desk to see what she could find. She was not positive, but according to some notes, it looked like some tests were completed, but some were never run. After holding and speaking to Ann for about 20 minutes (see, I told you 10 minutes was never long enough), William was provided with nothing concrete. She assured him that Sarah would return a call to him the next day with information.

William did not wait to hear from Sarah. He phoned her at around 10:00 the next day. Apparently, Ann did very thorough detective work. A few of the tests were completed, but several were not because the phlebotomist did not draw enough blood. "I told you so," does not seem like the right response to these circumstances because I had no desire to be right about interpreting the blood script. On the contrary, this was one of those instances where I would have been happy to be mistaken. Sarah explained that I had to go back to the blood lab in order to get additional vials drawn, which would enable the doctors to analyze the results and finally report their findings back to me.

In the meantime, six long days had passed since the last insemination attempt. Once again, my psyche analyzed each pang and movement inside my nervous system. I stared at every part of my body in the shower, especially the breasts. I pleaded with anyone out there to give me back those pregnancy boobs, and for nine whole months this time. I did not see any signs for long, but every glance or so, I could swear they looked different. On day 12, I had no signs of my period. Although there was a piece of me that hoped against hope that no period meant what Dr. Warren told me it meant, I did not feel pregnant.

I had already been through plenty of unnecessary pregnancy tests, so I was in no rush to take another one. I decided to wait two additional days. Two more days, two more progesterone pills, and still, my period had not arrived. Although I was beginning to feel hopeful, even calculating my new due date in my head, something seemed off. Then, as I was trying to go to sleep that evening, I remembered something. When I had gone through my two in vitro insemination attempts, I was told to go off the progesterone medication in order to bring on my period. What if the progesterone was what was preventing my period from showing its ugly presence and not a pregnancy? I decided I had to take a pregnancy test right away. If it was negative, I would stop taking progesterone, if it was positive, I would keep taking it.

After digging through my drawers and locating another box of tests, I barely had enough urine left in my bladder to test. I managed though, and the results were exactly what I imagined they would be: Negative. I took myself off the progesterone, and called the doctor's office. Now I had to wait for my period to arrive, again. Even though I had suspected that I was not pregnant, I couldn't control myself from crying like a little girl for the next few days. Would I ever get pregnant? Seriously, would it ever happen for me? I really doubted it.

My period arrived the next day, and the following day, I found myself back in the fertility office. Dr. Warren was the doctor on call again and came into the exam room with a sad expression. He empathized, "I was hoping not to see you this month because I was hoping you were pregnant. I really thought it was going to work"

My response was light and airy, although my heart was crushed as I replied, "Well, I was hoping so too." Within a few minutes, I found myself receiving another internal ultrasound, as he, yet again, pointed out my uterus and my ovaries. I was intimately familiar with them at this point. It sounds crazy, but I could not help but feel hopeful each time I viewed them on the screen. It was as if my uterus was just waiting patiently to form a life.

Since William was in the waiting room, I felt the freedom to ask questions that I would probably not ask in front of my protective husband. Since the Clomid had allegedly thinned out the lining of my uterus, I asked him which alternative drugs he was going to put me on this month. He reported we would try a medication that was like Clomid called Femara and he then started to suggest other injectable medication like Gonadotropins. The problem with the injectable medications was they had to be ordered in advance, and there was not enough time to do that. The other problem with the injectable medication was it was the same medication that caused my hyper stimulation in my previous two in vitro cycles. Suddenly, I could care less about OHSS. I was willing to put my body at any risk to have a baby.

Before I knew what I was saying, the following words escaped my mouth, "Give it to me straight Dr. Warren, I am about to turn that horrible age of 35 when supposedly all of my eggs will dry up and all babies that form are practically guaranteed to have birth defects. What would you recommend? I feel as though I may just be wasting time."

Naturally, he recommended another round of in vitro fertilization. I shuddered at the suggestion, but managed to shut off my doubts long enough to listen to what he had to say. He theorized that the reason the first round did not work was incompetence. Although there was an actual pregnancy with the second round, he suspected the reason it did not hold was because my "uterine environment" was damaged due to the OHSS my body had endured. He assured me that all of this could have been managed by waiting to transfer the embryos until my body had recuperated. Although I had debated this possibility with the second clinic, it was interesting to hear this point of view. Dr. Warren's ideas brought me back to reconsidering in vitro, something I promised William and myself I would *never* do.

Before I could entertain the thought any further, I reminded him that I had two frozen embryos that could still be transferred. I told him I wanted to wait until the summer to do the transfer (if nothing else worked before then) because I had plenty of time to come into the office. Dr. Warren informed me that an embryo transfer did not involve much more office time than insemination, which was news to me. Perhaps we could attempt that in a few months then, I asked? Dr. Warren assured me that it would be relatively simple.

As I exited the office, happy to have had someone speak so frankly and yet so gently with me, my head was spinning. As William and I drove back home, I began to replay my conversation with Dr. Warren. At the mention of in vitro, William became visibly upset. He said, no, absolutely not. Although I was in no rush to put myself through the process a third time, I felt compelled to explain how OHSS might be controlled. I also felt the need to explain Dr. Warren's beliefs that waiting a few months to actually perform the transfer might also make all the difference. I could feel William soften at the mention of a greater success rate, but there was still one issue remaining, the financial one. I admitted if it were covered by insurance, I would do it again in a heartbeat, knowing that my life was probably in better hands. William's response shocked me, "Don't let finances drive your decision. If you really believe that another round of in vitro will bring us a child and that your health will be protected, we will find the money."

Interestingly enough, I was balancing my checkbook the following day and realized that I could probably pay for one more round of in vitro fertilization. When William joined me for breakfast, we discussed the future. We decided we would try the regular old-fashioned way for the next few months. Well, not completely the old-fashioned way as we would still rely on scans, blood tests, Femara, and Ovidrell, but still, we would engage in intercourse.

If the next two months brought us no success, we would try transferring the two frozen embryos that were remaining. Assuming that either of the embryos would be viable when unfrozen, that is. If pregnancy continued to elude us, we would discuss in vitro in July, with a transfer possibly in September or October. In this scenario, I hoped against hope that we would find ourselves blessed with a child before having to consider another round of in vitro, but I knew in my heart of hearts, that we would ultimately be faced with that choice. I knew my body, I knew our luck; I knew that Murphy continued to live on our street. I absolutely knew, 100% that I would be back with many injections in a matter of months. Of course, if that one didn't work, we would have to give up. Our financial standings would not permit us to attempt in vitro for a fourth time. Something had to work; it just had to.

With my long-term plan in place, I was still hoping against all odds that I would not need to engage any plans because I would find myself pregnant sooner. And with that hope, I returned to Quest Diagnostic Center to put myself through another blood test to determine if miscarriage was predestined.

I do not understand what the deal is with Quest, but their employees all seem to be temporary. There were two women I had never seen, and I had been there often enough to recognize everyone. The woman who drew my blood had zero personality and even less interest in me.

She pulled out a regular old-fashioned needle, not a butterfly needle, which made me nervous. I did not want to sound as though I, a teacher, knew more about drawing blood than she, a professional technician, but I did gristle on the inside at the sight of the regular big, fat needle. She only poked me once, but then moved around the needle for about a minute until finding the vein. It was excruciating, but I was relieved when it was completed. My bruised arm showed the evidence of her handy-work, but in a few days time, I would know if my body worked against allowing me to sustain a pregnancy. The test was done on a Saturday and after the screw up of the previous test, the fertility office assured me that they would call me with the results as soon as they arrived.

My week at work was busy, but at any spare moment, I obsessed over the results. The following Saturday, on the twelfth day of my cycle, my legs were shaking in the waiting room as my mind raced with possibilities. My purpose for being there was to have my uterus and ovaries analyzed via an ultrasound again. Upon arriving at the clinic, we were happy to hear that Dr. Foster was on duty because we had not seen him in a while.

After getting my blood drawn, I let William know that he could come in with me, and we exchanged nervous glances while waiting for Dr. Foster to enter the room. When he walked in, he seemed extremely rushed, but was still somehow lovely and supportive. The ultrasound showed I only had one dominant follicle this month, which meant that the Femara did not increase my egg production. Although this was disappointing from an odds perspective, we did receive a piece of good news. My lining was nice and thick and even had some sort of white stripe, which indicated it would be in good shape to accept an embryo, should one, miraculously, form. I figured, like the previous two cycles, someone would call later and tell me when to take the trigger shot, and William and I would attempt to create a life the fun way. Instead, Dr. Foster shocked me by telling me that I had to return to the clinic on Monday morning for another examination.

I had been under the impression that this was the last appointment I needed for this cycle. It had not even dawned on me that I would have to return to the office. As far as my professional obligations were concerned, the timing could not have been worse.

For two weeks every year, students are bombarded with standardized tests. Think what you want of their purpose or benefits. I certainly do, but they are a fact of life. What people may not realize is that certified teachers must administer these tests. This means teachers are not permitted to have substitute teachers who do not possess a teaching certificate stand in for them during this time. In extreme circumstances, another teacher from a classroom in Kindergarten, first, or second grade (K-2 students do not take these tests), might be pulled to administer the tests. Regardless, it would be a logistical nightmare if I were not in school.

Standardized test weeks are probably the most important time in education, at least as far as public perception is concerned. What I am getting at here is that there was no way I could return to the fertility clinic in the morning during standardized test week. I told Dr. Foster that the tests were given around 9:30, so he assured me I would be able to leave the clinic by 7:15 am. The problem remaining was that I could not take a chance on being late to school. Besides that, I had to be in my building by 8:30. Considering it took about an hour to get from the clinic to my school, 7:15 was not a time that would ensure my timely arrival. I would be driving with traffic. It could take me two hours to get to work, and that was not an exaggeration.

As I tried to explain this problem, Dr. Foster kind of rolled his eyes at me. Okay, so he did not actually roll his eyes, but his response felt like a rolling of the eyes. To be clear, it was not a mean eye roll, it was basically like, "You know I would do something if I could, but what do you want me to do about it?" My priorities should have been focused on procreation, but I could not let go of my professional obligations. Dr. Foster did not have the ability to freeze time, although if he could, I am certain he would have for me or any of his patients. Instead, I asked him if I could come to the office in the afternoon, and he was agreeable to this, with one caveat, my blood work results would not be known until the following day. We could work around that.

I then moved on and asked whether or not my blood results had come in regarding the miscarriage test.

Dr. Foster responded, "Well, yes, and the preliminary results show that everything is fine, but I did not receive a copy of the lab report, so I can't confirm anything else. But don't worry, Dr. Warren, who did receive the report, will see you on Monday, so you can confer with him."

Knowing that the preliminary results looked okay was good, but not good enough. I wondered to myself, what does he mean I can speak to Dr. Warren on Monday? Where exactly are the lab results? Did Dr. Warren take them home? We are in the office for goodness sakes, why can't he retrieve the results? Before I had a chance to articulate my manic thought process, Dr. Foster reassured me that I had nothing to worry about. Perhaps there was nothing to worry about, but I wanted to see the results of the test to prove it. He smiled, wished us luck, and left us in the exam room. William and I sighed in unison, and headed out to the receptionist.

When I went to the receptionist (this was the nice receptionist) to schedule my Monday's appointment, I relayed the standardized testing conflict with Monday. She suggested that I visit Quest for the blood work in the morning. I was so happy to have an alternate option. Naturally, there were no appointments available on Monday at Quest until after 9:30, so I could take my chances, arrive when they opened, and hope against all odds that everything would work out fine. This was the plan, and I walked out of the office with the blood draw script in hand.

When Monday morning arrived, I left my house at 6:30 a.m. to try like the dickens to be the first patient in line. Daylight Savings time had occurred one day prior, so my drive to the clinic was in complete darkness. It also happened to be pouring rain outside, which did not make waiting outside the clinic door appealing. I pulled into the parking lot and sat quietly in my car, waiting for someone from the clinic to show up. Staring at the clock does not make time go faster, but at least it gave me something to focus on while I waited. At 6:59, a Quest employee pulled into the parking lot. I exhaled with complete glee, thrilled that no other patients had yet to arrive. The minute the Quest employee entered the building; I sprinted from my car, umbrella in tow, and stood outside the door willing a quick entry. The combination of the rain and the wind prevented my umbrella from keeping me dry, but at least I made an effort.

Meanwhile another two cars pulled into the parking lot. Two senior citizens, each in a different car, watched me from behind their windshields in fascination. As soon as the door was opened, the two senior citizens, one man, and one woman, joined me at the entrance. Although I had been waiting there for several minutes, I felt compelled to let the other two patients go ahead of me. Surprisingly, they politely refused my offer. They laughed and one commented, "Honey, anyone willing to wait outside in the rain for a blood test clearly has places to go. Yes, we're old and impatient, but even we can see when someone is truly in a genuine rush." They giggled and insisted that I have my blood work completed first. I gratefully accepted their refusal to go ahead of me, and I was out the door by 7:15.

At my appointment in the afternoon, I was shocked to learn that the surge was happening on its own. How did that happen? I thought my body did not ovulate on time; at least, that was one hypothesis. My one dominant follicle was the perfect size and ready to release the egg within the next 24 to 36 hours. I inquired if that meant that I could skip the trigger shot, but Dr. Warren dismissed my idea and encouraged me to take the shot anyway. He said it would ensure that nothing would prevent my egg from releasing on time. Not even a blood test with surging proof was enough to take one needle out of, at this point, what had become my monthly routine. I was instructed to have intercourse that evening and the following evening.

Receiving a prescription for sexual intercourse is how it felt. It is difficult to get excited about sex when you are ordered when and why you must have it. William felt the same way, and it was not easy to get him in the mood when there was so much pressure. Finally, my uterus was cooperating, and apparently, so were my eggs. His only job was to release sperm and hope for some magic. Unfortunately, the stress weighed heavily on William and it took a lot of, shall we say, coaxing, to get things started, and then continued. We had to stop midway and begin again, just from the stress. Eventually, we did have success, but I couldn't help but wonder if such a labor of love would result in my actual labor down the road. Although we repeated the sequence the following evening, I was not all that hopeful. Something inside me knew that nothing had happened, and after all that work.

I was told to take progesterone for the next 12 days, once again. On the third day, I couldn't do it. I felt nothing and I did not want to put a substance in my body for nothing, again. An argument raged inside my head. If I didn't take it and miraculously ended up pregnant, I would panic over the fact that I didn't take the progesterone. If I did take it and was not pregnant, as I suspected, I would be annoyed that I continued to introduce a weird substance into my system for 10 days for no reason. Surprisingly, my guilt over the possibility did not win over my assurance that I was not pregnant. I skipped the third night's progesterone and decided if I had any symptoms, I would begin taking it again.

As if to answer my question, a symptom arrived the very next day. My breasts were sore. At first, I thought I was imagining things, but no, they were in fact sore. They had not hurt since I had last been pregnant, so maybe I had been wrong. I started the progesterone again the next night.

As usual, the next 10 days dragged on. I didn't really feel any other symptoms of pregnancy, but my breasts continued to feel sore. I would constantly feel myself up in the bathroom or at any point in the day when no one was watching to make sure they were still hurting. On day 10, without telling William, I took a test. I stared at the pregnancy test and watched the line form for the umpteenth time. Once again, it was negative. That little plus sign that I had been praying for was nowhere in sight, or was it? When I looked at the test in the light, I could see the faintest of the faintest vertical lines; at least, I thought I could see it. The only thing to do was to wait a few days and take another test.

I couldn't help myself; I started hoping against hope that I was in fact carrying a child. The calculations in my head began again and I figured that I would have a baby in December if I were pregnant. The next moment, I would scold my brain for such foolish hope, but the minute following that, I would pray again that I was pregnant. When I walked my students to lunch, or to gym, I wondered. In between subjects, when we had a minute or two of transition, I would wonder again. Even when I was teaching, the thought would pop in my head, but I would quickly dismiss it in order to focus on my lesson. The drive to and from school was torture because I could think of nothing else. Yet, all the while, I said nothing to William for fear of getting his hopes up as high as mine were. Although it was only an additional two days, it felt like 20.

My hands were shaking a mile a minute as I unwrapped the pregnancy test stick. I prayed and prayed that the elusive plus sign would appear, and felt the pain of disappointment, yet again, when a big fat negative showed up. There was no mistaking it, I was not pregnant. I didn't even see a mirage of a vertical line this time. It was probably my imagination on the last test and my unabashed hope that made me see it like an oasis that a thirsty person in a desert would see. Here we go again, I thought.

At that very moment, I found myself at a crossroads. How much longer could I continue on this path? Every moment I was alone for the next two weeks, I cried. Sometimes, I found myself almost losing it in front of my students. As my pregnant coworker and friend would come visit me, I would stare at her belly with unrelenting jealousy and sadness. Why couldn't I join her in maternity bliss? I began to realize, once again, that my chances of becoming a mother were dimmer and dimmer each month. And this month in particular, was the month that I was due. My baby was due in March, and it was now March. Not only was I without my baby, I feared my chances of motherhood were escaping me. The sadness gripped me with unimaginable intensity.

I didn't know how to handle anything. If I had bothered to visit a psychiatrist, I am certain I would have been diagnosed with situational depression. I did not feel as though my life had meaning. What was the point of going to work each day, coming home, cleaning the house, day in, day out, for the rest of our lives? What was the point of anything? I knew my desperation to become a mother had officially clouded my judgment on a logical level, but I had no idea how to get past it. The only solution, in my mind, the only cure, was to become a mother, no matter what. Perhaps a third round of in vitro was necessary after all. Suddenly, putting my life in danger did not seem to be an issue. My life was in danger as it was, because I was living without hope.

In-Vitro — Round 3

BEFORE IT WAS time to revisit the in vitro process from start to finish, it was time to begin the transfer process. Two embryos had been waiting for us to try to use them for over two years. The beginning of the transfer process included a very unpleasant cleansing. I refer to it as a cleansing because it is the nicest way to put it. Once again, my uterus and tubes had to be sprayed with saline to ensure a perfect environment for the embryos. When the appointment time came, I was less than excited. For the life of me I cannot explain the pain that was involved during this sonogram. It was excruciating, but sweet William held my hand and put his face on top of mine throughout the procedure. He kept telling me that he loved me and I threw out one sarcastic comment after another. I asked him why he couldn't be the woman, just this once. I reminded him how much I hated this procedure (as if he didn't know) and told him that I needed to pretend that I was a yoga expert and knew how to breathe.

Dr. Warren was as gentle as possible and narrated the entire procedure, but we pretty much ignored him the entire time. We did not ignore him when he said, okay, I am going to remove the balloon and the catheter now. While he was "in my uterus" he also mapped out the best route. I found this hilarious. Apparently, there is a sharp right hand turn somewhere on the way to my uterine cavity. Maybe that was the reason I had only become pregnant once on my own. Perhaps William's sperm could not follow such a windy and curvy path.

On the way out, Dr. Warren grabbed me a two-month supply of birth control pills. I was instructed to also begin a regimen of baby aspirin and await the protocol the following day. I imagined there might be an ultrasound and a blood test, but Dr. Warren had already informed me that I would not have to make a lot of office visits for a simple embryo transfer. So, I waited for the protocol, eager to begin with actual fertilized embryos. Maybe this time, just maybe, it would work.

A few days and e-mail exchanges later, I finally received the protocol. It was unbelievably complicated. There seemed to be very little difference in medication amounts when compared with my two in vitro attempts. I would be receiving injections for about a month, followed by antibiotics, steroids, estrogen tablets, progesterone injections and vaginal supplements. I read and reread the protocol with a pit in my stomach. If I subjected my body to all of these medications and injections and the embryos were found (on the day of the transfer) not to be viable, I would not be able to recover from that. Instantly, I decided if I was going to go this far, I might as well go all the way with another round of in vitro fertilization. William understood my logic, but he was not looking forward to watching me go through such a procedure, again.

I responded to the protocol (which was sent by the patient coordinator named Jessica) with my consideration of going through one more round of in vitro. She was stunned and informed me that I had to speak with Dr. Foster because this would change timing and all sorts of other issues. I explained that I was fearful that my embryos would not be in great shape, even if they survived the unfreezing process. Upon hearing my new idea, Dr. Foster cancelled a meeting and squeezed me into his office the very next day.

Dr. Foster began by asking me if anyone had ever discussed the significance of my FSH level. I had heard of those three letters, but I did not know what he was referring to. Apparently, a woman's FSH level rises as she gets older, which is a reflection of her egg reserve decreasing. So, as FSH levels increase, egg reserve decreases. For someone who was about to turn the evil 35, a normal FSH level was around 9 or 10. Mine was a bit higher, at a 12.2. He explained that my FSH level reflected a typical 39 year old woman. Well, this freaked me out beyond belief. Apparently, a few years before my level was at a seven, this meant that my levels rose very rapidly in just three years' time. Dr. Foster suggested a very aggressive protocol of fertility medications to ensure the best possible egg quality on a woman with eggs of a 39 year old. Panic struck me immediately. William misunderstood and thought that Dr. Foster was suggesting a gentle protocol, and I had to explain that he was suggesting quite the opposite. Dr. Foster agreed with me and assured me that I would not over hyperstimulate this time because of my FSH level. Apparently, my eggs were too old to cause life threatening hyperstimulation.

While we were in the waiting room, I had glanced at the pamphlets and spotted one with information about egg donation. This clinic had a bank of embryos and women ready to donate them to needy couples. Before I knew what was coming out of my mouth I asked the doctor if we should just skip the IVF procedure using my eggs and consider using donor eggs. He was quick to respond that I did not need to consider egg donation. My chances were about 40-50% in my favor, which, quite frankly, did not sound encouraging to me at all. However, he posited that an egg donor's donation to an embryo increased the chance of pregnancy to about 80%. I wanted the 80% and turned to William and asked him what he thought. He thought we should use my eggs, which made Dr. Foster jump in to the conversation, adding, "Egg donation increases the cost quite a bit, around 12 to 25 thousand dollars, depending on which package you choose."

It may sound strange, but the additional cost actually swayed me toward interest in egg donation. If we went through a regular cycle and it failed, we would be faced with the prospect of paying for another cycle and possibly the egg donor on top of it, which we could probably never afford. If we just paid additional money for the egg donation now, it would be a smaller financial risk. I rationalized that we could take out a small loan to pay for an IVF cycle with an egg donor. If we were going to go through this process, I really wanted the 80% chance over a 40 to 50% chance.

I asked over and over again if we should use an egg donor and Dr. Foster urged me to hold off on that option. He insisted that it could be something explored down the road, but for now, since he had not yet had his own in vitro experience with me, he really wanted the chance to create our genetic baby for us. Both William and Dr. Foster argued with me and I responded with tears. Embarrassed, I pleaded with the doctor to convince me that he was the best there was in the business. The thought of going through this process a third time and it not working was too much to bear. Although he was humble and would not claim credit as being the best, he theorized that my past two cycles appeared to be "cookie cutter" in vitro recipes by clinics that clearly did not investigate my specific needs. He promised he would do better in those regards. It was somewhat reassuring, but not enough to make me feel optimistic. As we left the office, I lamented my fears and pessimism over and over.

When we got back to our house, I started looking at the egg donor information on the fertility clinic's website. Although an access code was needed to view profiles, a sample profile was included. The sample profile provided a picture of the donor as a baby and as an adult, SAT scores, college attendance, hobbies, health history, and more than I would have expected. Without checking with William, I shot off an e-mail message to Jessica and asked her if we could use an egg donor as a backup for our cycle. I was still willing to go through the extraction process, but in the case of my eggs being as old as my FSH level claimed, I wanted an embryo insurance policy. She did not know if it were possible and promised to get back to me.

Jessica did get back to me, and not with the news I was hoping to hear. She was told that the timing of the cycles could not be coordinated and that at least three months were usually needed when using a donor, even frozen eggs from a donor. There were quarantine rules that required testing and retesting on eggs before usage. This made very good sense, but it also meant that my insurance plan had disappeared before my eyes. William and I had two choices. We could wait for donated eggs to be ready and then go through with the entire in vitro process, or we could go through the in vitro process without donated eggs. If that didn't work, we could subject ourselves to another round of procedures using donated eggs months down the road. I really did not want to subject myself to the procedure again with such overwhelming statistics and the sixth sense that it would not work. But at the same time, if I was going to use my own eggs, I did not want to wait. Since my FSH levels were already too high for a gal my age, a few more months could make all the difference between success and failure.

William had been hesitant to use a donated egg for this cycle, and advised that we go forward, and so the decision was made. I contacted Jessica to let her know that we had reached a plan. She agreed with our decision and hoped that we did not need to pursue an egg donor at a later date. Financially, I did not think that would be an option down the road.

Down the road would not help me now. It was time to focus on this cycle. And on that front, I was ordered to begin a new packet of birth control pills on the third day of my period, which was two days from the day I spoke with Jessica. The pill packet was to be consumed for a full three weeks. When the pill packet was used up (the placebo week was not necessary) I would wait for my period and the fun would begin, again. The fertility medication would begin on the third day of my next period. Oh please, I prayed, let this finally work.

ACUPUNCTURE, REALLY?

IN THE PIT of my stomach, I feared that another round of IVF was a complete waste of time. I could not begin to explain why it was that I felt so negative, I just did. But, being the proactive, take charge type of person that I am, I wanted to do anything and everything I could to increase my chances for success, so I decided to investigate acupuncture. With a quick search on the Internet, I found an acupuncturist who specialized in fertility treatments in my town. The problem that I saw was that at least 90 days were needed to have an impact on follicular development.

If anyone does light reading, it becomes apparent that three months is the magical time frame for both the sperm and the egg. This means that the eggs I released this month through IVF would have been developed three months ago. I considered postponing the IVF, but there was absolutely no way I could endure the invasive fertility treatments at the beginning of a new school year. That was out of the question. I contacted the acupuncturist named Sally via e-mail and asked her if it would waste my time since 90 days was not a possibility. She responded immediately and assured me that although 90 days is optimal, there were still many treatments that I could benefit from even within a few weeks. That was all I needed to hear, so I made an appointment later in the week.

When I walked into the office, it smelled and appeared like the many naturopathic offices I had already experienced. My digestive system had been a major problem for years of my life and I had tried every diet out there to fix it. Dairy free, wheat free, gluten free, sugar free, yeast free were some of the extremes I had tried, but none had made a difference. I tried them for long periods of time. I assure you I was not one of those people who tried changing eating habits for a week and then gave up when it did nothing. Months, even years were dedicated to curbing all digestive issues, but to no avail.

According to Sally's website, diet would be discussed, and I was not looking forward to having that conversation again. Recognizing the inevitability of the conversation, I braced myself. Sally emerged from the hallway almost immediately upon my arrival and introduced herself. She apologized because another client was running late and therefore, our first meeting would be delayed. My response was that it was not a problem, but considering I had rushed out of my classroom to get there on time, I couldn't help but reflect upon all of the tasks I could have completed if I had known that a bit of extra time was available. One part of my brain yelled at the other part of my brain to relax and focus on the hope that might be available to me within the office, and I waited for our session to begin.

The first session was unlike any doctor appointment I had ever had. Sally sat with me and interviewed me about everything from my libido, to the temperature of my hands and feet, back to my diet, sleeping patterns, and of course, my past history of ART (Artificial Reproductive Techniques). She said fertility comes in many forms and that even if after many months of working with her I found myself without the ability to carry a child, acupuncture and Chinese medicine would teach me to embrace the gifts that I had and I would still emerge as a happier person. Inside, I balked at such a trite statement. As if I needed one more person to tell me that my life could still be meaningful without the ability to become a mother. What she was talking about was acceptance, and to me, that was the last issue I wanted to embrace. Regardless, my head understood that I would have to move on eventually, I just was not ready to do that, nor did I want to contemplate the possibility of its necessity. If I had, why would I have even made the appointment?

Sally was doing and saying what she needed to say. She told me that she didn't have any magic fairy dust and if she had possessed it in any form, she would have sprinkled it all over herself. Acupuncture, she admitted, was no miracle cure, but it did wonders with the mind and the soul for everyone who took it seriously. There were three additions to consider ensuring the success of acupuncture: diet, stress levels, and herbal supplements. She took me into another room and checked my pulse for what seemed like an eternity. She asked me to stick out my tongue and she analyzed what the color and texture meant, and then she began my first treatment.

Before she poked me with any needles, she diagnosed me (based on the interview, my pulse, and the color/consistency of my tongue) with a Spleen Qi deficiency. I did not understand what that meant, nor did I ask. Sally presented me with a few sheets of paper and proposed that I change my eating patterns to improve my Spleen Qi. I was urged to avoid processed foods and all dairy products. Not again, I thought.

Sally asked me to raise my pant legs and my shirt so that she could insert needles into my legs and stomach area. When she looked at my stomach, she criticized me for having tight abs. I laughed because I thought she was kidding, but she wasn't. My abdominal area is really not impressive, seriously, but she pulled out a statue of the fertility goddess and pointed to a round belly. She critiqued, "This is what you want to aspire to have."

"So let me get this straight, I am supposed to aim for a jiggly belly?" I asked in astonishment.

"Not jiggly," she corrected, "soft."

I was dumfounded. Why did my belly need to be soft to create a good environment for a baby? What about all those articles encouraging women trying to conceive to get into good shape that I had poured over in my initial procreation research? Just like every other experience regarding fertility, contradictions were everywhere. And here was another question, how was my belly going to get softer if I eliminated all yummy/fattening foods from my diet?

The diet was not the only concern I had at that moment. Even though I sought out acupuncture to increase my chances of fertility success, the acupuncture process frightened me. I did not like the idea of having needles stuck in all parts of my body, but before I had an opportunity to back out, it was time for the needle insertions. The first few acupuncture points did not hurt all that much, but when she reached my leg and inserted a needle in a specific pressure point, I felt throbbing throughout my entire body. Sally informed that the spot that throbbed was my stomach pressure point. Naturally, I thought. The only other needle to throb again was my ovary stimulation point. I was excited and a bit freaked out by my reaction. Perhaps I was just getting excited for nothing, but it felt like a positive step. She left me alone in the room, covered in needles for about 30 minutes or so, and with that, my first session was complete.

On my way out of the office, Sally handed me a few books, a list of herbal supplement suggestions (which was accompanied by data touting their effectiveness), and pamphlets about diet. She told me to try to give myself a Femoral Artery Massage three times a day and demonstrated how to accomplish it. In a nutshell, I was instructed to press down on my Femoral Artery for about 30 seconds, then slowly lift my fingers and feel the blood flow return. Apparently, this helped the quality of eggs, but I had no idea how or why. She suggested that I read the literature before I returned to her office in order to commit myself to her practice and improve my fertility chances.

Before I could read the literature, I had to purchase the herbal supplements on her suggested list. The first of the many prescribed supplements was Resveratrol, which had received a bit of publicity over the years. Supposedly, it offered all of the benefits red wine boasted without having to drink a drop of alcohol. Basically, all of the studies that were encouraging people to consume a glass of red wine existed because of the ingredient in Resveratrol. In addition to lowering blood sugar and improving the immune system, it apparently provided overall health benefits, which would ensure that egg production was given every advantage as well. She prescribed specific brand names and doses for vitamins B and D, Zinc, Calcium, fish oil, and digestive probiotics. In addition to swallowing the seven caplets and capsules from the various pill supplements, Sally prescribed me to swallow royal jelly three times a day. In one of the studies she handed me, it explained how royal jelly helped a woman's ovaries with optimal egg production. I had never heard of royal jelly, but was excited to hear the word jelly was part of the prescription. Royal Jelly received its name as it was created solely by bees and fed only to the Queen Bee. Apparently, the jelly helped the Queen Bee produce more bees.

Although it seemed improbable that the supplements held the key to a pregnancy, I ran out immediately to buy all of the products as instructed. I knew it seemed unlikely that these supplements would necessarily make a difference between me getting pregnant or not. I figured I had already changed my diet and endured needles; why not complete the trifecta of insanity? Did I mention the costs? One supplement cost more than the next. Standing in line, doing the quick math in my head, it couldn't be right, could it?

$550! As outrageous as the cost of the supplements were, and believe me when I say I have never spent any dollar amount close to that on vitamins before, the cost did not hold a candle to the total amount of money the in vitro procedure would ultimately cost. I justified the dollar amount by reminding myself that I was just doing everything I could to increase the probability of the in vitro procedure working, so it was an investment. Regardless of my justification, the conservative spender in me began reflecting on the total dollar amounts of everything related to fertility treatments, and it was astonishing. One bottle of Resveratrol with a 30-day supply cost $75. The various vitamins and probiotics totaled $350 for a 30-day supply. The Royal Jelly cost $125 for a 30-day supply. Supplements aside, the acupuncture treatments cost over $900. The required diet and special organic food products increased my grocery bill by hundreds of dollars each week.

Before beginning the regiment of supplements, I wanted to read Sally's books about fertility and acupuncture. When the weekend came, before my husband or even dogs woke up, I curled myself up on the couch with the books and educated myself in Traditional Chinese Medicine. The message in the book made a lot of sense. It explained that Traditional Chinese Medicine differed from Western Medicine in that it tried to find the route of the problem and change your body to bring it back in balance. The body was either in balance or out of balance, according to the author. If the body was out of balance, symptoms arose, such as digestive, fertility, skin problems, headaches, and so forth.

Western medicine treated symptoms, but did not solve the problem. This comment made a lot of sense to me as well. If you have a headache, you take an aspirin, but whatever caused the headache was not cured with the aspirin, but perhaps the pain was cured. As clear-cut as it sounded, the book championed Western Medicine as a great partner with Traditional Chinese Medicine, instead of touting one over the other. This was another point that appealed to me. I have never been the type of person to believe in only one thing, whatever it may be. In my classroom, I use a little of this technique, and a little of that technique. I use a range of strategies. I do not believe in any one best teaching method, but the combination of lots of methods.

In addition to the philosophy behind Traditional Chinese Medicine, the author preached about reducing stress and questioned the type of people who say yes to everyone but their self. That one stung a bit, as I definitely fit into that category. It pointed to all of the meridians in the body, educated about proper breathing techniques, and the power of positivism. Reading the book almost felt like a religious experience as no one had ever focused on fertility issues with data that so closely matched my own experiences, weaknesses, and triumphs. Of course, the book kept referring to that magical three-month time line, which made me crazy. Trying to follow the book's message, I tried to let go of the guilt of circumventing the ideal three-month trial of treatment before IVF, but it hung like a black cloud over my head.

The black cloud followed me as I investigated the dreaded nutritional topic. I learned the Spleen Chi Diet was a diet where one was required to avoid raw fruits and vegetables, all sweets, eggs, refined carbohydrates, soy products, any food that came out of a refrigerator or freezer, all food that was heated by a microwave, and any beverages with meals. I immediately became terrified of food. What could I eat? Meat was permitted, but must be organic, perhaps nuts, steamed veggies, and that was pretty much it. I had lots of questions for my next appointment, but in the mean time, I worried that anything I put in my mouth would ruin my chances of procreation. Although the author was telling readers to focus on all you do well and ignore guilt, food was something else to feel guilty about.

The days following this information overload left me clueless and pretty much starving and thirsty at all times. I searched online for a Spleen Chi diet guide, but could not find a suggested plan for breakfast, lunch, dinner, snacks or anything remotely close to a suggestion. Scouring for a Spleen Chi cookbook did not yield any greater results. In addition to my diet woes, the supplements required were no picnic either. Although my taste buds were angry with me over the lack of enjoyment they were receiving on the Spleen Chi diet, they were outright enraged with me the first time I swallowed a teaspoon of Royal Jelly. I truly believed that the Jelly would be enjoyable. With the name jelly built into the product title, I assumed it would be a quick and sweet treat.

Boy was I off base. Royal Jelly actually burns your throat. It was like ingesting poison. The three times a day I swallowed the jelly were the worst points of my day. The only way I was able to get it down at all was by brainwashing my mind about quality egg production and babies. Truthfully, I cannot handle cough syrup. If I am hacking up a lung, I search for products that come in a capsule form to avoid the horrible 10-second experience of tasting cough syrup. However, this disgusting goopy substance might increase my chances of having a baby, so I did it, but it was not easy for a wimp like me. All I kept thinking was that all of this had better result in making me a mother at last. The thought of eating the bland food, burning my throat three times a day with Jelly, keeping countless supplements straight each day, and having needles stuck in every area of my body had to result in fertility progress.

Since Sally could not do anything to change the taste of Royal Jelly, I did not mention my disdain with it, but at my next acupuncture visit, I complained endlessly about the diet requirements. Within that week, I had received two boxes of my favorite chocolates in honor of teacher appreciation day, but I could not eat them. My friends all wanted to go out for dinner or lunch three different times, but I was too concerned about eating anything that was not prepared by me from scratch. My husband wanted to take me out to a nice dinner, but I turned him down, citing our future fertility was at stake. Our very social society, which centers on eating, was suddenly my Achilles heel. It does not sound like a problem, and believe me, I know these problems are laughable to most, but the issue bothered me nonetheless.

Sally did not judge me for my sadness over two uneaten boxes of chocolate and assured me that I could have one piece a day. She also added that I did not have to give anything up completely. That made me happy, but I still did not know what I was supposed to eat on a day-to-day basis. I criticized the lack of information offering clear-cut diet suggestions to improve the Spleen Chi. Sally disagreed with my criticism, but did not really inform me of anything in existence that would help me figure out what to consume. She suggested steel cut oatmeal with honey for breakfast and encouraged that I think outside the box. I hate oatmeal. The only good thing to emerge out of this diet was that my belly was flat. Of course, I liked this side effect; but Sally criticized me for being too skinny. My argument, again, was that if my diet were so limited, I certainly would not gain weight. She assured me that I could eat as much fish and chicken as I wanted. That was not an exciting prospect.

I reminded myself that at least I had a choice. I was not suffering from a disease like Celiac disease, which I had been previously tested for. Celiac disease would require me to cut out all gluten from my diet forever. I was not suffering from diabetes or any other life threatening illness. Through my desperation to have a child, I, on my own accord, had sought out acupuncture treatment, which health care did not pay for. So, in addition to my seeking out the alternative medicine, I also was paying money to be told things I did not want to hear. I did not have to follow what she said, but if I wanted to truly try to transform my body with Traditional Chinese Medicine, I needed to embrace every aspect as an opportunity of turning my fertility status around. In simple terms, I had to stop whining like a brat and suck it up and try the treatment that I was investing in. Of course, I did not have to enjoy it. But oh, was I hungry!

HERE I GO AGAIN — ROUND 3

BEFORE I KNEW it, my birth control packet was completed. So there was nothing to do but wait for my period. The first real day would mark the beginning of the new in vitro cycle, as long as ovarian suppression was confirmed. I did not have a lot of realistic hope that the cycle would work. As I went forward with this cycle, I hoped I would be wrong. Perhaps a lack of optimism would save me from crushing devastation.

I tried to organize my classroom materials to ensure that my students would be taken care of in the event that I missed a week of school or more. I spent extra hours running off copies and creating lesson plans that would run themselves. There was nothing more in my control, and that frightened me more than anything else. And once again, the every other day doctor appointments began.

My first appointment was a typical nightmare. Naturally, the phlebotomist could not find my veins, which took a lot of time. In addition, the ultrasound technician was late. I did not get out of the office until 8:15, and I had to be at school by 8:55. My heart pounded and my pulse raced over the unfortunate traffic and time combination on the return drive to our home. We ended up behind a school bus, a very slow driver, and a flatbed truck delivering a 12-foot tree to a house with a gated and narrow driveway. The flatbed truck was what set us back the most. We were stopped dead in the road for at least 12 minutes, which, for the record, was about two minutes from my house. I arrived to work 30 minutes late and I am never late. Although I had another teacher covering my class, one of the few I let in on my secret, I was panic-stricken. How was I going to go through this traffic crazy time crunching schedule every other day for the next few weeks and stay positive and sane?

As I reiterated this story to Sally at my next acupuncture appointment, she chided me for allowing stress to enter my body. She accused me of respecting my job more than my body and asked if my job would ever have the ability to hold an infant in its arms. Ouch. I understood where her comments were coming from. The problem was she just didn't get it. I had been down this road before. Three times in fact. The only tangible joy that was left in my life, other than my family, was my job. I had not yet been able to have a baby. What if I risked my job and motherhood still evaded me? The hours I pour into my job are excessive, but it is my passion and I am privileged to have the job, and I know it. Who was she to criticize?

As I felt guilty over something new, William stopped my self-critique with four words, "She is an idiot."

I giggled but he continued, "You have worked too long and too hard to establish yourself to listen to such nonsense. Seriously, she is an idiot."

Of course it was exactly what I needed to hear, even if Sally had been a little bit right.

The day after my first blood test and ultrasound scan was the day to begin the new injections. This time, I was on a different round of medication, Menopour and Follistim Plus. The Follistim Plus was not new, but the Menopour was new and it was vicious. It burned and twisted my insides with each injection. How many days of this do I have to endure, I wondered? I couldn't remember. Was it 8, 9, or 10? And of course, as I moved along, there would be three injections instead of two.

The daily injections and constant blood tests and ultrasounds would make every day seem like 12, but my follicles, estrogen levels, and uterus all looked well with each appointment, according to the doctor. Our biggest issue was with the very rude receptionist. If we were early she would criticize us for being early. If we were on time, she would shoo us away from checking in and ask us to take a seat. When we tried to book an appointment, she barked out the times. When we showed up for the appointments that she booked, she claimed that we did not arrive at the scheduled time. I am not a violent person, but I wanted to deck her.

Regardless of Little Miss Attitude, the true test came 12 days after the first injection. I was a bundle of nerves waiting to find out whether or not the extraction would in fact take place in two days' time. It was determined that it would, and there was a "trigger" shot that had to be delivered intramuscularly at exactly 10:00. The lovely nurse from my school volunteered to administer the medication, so William and I arrived promptly at 9:45 p.m. for the beginning of another fertility cycle of hope, waiting, and more likely than not, eventual devastation.

The day before the extraction, the hours passed more slowly than they ever had for me at a day at work. I wanted this trial to be over and I wanted to be pregnant. Although I did not hold out a lot of hope, the doctors had been very encouraging during this cycle. My blood work was perfect, they told me. My follicle count was tremendous and the expectations were that 15 to 20 eggs would be retrieved. It was time to complete this attempt and for me to become a mother.

I was not nervous the morning of the retrieval about anything except for the quantity and quality of the eggs. I had been through the procedure twice already and knew what to expect. When the doctor welcomed me, he introduced the anesthesiologist and invited William to sit next to me and watch the I.V. insertion. The anesthesiologist explained what the drugs would do to me and it was quite different from the other two protocols I had endured previously. He kept saying, this will work, you will get pregnant, and I tried not to join in on the optimism, but couldn't help myself.

William was eventually whisked away and it was time to get up on the gurney with the stirrups and display myself once again. It was over rather quickly, and when I was completely coherent, which occurred only a few minutes after the procedure, I was asked about pain levels. On a scale of one to ten, I claimed I was about a three, so the anesthesiologist bid me adieu and I was left with the nurse. The doctor soon came back and asked if I had learned how many eggs were retrieved yet and I shook my head. Within a few minutes, my pain level rose to about a 12, but there was nothing offered but Extra Strength Tylenol. The nurse returned and announced that they had extracted nine eggs.

It was a crushing disappointment. She said nine was great, and Dr. Foster came out and cheerily supported that claim. I countered that Dr. Warren had anticipated 15-20, so nine eggs did not seem like a victory, especially since I did not know if any of them were mature. Dr. Foster reminded me that my other two attempts, the first with 19 eggs, all of which were immature, and the second with 11 eggs, did not fare much greater results. Although that fact was true enough, it was too early to know whether or not any of the nine eggs were any good. Even worse still, no one would call me until the next day to let me know the fertilization status.

Eventually, I was wheeled out of the office, depressed out of my mind, and on my way home. William was disappointed too, but reminded me that this was completely out of our control. The rest of the day and evening were pure torture from an emotional and pain perspective. I remembered the anguish of the hyperstimulation that followed the last procedure, but I did not really remember the intense uterine/back/ovarian pain. Every time I moved or my husband sat on the bed, I winced. Going to the bathroom hurt, breathing hurt, sitting hurt, everything hurt. And for what, I cynically reminded myself? Probably for nothing.

Every hour throughout the evening I stared at the clock wondering when my questions might be answered. Would they call at 7:00 a.m., 8:00 a.m., or after 5:00 p.m.? When morning finally arrived I pulled the phone off the base and sat it next to me in bed. I showered with the door open still hunched over in pain, but feeling the need to be clean, to listen for a telephone ring. At 10:00, the phone rang and I nearly jumped out of my skin. I picked it up and was crushed to hear my sister's voice. That is the rule, when you are waiting for a specific phone call, everyone but the person you are waiting with bated breath to call, calls. I cut her off and told her we were waiting to hear from the embryologist. A few hours later, the phone rang again and it was a wrong number. At least I was pretty sure it was a wrong number. They had asked to speak with W.G. something or other. After I hung up the receiver, I couldn't help wondering if it was the clinic calling the wrong name out with my results? Could they be that incompetent? Lord, I hoped not. I continued to wait, and worry, and was certain that the news would not be welcome.

Finally, the phone call came, and six of the nine eggs were mature, five of which fertilized. Okay, this was not terrible news, but greedily, I hoped that all nine eggs were mature and fertilized and wonderful. The embryologist told me they had to use ICSI because William's sperm count was only at 6 million. When it was important, the sperm count never seemed to be very high. Poor William handled the stress in different ways. I did not care that ICSI was used; I just wanted to have a baby, by any medical intervention necessary. At the end of our very quick conversation, the embryologist informed me that I would not be receiving a phone call for another two days. To try to keep them undisturbed, the policy was not to take out the embryos every day. This meant that I had another 48 hours of waiting and wondering.

Within the 48 hours, my husband received a phone call at work from the fertility clinic. One of the nurses explained to William that we would be receiving a phone call the following morning with instructions. We would either have to go in to the clinic for the transfer at 10:00 in the morning, or we would wait until Monday for the transfer. Naturally, I wanted to wait until Monday because that would mean I would have the deeply desired five day blastocyst transferred, which had been, according to my research, more likely to implant and therefore lead to a baby. Somehow, I knew that we wouldn't be that lucky.

Unfortunately, my instincts were right on the money. At 8:08 in the morning, as I was sitting on my couch with the phone next to me, I received the news that there were 3 embryos they wanted to transfer that day. Then they asked if I could be there at 9:00 instead of 10:00. Considering I lived about an hour away from the clinic, 9:00 was impossible, but we said we would do our best to get there as quickly as possible.

To say I was devastated is an understatement. I went from nine, to five, to three within a matter of three days. There was no doubt in my mind that they wanted to perform the transfer sooner rather than later because the doctors were convinced that the embryos wouldn't make it another two days in the lab. I tried to hold back tears on the ride down to the clinic.

Upon arrival, we were ushered back into the same operating room with the same directions as before. I was instructed to remove all clothing, put on the robe, special socks, hair net and then meet the staff in the surgical prep room. I did as instructed and the nurse reassured me that there was still a great chance for success. Appreciative as we were to hear her optimism, it was difficult to believe. But when the embryologist and Dr. Foster came out, they were both very hopeful.

It turned out that I still had five embryos, with three of them identified as "A" quality, and the other two embryos were deemed B and C quality respectively. Therefore the recommendation was that they transfer the three "A" quality embryos. Because of my history, Dr. Foster offered me the option of transferring all five embryos. I kept picturing the "Octo-mom" and those other parents of multiples and rejected the idea. He agreed that the three were my best bet. A picture of the embryos was shown to me on the computer screen and they looked (text book wise) great. They had eight cells and were all pretty much the same size cell, which is what you look for in good quality embryos. Still, I had a negative feeling that I couldn't let go.

Perhaps my full bladder torturing me that was required for the procedure did not do anything to dissipate the negative feeling. This clinic did not instruct me to drink 64 oz of liquid or 32 oz of liquid, just to drink. That tiny alteration actually made it a lot less stressful, but of course, I was concerned that I might not have consumed enough liquid to make my bladder as full as necessary. Within minutes of the ultra-sound, the doctor pronounced that my bladder was nice and full. That was one piece of good news.

William watched through the window and was able to see the three embryos, as Dr. Foster pointed out, which looked like three little ducks in a row, on the television screen. The procedure was over relatively quickly, and I was told that I did great. This made me laugh. Seriously, all I did was lie there and not move. Was that considered some sort of performance worthy rating of any kind?

When the procedure was completed, Dr. Foster removed the speculum and waited for the "All clear" word from the embryologist. He explained that sometimes one gets stuck, so they wanted to make sure that the tube was empty before calling it a day. As he stated this, I hoped the speculum would not need to be reinserted because it was a prospect that was less than appealing. Fortunately, the all-clear statement was made and I was instructed to lie down for the next 10 minutes.

Because the embryologist and nurse chatted with me, the 10 minutes flew by. I learned that the embryologist had endured fertility assistance as well, but she pointed out that she never had to endure an egg extraction. Still, she had to put up with timed insemination, trigger shots, and progesterone injections. Somehow, she gave herself the progesterone injections. They were brutal enough when William administered them. I could not imagine giving myself progesterone shots.

She eventually gave birth to two children which made me hope that I would also be able to have my happy ending. At this point, I had three in vitro attempts, five insemination attempts, four months of Clomid, one month of a Clomid alternative, three months of timed intercourse with ultrasounds and trigger shots, not to mention years of trying with ovulation test kits and of course, in my initial optimism, just when we "thought" timing was right. Wasn't it my turn?

Instead of focusing on the positive, I tried to wrap my head around hearing that the pregnancy test would turn out negative. It was too cruel to imagine, but my mind pictured it easily. How would I bounce back from another disappointment? I tried to think positively. I went to receive an acupuncture treatment following the transfer to increase my chances. Sally looked at the images of my embryos and pronounced that Dr. Warren and Dr. Foster did everything right. I asked her what magic foods I should eat and she told me to stay away from sugar and salads. I wondered why salad was something to stay away from, but I planned to oblige. And, here I was again, every time I felt a certain uterine twinge, I smiled, but when I didn't feel another one, I soured. Once again, it was going to be a long two weeks.

In the meantime, I did not return to work. I got winded going down the stairs, and I mean really winded. I had to bend over and catch my breath. Less than a week prior, I engaged in daily semi-rigorous workouts without incident. Clearly, IVF took a massive physical toll on me again. I missed my students and would have happily welcomed the distraction, but I was not well enough to return to my classroom. The pain added to my mantra of "This is a lot to endure for nothing, again." I shuddered at the great possibility of another fertility failure and fantasized about feeling healthy again. Over the next few days my symptoms continued to get worse as did my mood. My stomach protruded by about seven inches more than before the procedure. Pressure took over my every breath. I wanted to take a giant pin and stick it into my abdomen. Fantasies of liquid spurting out from my abdomen abounded, but I knew it would be painful, not to mention stupid to try anything of the sort.

Meanwhile, William called the doctor's office each morning and reported my ridiculous fluid retention and bloating. The staff did not seem all that concerned and I was put off by that fact. Knowing my history, I imagined that the doctors would insist that I return to their office immediately. Every time we called, they were supportive and lovely, but they did not ask to have me come in so they could check on me in person. Perhaps that is because William and I had been overreacting a tad.

I had to get my first blood test to check my hormone levels at the one-week post extraction mark. Although I had the test first thing in the morning at Quest at 7:40, by 4:00, I had not heard any updates. William called the clinic and asked them if there was any news and 15 minutes later, I received an update. The nurse reported that my hormone levels were wonderful and that I should remain on the current dosage of progesterone. Cheerfully, she added, "I'll speak to you again next week with the results of your pregnancy test."

"Yeah, great," I replied.

I confessed that I had not felt any symptoms of pregnancy and was not looking forward to the pregnancy test. This, of course, made the nurse do what all people do when they are uncomfortable with the truth; they shine fake optimism your way.

Attempting to encourage me she resorted to sharing an anecdote. "You know, just last week I was speaking to another IVF patient who claimed that no symptoms were felt and she wanted to stop the progesterone injections. I urged her to keep taking the hormones because you never know, and she had a positive pregnancy test. Don't give up."

The nurse was sweet and supportive, but I was not in a proper mental state to receive such support. Without physically rolling my eyes, I did so emotionally because I knew my body. I had experienced two previous pregnancies. Of course those pregnancies were both short lived, but I distinctly remembered how they felt. With longing, I recalled the fluttering in my ovaries and the electrical type impulse that was likely implantation. Nothing even close to that had appeared and I knew the truth; I was not pregnant. But of course, to be polite, I commented on hoping that lighting would strike twice and rushed to end the belabored conversation.

My mood was infinitely negative and my stomach was outrageously bloated. I had one small ounce of hope left, which I tried to squash for my own benefit. The Traditional Chinese Medicine book claimed that a slippery pulse was a sure sign of pregnancy. When my fingers pressed against my wrist, it was clear that my pulse was definitely stronger than previously. I could not really say for sure that the pulse rate was stronger after the transfer, but it was certainly stronger than it used to be. Of course, that might have been my dietary changes, the acupuncture effects, or a coincidence. What I did suspect was that Sally would be able to tell immediately whether or not I was pregnant by my pulse.

My acupuncture appointment marked my first driving venture since the extraction and the transfer and the ride hurt. Every bump was torture on my bloated belly. I was hopeful that Sally would relieve a bit of my pain, but even more desperately I hoped that the words "slippery pulse" would emerge from her lips.

Without informing her of my intentions, I confessed that I felt no symptoms this time and was certain I was not pregnant. As she felt my pulse rate and my meridians, her body language confirmed my suspicions. And so I endured another torturous round of acupuncture needles hoping for relief from the hyperstimulation and fighting back tears.

As soon as I drove away from my appointment, I stopped fighting and the tears flowed freely down my cheeks. It was time to admit, with 100% certainty, that I was not pregnant. Immediately, anger took over where sadness left off. Earlier that morning, I had heard about a Hollywood starlet who found herself unexpectedly pregnant. The examples continued to prove the rule. I never met this particular starlet, or the dozens of others who had reportedly found themselves in the same situation over the past several years. It is possible that all of these women are lovely people who make great mothers, but at that moment I heard myself whining about how yet another woman could get pregnant without even trying or necessarily wanting to have a child, but someone who sacrificed her body, money, and time, someone who wanted to be a mother more than anything else in the world, could not. It was not fair, and the reality hurt far more than it should have at this point of my infertility journey.

Regardless, the anger built up over the rest of the evening. I was increasingly angry with William for his inconsistent sperm count. I changed everything about my lifestyle, including my diet to try to make baby making possible. I digested royal jelly twice a day for goodness sake. What did he do? He did not do anything I decided, at least not to his own body. Even though we ordered specific supplements to increase his sperm motility, he refused to take the recommended dose. He consumed far less because he felt he should. He did not cut out artificial sweeteners, alcohol, or junk food. Since this attempt clearly failed, yet again, we contemplated moving on to an egg donor, but did we need a sperm donor as well?

When William returned home that evening, I shared all of my reservations and anger with him through tears. He did not react with anger, although, clearly, he was offended by my theory. The offended reaction was in his eyes, not his words, for he did not articulate whether or not he believed his sperm were damaged goods. I could see my remarks impacted his male ego though. The ego is a fragile entity, and I understood that a man's ego, especially when his sperm was under consideration, was very sensitive. I preceded this admission by admitting to my own shortcomings in the fertility department. Clearly, my eggs were damaged goods. The embryos would not stick to my uterus, even though they were "Grade A" and there were three of them and my uterus was in wonderful shape. Would any embryo ever stick to my uterus? I wanted to hope that a very good quality one would, but only time and additional attempts would reveal whether or not it would.

Meanwhile, William chastised me for giving up before the official test results were in, but I knew my body. Regardless, he went online to try to dispel my negativity.

With unabashed hope in his eyes, he shared that many websites supported the fact that it was too early to feel any symptoms of pregnancy. Although I appreciated his optimism and deep-seeded desire, I reminded him that I knew my own body, and tears welled up in his beautiful eyes. He was ready to accept that it did not work, but clearly neither one of us was 100% ready to accept it, because the progesterone injections continued.

As I played down any optimism that showed its ugly head, I found a medical website with a number of women who were facing similar issues that I was facing. All of our stories had striking similarities, but were unique as well. Regardless, there was a discussion thread revolving around home pregnancy tests. All of us were in the two-week waiting period. Waiting two weeks to find out whether or not you are pregnant feels like two years. No matter how you try to distract yourself, you cannot help but obsess over the question of whether or not you are with child. Every twinge in the uterus area leads to unadulterated joy, but any lack of a sign is a knife in the heart. I wanted to be proven wrong. A positive pregnancy test would happily disprove my theory of understanding my body the way I thought I did. I knew I still had a few pregnancy tests lying around, carefully hidden in my drawer.

Furtively, I grabbed one and ran to the downstairs bathroom while William was occupying the upstairs bathroom. I actually kissed the pregnancy test before I used it to try to bring myself some much-needed luck. As I carefully placed the cap on the soiled tip, my heart fluttered in anticipation. After the suggested time passed, I thought I glimpsed a very, very faint positive line, but I was unsure whether or not I was trying to convince myself of a positive line or if it was there.

Women who have gone through the IVF process are advised not to take a home pregnancy test because a trigger shot, or an hCG shot, that is used to begin the ovulation process, can remain in your system for 14 days. Since hCG is the same hormone released during pregnancy and in the trigger shot, it can compromise the results of a home pregnancy test. However, most of the women on the message board reported that they took home pregnancy tests after two days and were clear of the hCG drug. The question was: was this faint positive line a mirage, leftover hCG, or something to smile about? As much as I tried to let negativity keep my heart in its proper place, I started to smile. All of the women reported that with each day that passed, a stronger positive line showed up on the test. I resolved to take another test in the morning and seek out the darker line.

Sleep was out of the question that night. As the hours ticked by, I tried to envision a big, fat, positive line emerging with the next test. I rubbed my belly and urged it to move, twinge, or give me some sort of positive sign. My belly did not respond to my request and my heart sunk. I finally fell asleep for a little while and dreamed of a big fat negative result on my next test.

The morning finally arrived, and I tore apart my drawer searching for the other test in the box. I yanked it out and snuck into the bathroom as William slept. I prayed for a positive line, but I truly believed that a negative result would show. Unfortunately, my instincts were correct. There was no trace of a positive line on this test. I knew I could not possibly be pregnant.

I confessed my pregnancy test taking to William and he resigned himself to the fact that this third IVF cycle had not succeeded. Regardless, he insisted that I continue to take the progesterone injections for the next few evenings, just in case. He rationalized that if I were incorrect, I would be in a full-blown panic if I had missed even one dose of progesterone. He did know me well, so I reluctantly agreed to have my poor, sore bottom tortured for a few more evenings. Ouch, was it rough.

The morning of the pregnancy test finally arrived and I was a little sad. Although I was certain that the results were negative, the official confirmation from the doctor's office would end my dream and finalize the repeated failure of my body. My horoscope, which I never read or took seriously, warned me not to get bogged down by the bad news I would inevitably receive. All signs in my body and apparently, in the stars, pointed to a big fat negative. I drank my usual big glass of water to try to help the phlebotomist find my veins with a bit more ease. My appointment was at 7:30. Before leaving for the appointment, I turned to William and said, "There is no chance that this worked, have you accepted that?" He nodded his head and told me he loved me.

I marched into Quest to a full house. Although I told the receptionist that I had a 7:30 appointment, I watched one patient after another walk in before me. Finally, at 8:15, my name was called. Since I was only 15 minutes from work, I did not panic over the delay, but wished it were over already. A final insult to the IVF cycle nightmare was the inability of the phlebotomist to find a good vein. In addition, she tried using a regular needle, not a butterfly needle. I told her most doctors were less than successful sticking me without a butterfly needle, but she balked at my advice. After she poked the first giant hole in my arm and moved the darn thing all around for a few minutes, she pulled it out and gave up.

Ironically, she began running around the clinic to try to locate a butterfly needle. When she returned, she explained that Quest Diagnostics was very stingy with butterfly needles, which was why she did not try to use one right off the bat. I cannot imagine that the butterfly needle costs that much more than a regular one, but I have nothing to base that assumption on. The butterfly needle eventually produced a blood sample, but not without a great amount of torture to go along with it. I fought back tears with the irony that I was going through this agony to go through additional agony when the results came through later in the day.

My school day crawled by slowly. Every time I thought about the official test results, my heart sank. I had asked the clinic to leave a message on my cell phone. Of course, I received no cell service in my school building, so I would have to wait until the end of the day. Sometimes, you could get a tiny bit of reception in the parking lot, so I vowed to wait until then.

To prolong the awful truth, I did not run out to my car when the day was over. I stayed in my classroom fixing one thing, cleaning another, until I knew it was time. I stopped in to say goodbye to my friend next door, and with my cell phone in hand I headed for the car. Carefully, I looked around the parking lot to make sure that no one would watch me as I listened to the message. There were two messages. They were both from Dr. Warren.

The first message he left asked me to call him back. I thought, well, he didn't want to leave the bad news on my voice mail. The second message was also from Dr. Warren. Apparently the patient coordinator informed him that I requested that a message be left on my voice mail. He was sorry to say that the hCG was negative and I was not pregnant. He explained that there was no known reason as to why I did not get pregnant. He reminded me that my embryos were top quality, all three of them, my uterus looked great, and therefore, they could not explain the negative outcome. At the end of the message, he asked that I call him.

And so I did. I explained that although I was devastated by the outcome, I had suspected that I was not pregnant and was at least not surprised by the bad news. We talked about different protocols in the future, including using an egg donor, but with my track record, and now serious lack of funds from this past failed attempt, I did not see how I would be able to afford another cycle, regardless of the protocol. As I reflected on the world of fertility assistance, I cynically started to compare all fertility clinics to casinos.

William and I had gambled a great amount of our money on what we were pretty sure was a safe bet. Yes, we knew there was a risk, but if we followed protocol perfectly, especially on this third round, we thought our chances were wonderful. The fact of the matter is when a cycle fails at a fertility clinic; the fertility clinic still wins because they receive all of their patients' money. They also win if their patients end up pregnant, because, once again, they still get their money. In addition to the money, if their patients end up pregnant, the clinics can boast about their incredible statistics for their future clientele. Either way, they collect their big payday, regardless of the patient's fate.

The difference, naturally, was that fertility clinics, this one in particular, deserved every penny they received. Dr. Foster, Dr. Warren, and their entire staff worked tirelessly to try to get me pregnant. My analogy was unfair to them and I knew it. I was just angry at the loss of my income with nothing to show for it.

If we were to gamble again, even with a safer bet of using an egg donor, there were still no guarantees. We could end up completely broke and remain childless. If it failed again, and a birth mother finally selected us to adopt her child, we would no longer have the adoption money in the bank because we would have spent it all. We would go into debt trying to start a family, and would that be any way to begin the responsibilities of having a family? I found myself at yet another fertility crossroads.

SOMEONE ELSE'S EGGS

WILLIAM AND I have never been gamblers; by nature we were conservative spenders. We never purchased lottery tickets or visited casinos. We were rarely extravagant with what little money we earned. We bought a very modest home in need of millions of repairs because we did not want large mortgage payments, in case one of us found ourselves unemployed. We fixed one part of the house at a time, but only after we saved enough money to pay for the remodeling outright. When the money was saved for repairs, we made the repairs ourselves, or rather, William did. We barely went out to eat or to theatres to see movies. For a couple as conservative with money as William and I had been, risking it all, even for a child, was perhaps too much of a gamble. As I mentioned, we were not risk takers with money. Were we suddenly about to change our ways?

Of course we were. When an obsession overtakes your life, you will disregard any and all beliefs that once defined you for a chance at getting what you want. Make no mistake; becoming parents was now a full-blown obsession for both of us. As easily as we were willing to change our ideals, we were not prepared to throw them out completely. Once again, the Internet search for options resumed.

Beyond the search for egg donors, which I became obsessed with, I decided to enter key words into Google such as "money back guarantee" and "IVF." Surprisingly, after a multiple hour search, there were results that appeared. A clinic based out of Washington D.C. offered a package called a shared risk program. The shared risk programs that this particular clinic offered were varied. The basic principle in a shared risk program is that the clinic and the patient are sharing the financial risk of an IVF cycle. This translates to the patient putting up more money upfront and the clinic offering a partial or full money back guarantee if the cycle does not result in a baby after six IVF cycles. One point worth reinforcing is that the clinic guaranteed a live baby, not just a pregnancy. This meant if a patient did get pregnant, but the pregnancy was followed by a miscarriage, she would still get reimbursed by the clinic. A beacon of hope had arrived.

I placed a call to the clinic immediately. It was as if my phone dialed itself, but it was during the clinic's off hours. Since I could not speak with a person, I had no choice but to leave a message and wait for a response. Meanwhile, my follow up appointment with Dr. Foster was scheduled for the following day. I had thoroughly perused the Washington D.C.'s website and had already obtained a great deal of information about the clinic and the conditions of their shared risk program. Although it pained me to leave Dr. Foster's clinic at this point in our journey, our decision had to be financially driven, plain and simple. I dreaded having to explain our reason for leaving Dr. Foster, but it had to be done. If there was a chance that someone would guarantee me a baby or give me my money back, I needed to pursue it further.

As I rehearsed exactly how I might "break up" with my doctor, I walked through his office door and felt my heart beating in that panicky way that makes the fluttering reassuring. He warmly welcomed us and apologized that the procedure failed. He presumed that William and I were not done with our fertility attempts and asked what we had planned next.

I agreed with him that we were not done, but maybe we were done trying to achieve a pregnancy with my eggs. Dr. Foster smiled and reminded us that it was not impossible to use my eggs. He acknowledged that an egg donor might increase our chances if we were truly comfortable pursuing this avenue, but it was not something we needed to do now. Either way, he was very confident that I would be pregnant in no time. I smiled at him and tried to break the news as gently as possible that he would not be the one to knock me up. The best method was direct, so I just blurted out that we were looking at using another fertility clinic. In my break-up line attempt, I mentioned that our decision was purely financial and that we truly felt that Dr. Foster and his associates (except the one snooty receptionist) were wonderful.

Surprisingly, Dr. Foster offered us a competitive shared risk program to entice us to stay with him. He was very confident that he could successfully bring us a child. He confessed that this was not something he offered most patients, but would do anything he could for us because he wanted to help. He told us that we were really nice people, great patients, and that we deserved success. William and I were really touched that he wanted to help us so much. Obviously, we were not going to need to travel to Washington D.C.

Knowing we were continuing our fertility journey with Dr. Foster, we asked him if we could, at the very least, investigate the egg donor option. He accommodated our request and swiftly directed us to the egg donor coordinator's office.

The egg donor coordinator's name was Lynette. She excitedly began to tell us about a donor who was eager to be selected and would be an excellent match for us. She had blond hair, blue eyes and was intelligent. We could be trying again as soon as August she declared. Wow, William and I thought such a prospect was wonderful! Enthusiastic, we followed Lynette over to her office that was about to get repainted. The furniture was displaced and plastic covered the floor. She apologized profusely for the mess, but we didn't care. The office matched our own identity; we were rearranging ourselves as well.

After waiting in a corner for several minutes, she invited us over to her desk to take a look at the blond/blue eyed egg donor number, who was identified as donor number 1543. We took one look at her and said, no. It was not that she was unattractive, but there was something about her that rubbed us the wrong way. I know, I know, one should never judge a book by its cover, but you know what, I don't agree with that cliché. There are plenty of books that are judged accurately by their covers and plenty of people as well. We told her we did not get a good vibe and she promised to send us some other egg donor candidates later that day.

Since William and I had obsessively been searching for egg donors through many national websites, we had found a few that we felt a connection to and asked about the prospect of using an outside agency. Lynette immediately cautioned us and tried to talk us out of such a prospect. She explained that often the women from these agencies are unreliable and do not follow dosage instructions or anything else they are supposed to do. In fact, many just sign up to collect money. We never thought that someone would actually sign up to be an egg donor to only stop short of following through with the medical instruction. This made us nervous.

She printed out the financial burden of a cycle for us and we were staring at a price tag of (minimally) $35,000. Since Dr. Foster had agreed to match the shared risk dollar amount, we did not think this price tag was accurate. Unfortunately, it was, and then worsened when she commented, "Of course that price does not include the medication or donor fee, so you need to add about $10,000-$15,000 each time you go through a cycle."

What was there to say? William and I did not have that kind of money to spend on a procedure. Speechless, and because I had somewhere to go and felt like I had been slapped, I kind of nodded at the information and walked out. When we got to the car William questioned the dollar amount and I went right down the astonishment path with him. They were trying to tell us that $50,000 would match the Washington D.C. shared risk program? We both doubted it, but William reassured me over and over again that all we would need to do was get an actual price from the D.C. clinic and contact Dr. Foster directly. I had gone from elation to despair; now why was that cycle so familiar? Regardless, there was nothing we could do until we received a comparison from another clinic.

I went back to my weeklong intensive workshop on teaching strategies and William went home. While he was home, he received a call from the clinic in Washington D.C. and he asked them about pricing. He explained our situation, well, most of it, and the egg donor coordinator from that clinic promised to send him a PDF of the various financial packages and options. He was perusing it when I returned from my class. He had a big smile on his face. "Look what I got!" He sounded like a devious little boy.

We started to decipher the different options and our eyes became crossed. I took over when he had enough and created an Excel spreadsheet of all of the different options. Although it was all unbelievably expensive, it was clearly much less than our current clinic. If Dr. Foster kept his word and truly matched their pricing, which we knew he would, we would definitely stay with him.

The options were very different. Patients could choose a non-shared risk program, which was less, but would receive no money back upon six failures of IVF. There were programs that cost a bit more and just the price of medicine would be reimbursed if no baby were produced from the events. Then, there were options where a patient could decide which part of the medical procedure she wanted guaranteed, and receive that amount back if all failed. There was also an all-inclusive offer where all money would be reimbursed after six failed IVF attempts, but that cost a lot more for obvious reasons.

My head was swimming. I looked at the risk on both ends of the spectrum. If it failed I would lose a specific amount of money, if it succeeded after one cycle I would lose a different amount of money. There was so much to consider. My analogy about the clinics being a cloak and dagger version of a casino seemed truer with each mathematical computation and comparison I made. By the end of the evening, I was exhausted and scared. No matter which way we went, this was a lot of money to spend at one time, a lot of money. What if it failed? What if it worked?

As I continued to play countless scenarios in my head, I received an e-mail message from Lynette, which contained access to egg donor profiles. She sent me 15 profiles. After searching through hundreds in most agencies, 15 egg donors seemed as if the number was an astonishing few. Of course, it only took the right one, so I began to open each profile with bated breath. None of them struck me as people that I might be a friend with in real life. This sounds bizarre, but that was what I was searching for with each click of the mouse. For whatever reason, I convinced myself if I found someone that looked like someone I would hang out with in my everyday life then the genetic mix would work out well. In addition to the physical snapshots provided, none of the women's personalities were anything like mine.

I know I sound greedy here, I really do understand that. The fact that any woman is willing to donate her DNA to help a fertility challenged woman like myself have a baby is beyond generous. Granted, they do receive a hefty stipend, but being someone who had endured the process three times, I believed that they more than earned such a fee. Regardless, I would be forking over huge sums of money to try to create a genetic half to our child; I was looking for that special connection. After searching all the national databases, it was tough to find someone we felt would make up one complimentary genetic half of our child. There was one donor that William and I both liked on the fertility clinic's website, but that was it.

I responded to Lynette's e-mail and reported that there was only one donor that we felt comfortable using. She was very excited because the one we had chosen was about to start cycling the next month. Lynette explained that we would learn whether or not she produced a pregnancy for another woman before I would possibly use her, but of course, the earliest I would be able to cycle myself would be in about four months.

After trying to have a baby for five plus years, an additional four months sounded like an eternity. William and I decided to ignore Lynette's advice and looked even more carefully at outside egg donor agencies. To the inexperienced infertility person, four months does not seem horrible, but it is far worse than only four months. Let's say that four months later, I was finally able to begin cycling. The cycling takes about six weeks, which would mean we would be into the sixth month down the line.

After waiting two additional weeks, which would be the end of the sixth and approaching the seventh month, we would find out if we were pregnant. If we were and the pregnancy was sustainable, all would be well with the world. If it did not work and I was not pregnant, we would have to wait an additional three months to try again. Permission to try again would only be granted if there were extra embryos from the first attempt. If there were not, we would have to start at square one again where the process would take six weeks and so on and so forth. This is why four months was so long. We understood that using someone else's eggs that were proven to work would make the four month wait worth it, but we had no patience left.

We found someone through one of the on line agencies that shared a lot of similar physical and personality qualities with me. She was petite, blond, blue eyed, loved dogs, and enjoyed cooking. There were many other aspects to her personality that she shared that were spot on with mine as well, such as her deep desire to avoid confrontation and to do all she could to make it on her own.

When any DNA mixes, one can never predict what one will end up with, but when creating the concoction, the most logical ingredients are identifiable. Plain and simple, we wanted the woman to be similar to me. We really wanted the woman donating her eggs to be me, but this seemed to be the next best alternative. William and I discussed the different options obsessively for several days. When it came down to our reaching a decision, it evolved out of a combination of financial and emotional factors. If we were about to plunk down our entire savings to try to make our own baby, we wanted the best. Paying an agency a bit more was a risk worth taking. Period.

I spoke to a patient coordinator named Kathleen about the blond haired, blue eyed donor number 2822 and was thrilled to know that she was available and excited to be selected. The final price tag for using this donor would run somewhere around $16,000, which would be in addition to the huge fee at the clinic. It was only this low because the egg donor was willing to take a smaller fee since she had not yet been a proven donor. Of all the people to receive less money, I felt enormous guilt over the fact that it would be the woman who might ultimately be the reason I was able to have a baby. Of course, when faced with such a large financial undertaking, I was willing to accept anyone else's sacrifice without issue. I started to have heart palpitations as I considered parting with such a huge sum of money that was, once again, a giant risk. All of our investments had failed; would this be any different?

Before I could consider making a down payment on the donor, I needed to know that my fertility clinic was willing to work with the egg donor agency and me, and follow through on the promise of competitive pricing. We also would have to contact our bank for a loan. At 5:30 p.m. I shot off an e-mail message to Lynette to explain our decision to go with an agency egg donor. I was explicit as to why I wanted to go with this particular egg donor and hoped that she understood and supported us every step of the way. As I pressed the send icon, I felt the butterflies in my stomach while trying to envision her next day response.

After the e-mail was sent, I pulled out my checkbook and my financial statements wondering how we were going to be able to afford this prospect. As I continued to reflect on our finances, I questioned the long-term repercussions of using an egg donor. Would our child resent us for using an egg donor? At least with an adoption, a child can know her genetic mother in some way. That is not the case with anonymous egg donors. I would love and cherish any child, but would that mentality be mutual with our child? For the first time, I stopped and thought about the process from a new perspective. Suddenly, I felt conflicted about using an egg donor.

There have been stories circulating about making a designer baby for years and apparently, I had just joined the ranks of such stories. I had read blogs on the Internet from people who thought people pursuing in vitro were horrible people. I remembered one entry in particular where someone stated, "IVF makes the lab techs the arbiters of life. Playing God is expensive, apparently, but the full cost is going to be felt by a society that loses its sense of our limits and ethics." This was beyond IVF; this was IVF with someone else's eggs. What would perceptions be in this scenario? Long term, what would be the impact of choosing a stranger's eggs to make a baby? Perhaps if I knew someone willing to donate her eggs it would make more sense. As good of friends as I had, would anyone actually consider donating her eggs to me? Even I would not go to such lengths for a good friend. It was too complicated and weird.

While I was heavily debating myself, the phone rang and it was William. I let him know about the e-mail I had sent and he was happy that I continued to keep the ball rolling. Of course, I began sharing my sudden concerns about using an egg donor. After all the disappointments along the way, we were now programmed to keep trying new alternatives. However, we had begun to behave rather impulsively. Instead of practicing our usual well-researched and careful thought processes that were applied in every other aspect of our lives, we had stopped thinking any of these details through. During that conversation, we recognized that we needed to stop and think before making any moves, but we really found ourselves without any reasonable solutions. Besides, the doctor had assured me that there was still a chance for success with my eggs. Shouldn't I try again with my eggs? Did it really matter either way?

As our conversation continued, I reminded William that I was going out at 6:30 with my friend and he started to tell me about something that happened at work. I had to interrupt him in the middle of his story due to the dreaded beep of call waiting. In all honesty, I ignore call waiting about 80% of the time because I just find it rude to take another call when you are talking to another person. However, since I had plans and did not have caller I.D., I thought the phone call might be from my neighbor, so I put William on hold.

THE UNEXPECTED CALLER

INSTEAD OF MY friend, the caller was our social worker, Trudy, at the adoption agency. I knew why she was calling. William and I had not attended any of the meetings that they continuously offered regarding adoptive practices because, quite frankly, we found them entirely too painful. Although she rarely e-mailed us to find out how we were doing, she did call every once in a while to check in with us, not often, but once in a while. Since we had not spoken in a long time, I felt obligated to update her on the latest and asked her to hold for a minute so that I wouldn't leave William on hold for several minutes.

When I returned to Trudy, I apologized for placing her on hold and explained that William had been on the other line. She responded, "Oh, he's not home yet?" She seemed disappointed, but went on without missing a beat. "I am just calling to tell you that a pair of birth parents in Massachusetts has selected you and William to be the adoptive parents of their baby girl. She is due in October."

Everything stopped at that moment. Instead of focusing on the words coming out of Trudy's mouth, my mind drifted to the fear of using egg donor 2822 and my own body going through pregnancy with someone else's DNA, if able to go through pregnancy at all. Then I started to consider the painful progesterone shots, the nausea, the uncertainty, and the past heartbreak and slowly, I began to comprehend that this would mean the ability to avoid all of that and still be a mother. As she rattled off the medical backgrounds of the biological parents, I listened without prejudice. When the words bipolar, dyslexic, and asthmatic were shared, they barely made an impact. What the parents looked like, sounded like, or behaved like hardly mattered. What mattered was that they chose us to be the parents of their baby, and in that moment, that was more than enough for me. Obviously, the universe was stopping me from pursuing pregnancy with an egg donor. The debate in my head was resolved in the most wonderful and unexpected way.

I was bursting at the seams with happiness. Trudy explained the reasons why the birth parents chose us. They chose us, according to Trudy, because of my love of music, my volunteerism, and William's and my traditional values. I was kind of confused which traditional values were being referred to, but I loved being described as traditional! Although there were some genetic issues with both sides of the birth parents, I remained unfazed. Truth be told, if I carefully analyzed my genetic history or William's we would find red flags as well.

The more I heard, the more excited I became. I told Trudy to tell me what William and I needed to do and it was as good as done. She told me that the next step was meeting the birth parents, and I was more than eager for her to set that up. She said it might take a few days to establish a meeting, but before that, she wanted to make sure that William and I talked everything through carefully and decided together before any additional steps were taken. Was she kidding? What was there to think about? A healthy baby girl (her words) was due in a few months and meant for us. However, I understood what she needed to hear from me so I told her that I would discuss it with William immediately and call her the next day.

Meanwhile, I had about 10 minutes before my friend was set to pick me up for the movies and a book-group type meeting immediately following the film. Nothing appealed to me less than going off to the movies when all I wanted to do was be with William and bask in our sudden and shocking good fortune. If history had anyway of repeating itself, I knew better than to spill the beans to anyone other than a select few. It was too premature to say anything; I hadn't even met the birth parents yet! Instead, working against the clock, I dialed William's number.

He was unable to get much out before I blurted out that Trudy had called because we were chosen. I think he said something like, "Come again?" He could not believe it either. He agreed that there was nothing to think about and was over the moon with joy. I bemoaned the fact that I had to go out and would not be home when he arrived and he joined me in that disappointment. He decided to clean everything up at work and rush home anyway, because he knew there would not be additional work accomplished with this earth shattering news.

With the five minutes I had remaining until my neighbor's arrival, I quickly called my sister and told her that I was on my way out, but had to call her to tell her that I had just received "THE phone call." She did not initially understand what I meant, even though we had discussed the possibility numerous times. I rephrased it, "The magic phone call...baby." Screaming ensued, and I quickly reiterated the same conversation I had with her as I had with William. Before we had time for any additional conversation, my neighbor was pulling up the driveway, so I hung up with my sister, blew kisses to my dogs and ran out the door with a huge grin on my face.

It took every ounce of willpower I possessed to keep the news inside, but I was beaming. An overwhelming amount of joy emanated inside and outside of me, and I could hardly contain myself. The movie was an absolute delight, but I am not sure if it was due to my wonderful mood or the direction of the film. Regardless, I could not recall feeling such joy, wait, I could, and it was the last time I found out I was pregnant. I reminded myself that this was different. The birth mother was already almost six months along and the baby was healthy. She would not miscarry like I had. This baby was real, and she might be ours, and the elation grew.

I was so excited about finding out that I was finally going to be a mom I could barely contain myself. I wanted to tell anyone and everyone, but Trudy warned me that biological parents often changed their minds and that I should not get too attached or excited about this baby. Although my brain knew that her words made sense, my heart was speaking in another language, an optimistic language, and I desperately wanted to listen to my heart instead of my head for a change. The timing could not have been better. This timing seemed fated. It was as if the universe provided me with an answer I had asked for just moments before. How could this not work out? Hadn't we been through enough? Wasn't it finally our turn?

I decided to tell a few people, but a very limited circle. After letting my sister know, I hesitantly shared the news with my parents. We considered keeping the news a secret from them in case it did not work out, but in all honesty, whether it worked out or not, we knew they needed to know. If everything fell into place, my parents would need advanced notice to get plane reservations to fly out and meet their granddaughter. If the process fell apart, I did not want to have to cover up my emotions with them every single day for however long it was necessary.

William and I weighed the pros and cons carefully and eventually reached the conclusion that they needed to know. They had been on a cruise when I had received the phone call from Trudy. When my father called me from a port, I thought it best to blurt it out. Thousands of questions followed, excited questions, hopeful questions, but I could only share as much as I had learned. Since I had not met the birth parents, there was very limited information available.

After the conclusion of their trip, my mother immediately insisted on knitting a blanket in my favorite color, lilac, for my future daughter. I pleaded with her not to get ahead of life's events, but she insisted that she would need to get started to ensure a ready blanket for her granddaughter. Although I argued with her and reminded her that my baby would be fine without a knitted blanket from the beginning, she would not listen to reason. My heart cringed at the thought of making too many plans in case the birth parents changed their minds, but there was no convincing my mother that anything was a bad idea.

A trip to the mailbox the following week resulted in a stuffed envelope from my mother. Although the envelope was nearly bursting open, the tape used to seal it kept its contents a secret until I ripped it open. As soon as the tape was removed, several images of knitted blankets stared at me from the many pages of her catalogue. Although I tried to ignore the mailings, she bugged me until I finally relented. Don't get me wrong, it was a lovely gesture, but I couldn't understand why she would not listen to my wishes to hold off until the child was actually placed in our custody. My mother is impossibly stubborn, so there was no way for me to win that argument. With the news barely a week old, my baby was already receiving custom made gifts.

Someone I knew I could trust who would never try to force knitted blankets or anything on me was my best friend, Julia. She had cried along with me during my miscarriages and prayed for my luck to change. Although I wanted to call her as soon as I knew, I really thought she deserved to receive the news in person. Since we often met for lunch during the summer months, I decided to drop the news during one of our lunch dates. While munching on salads, I quietly revealed, "William and I received the magical phone call a few weeks ago."

Julia's eyes welled up with tears of joy and she could not contain her excitement for us. I told her everything I knew and we began to fantasize about our children being great friends, just like we had been for all of these years. She wanted to throw me a baby shower on the spot, and I was honored, but I told her I really was uncomfort-able with making any plans until all was official. She understood completely, and then asked me about the birth parent meeting. Trudy had told us that she set up a date to meet the birth parents, and it would be in about three weeks time. It seemed like an eternity, but there was certainly nothing we could do to speed the process up at all.

The meeting made me insanely nervous. Every detail was important to me, includ-ing my outfit. Julia insisted that I wear something that made me look young, hip, and responsible. I had no idea what outfit would make such a statement, but after lunch was over, we went from one store to the next in search of the perfect ensemble. No store specializes in a birth parent and adoptive parent meeting outfit, so we ended up with nothing at the end of our search. She decided she needed to come to my house and pick something out for me, but she never got around to it. Since she had three children of her own and her own business, her schedule was impossible. I was lucky to get her for lunch as frequently as I did!

Even without my best friend's help, I knew her advice was spot on and that I needed the perfect outfit. I started trying on every shirt and every pair of pants I owned. Skirts were modeled, as were dresses, but no outfit satisfied young, hip, and responsible all at once. Even though there were two weeks to pull something together, it did not seem like enough time. Regardless, within that two-week waiting period, William and I were full of so much joy; we were both on the verge of bursting with happiness at any given moment. Although we knew we were supposed to remain cau-tious, we could not help ourselves.

Immediately, we began debating baby girl names. William had always loved the name Jennifer. It had been his favorite name since he was a child. Coincidentally, my favorite name had always been Jenna. In high school, one of my friends had dated a girl named Jenna. This girl did not attend our school, but when I met her, I thought she was beautiful and sweet and because of that, the name always struck me as the most beautiful name in the world. When my Grandpa Jesse died while I was attending col-lege, I knew I would name a daughter, if I had one; Jenna after my grandpa and it had been waiting ever since to be used. Eventually, we agreed that we would use Jennifer because it had so many options. I would call her Jenna, but if she wanted to go with Jenny or Jen or Jennifer, she could decide that for herself. It was the middle name that gave us the most attention.

There were many beautiful names, but to pick the perfect one was daunting. No doubt, every couple goes through this, but for us, it seemed especially important that our daughter have the most perfect name. William found a few website engines that were literally used to find the perfect middle name with the first name. We typed in Jennifer and let the website continuously make suggestions to us for weeks. Although we thought names like Addison and Amelia were beautiful, there was no way we would allow our child to have the initials JAP, as our last name was Porter. We also liked Jennifer Ava, but again, would not consider a middle name that started with the letter A. Each day, William would e-mail me middle name suggestions and I would save some for him when he returned home. Then one night, as we were going back and forth with middle name choices, he asked me how I felt about Violet, since purple was my favorite color. I really liked the name Violet, but responded, "Actually, Lilac is my favorite shade of purple, how about Lila?"

William's eyes widened and a huge smile emerged. "I love it! That is the name we have been waiting to find."

We said the name Jennifer Lila over and over again and were so excited. It was a beautiful name, and it was a name that we both loved dearly. I still had reservations about using Jennifer instead of Jenna, but either way, what a perfect name. A name that waited over 20 years to be used and we could not be prouder. William looked at baby announcement cards and typed in our baby's name. When we saw the name Jennifer Lila Porter, we felt like the universe had finally answered our longing. There it was, staring at us with pink font and it was perfect. The moment was too.

It was finally time to meet Helen and Walter (the biological parents) in Massachusetts. I made myself busy that morning in the house. For some reason, I felt the need to clean my closet and vacuum and perform my version of nesting. Upon leaving our home, William and I tried to inspire the other to imagine what Helen and Walter would look, act, and sound like. Try as we may, we could not come up with any ideas. Nervous energy filled the car, and although the ride down to Massachusetts was traffic-free, it felt like it took countless hours. The unexpected nature of the visit was eating away at us more severely with each mile on the road.

When we arrived at the adoption agency at 5:20, we only needed to wait an additional two minutes until Trudy drove into the parking lot. She got out of her car, took one look at me and exclaimed, "You look like you're about to throw up!" She laughed at me and I giggled in response. I honestly didn't feel nauseous, I felt nervous, but I guess the expression on my face was eerily similar to nausea. She promised us it would be fine and in we walked. She peeked into the conference room and announced that Helen and Walter were already there and waiting for us.

THE MEETING

MY HEART SKIPPED several beats as I took in the image of the birth mother, Helen. She was not exactly unattractive, but there was something about her look that I did not like, just like the egg donor that we had refused at our last clinic. I had a tough time pinpointing my disdain, but I had known many other people with a similar look at one time in my life or another and it had never been a positive experience. Was it her eyes? It might have been her eyes. They were a bit shifty and looked untrusting. She also had a nose ring. I do not hold a specific disregard against nose rings, I just happen to be very conservative.

I know what I sound like, and I have met other people with nose rings who have been perfectly lovely, but this had not been an image I was prepared for when picturing the biological creation of my child. Helen had brown hair, a little past her shoulders and was about 5 feet 6 inches or so. Walter was tall and thin with dark hair, hazel-brown eyes, a giant nose, and terrible acne and teeth. Immediately I wondered what the combination of their genes would produce.

I had pledged all along that it did not matter what the child would look like, but as I gazed at the physical representations of Helen and Walter, I could not help but be disappointed that they weren't younger preppy versions of William and me. Ridiculous to hope for such a scenario, but it was truthfully what I had been wishing. Again, I realize how this sounds, but these were the thoughts circling in my brain. Would the baby look like her mother or her father or an unimaginable cross between them? I closed my eyes and tried to feel her and picture her and somehow, was able to see the most beautiful being in the world.

I do not know how Helen and Walter felt about meeting William and me in person for the first time. They had already seen lots of pictures of us, so it should not have been a huge surprise. How could people like that pick conservative people like us? We could not have physically appeared to be more different. My nerves and fear kicked around my brain and my heart as I tried to protect myself in anyway from feeling a connection to someone who could, in all honesty, change her mind at any time during and even after the process.

Regardless of my first impression, what struck me as funny was that it turned out we were all extremely nervous at the beginning of the meeting. Slowly, to my delight and surprise, the conversation began to flow naturally. Helen told me that before she got pregnant with her baby, she dreamed of me. Then when she found out she was pregnant, she dreamed of me being the baby's mother. It was several months later when she was given our family portfolio and recognized my picture from her dream.

She said she knew that I was meant to be this baby's mother, even before her conception. The story gave me goose bumps and made me cry. It was that statement that silenced all of my concerns and made me feel that this was meant to be for all of us. She then told me that she loved her daughter so much and knew it was going to be hard to let her go. Helen teared up when she admitted how scared she was of the day she had to let her daughter go, and this made me uneasy. She gently patted her tummy and sighed, but then she explained how she reached the very, very tough decision to have her daughter grow up with someone else as her mother.

Helen and Walter were only 19 years old when they discovered that she was pregnant. They were very young. Neither Helen nor Walter had jobs, as they were planning to attend art school in January. Helen hoped to be a computer animator and work for Pixar. She shared samples of her artwork with us at the meeting, and they were a bit startling. I am from the wholesome Disney days, not the Japanese animation era, but she had an affinity for fairies and cosmic images, and they looked pretty good to my inexpert eyes. Certainly better than anything I could do; I have zero drawing/painting talent. Helen had even drawn a picture for her daughter and asked that we give it to her someday. I cringed at the thought of hanging such an illustration in a baby's room, but recognized that it would be the right thing to do. Truly, I wanted to hang it up the moment I returned home as a gesture of faith and love for Helen's sacrifice.

Helen and Walter had no college education and very few prospects. Helen explained that the baby was an "oopsie" but learned not to regret that this baby was conceived. Although she suffered from moments of depression about her situation, she loved this child. While looking at her artwork, she even showed us a picture she drew of her pregnant belly with baby's arms reaching through and anguish on the birth mother's face. It was a terrifying picture, but it was her outlet on how she had been able to deal with her pain.

Helen knew, very early on, that she was ill equipped to take care of the baby and herself. Helen grew up in poor conditions. She explained that her mom was a single mom and struggled throughout her life to keep food on the table and a roof over their head. Helen had many friends of similar age that had gone through what she was going through, but those girls kept their babies and did not pursue adoption. She admitted that knowing how these girls' babies were treated made her unbelievably angry, as they were not treated well. According to her observations, these babies had to live in squalor, were often dirty themselves, and lived without the most basic necessities. Helen emphasized that she loved her baby so much; she had to put her up for adoption and send her off to be raised with parents who would ensure the most healthy and wonderful future, which she was positive she could not provide.

Helen told me she was exceedingly picky in selecting parents for her daughter. She was worried she would have to compromise some of her prerequisites of the adoptive parents, but could not believe it when she learned about William and me. She said we had everything she dreamed of for her daughter and more. First and foremost, it was her deep-seated desire for her daughter to be the first born of someone else's family, since she was meant to be the first-born. She wanted her daughter to have music lessons, or art supplies, or dance costumes, which she knew she would never be able to provide. When she read that we owned a grand piano, her heart danced for her daughter's future. She dreamed that her daughter would learn to play the piano, as she had always wished to do and maybe the drums, which she had learned to do. Helen dreamed for her child to live in a house with a mother and a father at the end of a cul-de-sac, which, coincidentally, we did. Her hopes were that her adoptive mother would love to bake cookies, which I do, and prayed for her baby to learn to cook alongside her mom, which I could only hope my daughter would desire. She wanted this child to have a doting dad, because she felt like something was missing her whole life, without having a father, and wanted more for her daughter. Although she and Walter were in love, she had no intentions of marrying him anytime soon and did not want that kind of lifestyle for a baby.

Helen seemed to have a huge heart. Not only was she wanting to give her baby opportunities that she, herself, never had, she also thought it was unfair that loving people who wanted to be parents had somehow been thwarted from becoming parents. She explained how she wanted to give not only her daughter a better life, but people like me and William the opportunity to live life to its fullest by becoming parents. Helen was the answer to William's and my wishes and prayers. Her big dreams for her daughter were going to make our dreams come true as well. Helen was, in that moment and time, our personal hero. Knowing that our daughter would come from her made us know how special this child would be in life. We knew, because of the way this child would enter the world, that this baby girl was destined to make the world a better place, by being a part of it.

Walter had an excellent sense of humor and a lot to say. He was extremely talkative and clearly, very much in love with Helen. They had been together for about four years, since they were 16 years old, and were leaning on each other heavily. This child was certainly conceived out of love and possibly a little lust as well. When I asked Walter how he was doing with the decisions that had been made for their daughter, he said he was trying to focus on Helen's emotions, but he firmly believed that this was meant to happen. He also believed it was meant to happen to bring his daughter into this world and to send her into our world. He, too, seemed to have a huge heart. He loved computers and enjoyed writing even more. He was going to school in January for directing and writing and hoped to be famous some day. During our meeting, Trudy asked if he had ever considered becoming a stand-up comic, and Helen admitted that Trudy had not been the first person to suggest such a career path!

Helen's mother, Sara, was also at the meeting. Sara was outspoken and clearly an advocate for her daughter. She had a lot to say, and amused us as we witnessed them battling it out as mothers and daughters do. I had been told that the entire family was supportive of Helen and Walter's decision to pursue adoption, but the encouragement we received from Sara was far more than I could have ever hoped. She said that she too dreamed of me and truly in her heart of hearts believed that this baby girl was meant for William and me all the while. She expressed her opinion that it was God's plan and Helen was simply the surrogate.

She empathized over the four day waiting period we would have to endure while waiting for Helen and Walter to surrender their parental rights, but assured us that we had nothing to worry about. She opined that after meeting us, how could any of them change their minds? "What kind of people would that make them?" she asked. She added, "I will not let Helen change her mind. Not only does this little girl deserve a better life, but my daughter does as well." Walter jumped in as well and added, "I could be really stubborn too, and I will not allow this plan for the baby to change." I didn't know what to say, so I just smiled. Their words were exactly what we longed to hear.

After Sara finished expressing her thoughts and opinions with us, Helen wanted to change the direction of the meeting. She took out the ultrasound pictures and asked if we wanted them. Of course we did, but it was visibly tough to watch her relinquish them. I asked her if she was sure and she said that we were going to be the baby's parents in every way that mattered, therefore, we should have the pictures. I could see how much she loved her daughter and how very difficult it would be for her to say goodbye to her as she handed us the ultrasound pictures. I felt a wave of guilt, but it vanished when I looked closely at the pictures. Helen had her mind set to make sure that her daughter was adopted and I had nothing to feel guilty about because I desperately wanted a baby. She was doing what she wanted to do, and so were William and I. Everybody, as painful as it was all around, would end up with what they wanted for this child.

As we were about to part, the only question Helen still had was whether or not we had thought of a name. Although we had not planned to share our name with anyone, we thought it was the least we could do for Helen. We announced Jennifer Lila and felt more excitement, from sharing our big secret. Helen confessed that when she was going to keep her baby, at the beginning of her pregnancy, she was going to name her child Lily Rain. Although Rain was not in the running for our name choice, Lily and Lila, were eerily similar. This was one more sign to all of us that we were a great fit.

My first instincts were clearly mistaken. This adoptive scenario appeared to mean more and more by the moment. Helen and Walter told us at the end of the meeting that they always thought that adoption was the right path for them, but meeting us sealed the deal. I confessed that when I first found out that I could not conceive a child, I believed that meant that a child, somewhere out there, was meant to enter our lives through adoption. However, after all this time had gone by, I began to doubt that thought. Meeting Helen and Walter restored my faith and my joy in one day. We agreed to meet again in a month to discuss the hospital plans.

When we left the meeting, I called my family members on the way home, as planned. I replayed the meeting between Helen and Walter and William and me. We stopped at my sister's house on the way home to exchange all the details in person. My nephews were excited to know that they were going to have a cousin and wanted her to hurry up and be born already. I reminded them that the baby was not exactly ours yet, so they understood how adoption was not a certainty. Of course, being children, they heard this news and ignored it immediately. Truth be told, we all ignored such a possible outcome quite easily. How could we not with the conversation that was had? William was grinning from ear to ear. That evening, we both had trouble going to sleep. William said over and over again, "What a wonderful day!"

Our next meeting was set up for the end of the next month. It was at that meeting that we would discuss the hospital plan. A hospital plan sounded magnificent and frightening all at the same time. The fact that we would be discussing a hospital plan meant that the baby was that much closer to arrival. It also meant that we were that much more invested into the birth of this child, and fearful that the parents would have a change of heart.

The fear of the birth parents changing their mind remained over me like a dark, black, violent storm cloud. It followed me wherever I went. At the same time that this cloud lay overhead, I was also deliriously happy. The hope that I felt scared me, but I couldn't help feeling optimistic. Optimism had never served me well before, but it too, like pangs of fear enveloped me. It is a conundrum to simultaneously feel pure bliss and debilitating fear. This emotional combination propelled me to register for the baby, yet feel doom with each click of the Toys R Us merchandise scanner gun. William and I figured if the adoption did go through, we would not have time to figure out what we needed once the baby arrived. It made logical sense to go through with a scanner and carefully select the products that we thought we needed. That way, if the baby did arrive and begin her life with us, we could order the products online directly off our registry.

I also requested a meeting with my principal and human resources director to plan out my maternity leave. It turned out that since I was adopting, I was only allowed seven paid days leave from my classroom. According to our contract, when a woman physically has a baby, it is considered a medical procedure, which allows her to use between six to eight weeks of her saved up sick time. That is assuming that a teacher has been teaching long enough to accumulate six to eight weeks of paid sick leave. Although I had acquired such time, since this was an adoption, seven days was it. It was explained that since we were allowed two individual commitment days a year and since we were permitted to use five of our sick days per year for family members, the district had agreed upon seven days. As though I had not already been physically and mentally punished for lacking the ability to procreate, here was another insult. And yet, I did not care. After all of our years of waiting to be parents, if I did not get a paid leave at all, it hardly mattered. Meeting with my school officials and registering for baby supplies were smart and strategic moves, but each action stirred up fears that we were jinxing ourselves.

Speaking of strategic moves, we read that we needed a pediatrician selected before the birth of the baby. Again, I did not want to put any plans in motion, but if I didn't and the baby was born, I would be unprepared, and I couldn't have that. I already anticipated being completely clueless as how to hold a newborn, change her diaper, feed her, burp her, etc., I needed as much of the preplanning taken care of as possible. My best friend Julia, who was perhaps the only person in the world who was more excited than me for this to happen, gave me the name of her pediatrician. With the name and number in hand, I made an appointment to make one more plan for our baby.

Most pediatricians allow new moms or moms-to-be to make preview appointments. I had not known this before because I had previously held no reason to contain such knowledge. Since it was time to select a doctor for a child who would be in my care and hopefully, the rest of my life, I cursed all jinxes and dialed the phone with shaky fingers. When I made the initial phone call, the secretary asked me when I was due. I had to explain that I was not due because I was not pregnant. This was perplexing to her initially, but then I explained that I was adopting a baby. She seemed unsure as to how to progress, but as I offered her details, her understanding developed. She granted me a preview appointment with the doctor in a few weeks' time.

When the appointment arrived, I walked into the office and examined the waiting area. It looked like the once popular Disney store and Warner Brother's store merged to form some sort of conglomerate. In other words, it was the perfect setting. The office staff greeted me and asked me when I was due. I laughed and made a comment about never wearing the outfit I was wearing a second time. Again, I had to launch into the fact that I was adopting. The secretary asked me when and I gave her the due date of the baby. She grimaced and cautioned me that one of their other patients just went through a failed adoption and a shiver went up and down my spine. Why would she say this to me?

Believe me, I knew that Helen might change her mind, but I was trying very hard to think positively. Regardless, the negative energy was expelled into my brain and worked its ugly magic. As I waited for the doctor, I wondered if being in the office was going to jinx the situation. I had never been superstitious until my miscarriages. Now, anything related to baby making seemed doomed from the beginning. With all of the failures in the past to becoming a mother, I had turned into a crazy person. All I needed was wood to knock on and salt to throw over my shoulder to complete the picture.

The superstitions did not really matter; what mattered was that I had everything lined up as was required by the adoption agency. They required William and me to purchase a car seat, bottles, a crib, diapers, and more to prove that we were prepared. We were also required to have the name of a pediatrician to give to the hospital staff. Although I was doing what was expected of me, it felt wrong. It reminded me of the time I was in the doctor's office at six weeks of pregnancy and they asked me to pick a pediatrician for my unborn baby. I felt that was premature as well. It turned out that it was and I was worried that I was destined to repeat the mistakes of the past.

When the pediatrician called me in to his office, I felt stupid for even being there. Once again, I found myself relaying the entire adoption plan and story to a perfect stranger. He was taken aback by certain facts of the adoption process. For example, once the baby was born, I would not be allowed to leave the state of Massachusetts until an interstate compact agreement was made allowing me to do so. This meant that I would not be able to bring our daughter for a check up for several weeks to this doctor. He asked if there was any way around this but I explained that there were no ways around this at all. Once we got past the basic points of adoption, he interviewed me for the family history on the birth parents. I had not brought any records that I possessed because it had never occurred to me to do so.

It hardly mattered; I had memorized both the biological parents' family histories. The birth mother's sister was bipolar and lived most of the time at a special school. The birth mother had endured situational depression, dyslexia, asthma, and seasonal allergies. The birth father also suffered from situational depression. His mother suffered from bipolar disorder and his brother had severe ADHD. The doctor cringed with all of the depression on both sides of the biological family. He lamented that it was more of a concern if the biological parents suffered from bipolar disorder, but it was still a concern. He explained that signs of bipolar disorders often did not emerge until a child's teenage years or once puberty hit. We moved on to friendlier topics of conversation, such as how wonderful my best friend was and what I might see in the hospital when the time arrived. As I left, my head was swimming, but I tucked the worry and red flags of the situation away and wondered what it would truly be like in the hospital. We were meeting with the birth parents to discuss this very topic the following week.

When the day arrived to discuss the hospital plan, we were simultaneously struck with a combination of elation and fear. The car ride did nothing to dispel our shaky emotions as we got stuck in major traffic. If we arrived late to the meeting, would Helen and Walter change their minds because we were not responsible enough? All sorts of crazy scenarios popped into our heads during the ride. Would they want us in the delivery room? Would we even want to be in the delivery room? I did. William wasn't sure. A woman, practically a stranger, would be going through one of the most primal, painful, and personal processes, as we watched from the sidelines. As crazy as it sounded, I was secretly hoping for an invitation. I knew it would be unexplored territory, but I wanted to be present for the birth of my baby.

I am happy to report that we arrived on time. When we exchanged greetings with the birth parents, we both realized that we were not nearly as nervous as we had been previously. Trudy, our social worker, had also gotten stuck in traffic, and was running late, so we were there on our own with Helen and Walter and their social worker. We started idle chitchat, and then decided to get started without Trudy. I had brought a list of questions for Helen and Walter so that I could learn all I could about their personalities. I wanted to know the types of foods they loved, what fears they had, how they slept at night, and most importantly, what dreams they had for their child. I was nervous to ask whether or not it would be all right to ask the questions, but luckily, they were only too happy to oblige. They loved the idea of their daughter learning as much about them as possible and it was actually fun. We learned that we had a lot in common, which made us so happy that this child might be an excellent personality mix for us. It loosened the serious mood of the room and we all began to relax. When we were finished asking them questions, they asked if they could turn the survey around and on us, so then we answered the questions too. Laughter ensued and a connection was made.

After the merriment was over, it was time to get down to business and discuss the hospital plan. We were first told which hospital Helen would deliver and then who would be in the delivery room. Walter (obviously) and Helen's mother would be joining Helen. Then, they extended an invitation to us. I was jumping up and down for joy in my head, but before I was allowed to answer, they told us to take some time and think about it. Trudy had finally arrived by this time, and she encouraged us to be in the delivery room in order to tell our daughter what her delivery was like when she was older. Trudy felt it was important for us to be able to relay that story years down the road. Did she cry, was she alert, did she pee on the doctor, etc. We exchanged e-mail addresses with Helen and Walter and with that, the meeting ended. Collectively, we decided not to have any more meetings until the baby was born.

When William and I got into our car, we were in high spirits. We immediately began discussing whether or not we would be in the delivery room and, of course, we agreed it would be best for all involved. But then we started to wonder where we would stand? Would we stand near Helen's head or stand in a place with a bird's eye view of the action in the nether regions? I was unsure whether or not I felt the need to watch our daughter make her grand entrance through another woman's private area.

In regular circumstances, I would have been the one lying on the table and pushing out a baby, so I wouldn't have normally received an opportunity to watch. Of course, I have to be honest; I was not feeling too badly about skipping that part of the process at this point in my life. I decided the best strategy was to ask Helen and Walter where they might think they wanted us to be stationed and take the decision making process out of our hands. She deserved to make that call; there was no doubt in my mind. I figured we could discuss the details through e-mail messages. And so the communication without the agency began a few days later. I started the ball rolling:

PEN PALS

The following letters are excerpts from our e-mail exchanges. The excerpts appear in original form.

Dear Helen and Walter,

There is so much that William and I would like to say, but we don't know where to begin, and of course, if it is appropriate to share.

I am so filled with joy right now, I am literally bubbling over. However, at the same time I feel so much joy, I worry about you. You are unbelievably brave and selfless individuals and I cannot imagine how you are handling this situation. All I can tell you is that this child will be the center of our worlds, and I hope that sums everything up.

We are honored that you would invite us into the delivery room and would really love to be there. This leads to 101 questions. Where do we stand, or should we sit, or will you just want us to leave because you are going to be so uncomfortable? This is all up to the two of you, or maybe the three of you (Sara) to decide. Think about it. The last thing we want to do is make your delivery more stressful than necessary. Trudy suggested that we visit you during labor for just a few minutes, and then return when you are about to push. How do you feel about that? It is truly your call. There is a lot to consider, and we do not want to burden you on what is bound to be a very physically and emotionally trying day.

If anything pops in either one of your heads, don't be afraid to reach out. We are all in this together now.

Be well,
William and Emma

Walter responded immediately:

Dear William and Emma,

It was very reassuring to see so many similarities between us. Sara told Helen and I that you two were like us, several years from now. I'm beginning to think she's right. You're a couple after our own hearts.

This is indeed an incredibly...strange connection that the four of us hold. It's strange, because the more I get to know you both, the more I am certain we would be friends, had we met under different circumstances.

This is not to say that I am disappointed with the current circumstances. It is incredibly inspiring and, to be honest, uplifting to know that we are bringing such unbridled joy into your lives. This is not an easy time for us, especially Helen, but knowing how happy we have made you has made the burden considerably deplete.

I will be fair with you. None of this has been easy, or even close to it. It's been a long, difficult road, and now with the end in sight it seems to only get bumpier and more frightening. As things become decided, as plans are made, things begin to feel more real. It's a heartbreaking process. But I am someone who really does not do well with negativity, as Helen will be the first to tell you. While yes, there is pain, there is [sic] also INCREDIBLE amounts of joy knowing how safe, happy, and loved Jen is going to be with you two.

I have the utmost faith in you both, and I know you will both be wonderful, amazing parents.

If I have a problem, or need something answered, I will be the first to reach out. But the SAME goes for you. Seriously. Anything you need, ask.

I will speak to Helen about the delivery room business, but it shouldn't be a problem. Really. We're weirdos [sic].

Sincerely, and with the Utmost Respect,

Walter

His words could not be more reassuring, and they made me feel as though it would be okay to spill the beans to other people in our lives. William and I began to share our wonderful news with other friends and family members as the lines of communication continued.

Dear Helen and Walter,

Helen-This is a response to Walter's e-mail, but I thought I should send this to both of you.

I envision a great future for you and Helen. I cherish Sara's comparison of you and Helen to William and me. Perhaps I am biased in my opinion, but William and I have the best relationship in the world. Traumatic events can either pull people apart or bring them closer together. Every happy and tragic event has brought William and me even closer and filled our house with even more love, affection, and respect for each other. Seeing how you and Helen are getting through this situation together makes Sara's comparison all the more accurate. I know you and Helen have already made up your minds and I do not doubt for a second that Jennifer will be our daughter. I also do not doubt that she will inherit a lot of biological gifts from you and Helen and wonder how William and I got so lucky. I don't know why this happened, any of this. I always questioned why my pregnancies ended in miscarriages because it didn't make sense. I don't know why Helen and you found yourselves in this situation when you were about to pursue educational opportunities. I wish there was an easy answer. The "If it's meant to be, it will be" comes to mind, but I only put so much stock in that. Well, usually I do, but in our collective situation, how can it be anything but fate? The stars aligned for all of us. But still, I am at a loss as to why you have to experience the emotional angst of an unplanned pregnancy. The only thing I extracted from my inability to carry a child to term is how much I wanted to be a mom. With each loss, I was more certain I was meant to nurture a child. With your loss, and believe me, I understand that you will both be experiencing an unequivocal loss, perhaps you will leave the situation with joy that you were responsible for bringing Jennifer into the world. I think she will make the world a better place, just by being a part of it. I know she will make William's and my world a better place. She isn't even here yet and she already has done just that. We will do everything we can to help Jennifer find her own destiny, but whatever that may be, we all will be a part of the big picture. What a beautiful picture that is...

Warm regards,
Emma

Soon after Walter's response, Helen responded as well:

Dear Emma,

As I said before, this is going to be the most personal, impersonal experience we are all going to go through. I do wish that it be as personal as you would like it to be. As the birth mother I do not have as much freedom with questions as you do, nor would I want to cross my boundaries in any way, making you both feel uncomfortable with my words or actions. The agency makes it feel almost as if we're apart [sic] of a business transaction, a little silly if you ask me. However, for you both there is nothing you can say, do, or ask Walter and I that would be inappropriate or make us uncomfortable in anyway. What ever [sic] you want to know just ask and we would be over joyed [sic] to answer the question you bring to us.

I am so enthralled that Walter and I have impacted your lives as strongly as we did. I had no idea before this experience that there were so many couples unable to have children. The thought of it makes me clench up with anger and sadness. There are so many innocent children that are being born to young mothers that are unable to take care of themselves, not to mention a baby. I see them abuse themselves with drugs and alcohol, bad food choices, just bad choices in general. They keep their children knowing that all they'll know is sacrifice and suffering. Where is there[sic] baby in all of this? I think of these children, and then I think of you. Not only are these children going to grow up in poverty and hardship, but there are so many beautiful women like yourself [sic] unable to have babies. It literally makes me cry, knowing that women that should be having children can't, and little girls that shouldn't be having children can and will. I refuse to let that happen to you or my child, you both deserve each other and I am willing to sacrifice my own emotions to allow this to happen. Thank you so much for caring about my emotions, but there is no need to worry about me. Although this might be the hardest thing I ever have do [sic] for the rest of my life, I do not wish any different of this circumstance. Remember, I am perfectly capable of have[sic] a child in the future when I am set and ready in my finances to start a family. If I was given a choice from God himself to either continue this pregnancy or go back erasing everything that has happened, I would continue just because of the sheer fact that I'm granting someone the gift of life. I could not have picked a better set of people to be the parents of my child. The second I saw your portfolio I knew you were the ones, I guess you can call it ones [sic] intuitiveness. Talking and getting to know you better I must say was [sic] extraordinary.

As for the delivery, I promise that you won't be a burden to anyone. It's going to be a very time consuming process so feel free to come in and out when ever [sic] you'd like. To be honest, I'm not sure where you'll be standing or sitting. I will ask my doctor about it the next time I see her and will get back to you on the matter. As for my mother, she thinks that having you in the room would be a beautiful experience for all of us. I can assure you, there will be no extra added stress on me or anyone else from your presence. Everyone is more than happy to have you there with us.

It was so great to here [sic] from you!

With love,

Helen

I cherished each e-mail message as a way to stay connected to our daughter. Although Helen's disability reared its presence with each e-mail message, her words were still beautiful and touched me very deeply. I wanted to reassure her that I could hear her true depth and beauty with each communication.

Dear Helen,

Thank you so much for your letter. It is wonderful to hear what is in your heart and receive the opportunity to get to know both of you even better. Sometimes, there are no words. You both truly inspire me.

Sincerely,
Emma

Focusing on the new school year would be extremely difficult. How I was expected to concentrate on anything unrelated to becoming a mother was beyond me. And yet, my elation translated beautifully into my classroom. Since I was beaming from ear to ear, my students received the best of me. My plans were to leave my class when my baby girl arrived, so I thought it important to make every moment we experienced together count. As the school year got underway, I continued to receive e-mails from Helen.

Dear Emma and William,

Thank you so much for such beautiful compliments, I always liked to think I might inspire somebody one day.

Actually, I do have one small favor to ask of you, if it's ok with the both of you? When our socialworker [sic] was photo copying my ultrasound pictures, she accidentally missed the one of Jenifer's [sic] feet and the one of her bum. I was just wondering if there was a way you could send me a copy. E-mail, mail, it doesn't matter how, but if you could do that for me I would be eternally thankful.

Best wishes,
Helen

Hi again!

William said he would bring the ultrasound pictures to Kinkos on Monday and scan them into a PDF file so that we can e-mail you the missing images of the bum and the feet. He has back-to-back meetings on Monday, so it could turn into Tuesday. I hope that is okay. It was so generous of you to give us the original pictures; you should not hesitate to ask for such a small request. They are already in an album in order, waiting for the addition of her birthday pictures. Hmm. Would it even be okay with you and Walter for us to take pictures of Jennifer when she is first born? Would you want me to take a picture of the three of you together so that I could weave in your collective image to her adoption story? Perhaps pictures of us together might be nice? If any or all of this is too much, please tell me and I will drop the topic immediately. Still, it's better to allow you time to reflect on such questions now before bombarding you with questions (or a camera) on Jennifer's birthday.

Best,
Emma

This was a truly joyous time for me and I couldn't wait to send out the next letter. Trudy thought it was a good idea for all of us to get to know each other. According to her, strong relationships between birth and adoptive parents benefited an adopted child. Although we had been advised that such a personal relationship was a good idea, sometimes I worried whether or not it truly was in everyone's best interests.

Dear Emma,

Thank you, both of you, for getting a copy of those ultrasound pictures to me. It means the world to both Walter and myself [sic], that you are willing to help us complete our ultrasound collection. All I can say is thank you, and take your time; there is no need to rush. Do what you need to do, and when you have some spare time on hand, then send them, ok? I know you are very busy people and I don't want you to think you have to rush to get them to me. We still have almost 2 months left, just as long as I receive them, it doesn't matter when. It was really hard to give them up, but I figured you deserved to have the ultrasound pictures of your child. I thought that, maybe Jenifer [sic] would like to see them too. Looking through our albums when I was a little girl, seeing my ultrasound pictures intrigued me a great deal. I'd like that for her too.

Speaking of albums, feel free to take as many pictures at the hospital as you like. Mom is bringing a camera as well. I would be honored if you would take a picture of the three of us together. That would make my world. I would also love for all of us to take one together as well, [sic] I think that is such a great idea. Believe me when i [sic] say that non [sic] of this is overwhelming to me. Actually, it's the complete opposite, knowing that Jenifer [sic] is so thought of in everything you do makes me bubble over with happiness. For me, how could that be to [sic] much to handle? It's quite a relief if anything, so feel free to bombard me with as many camera's [sic] as you want when the time comes. Um, just one question if you both don't mind, and feel free to reject it, it's just a small thought that crossed my mind. Would it be ok if, with the picture I drew, I send home with you just one decent picture of Walter and I. I'd like Jenifer [sic] to see when she's ready of course, what we actually looked like? [sic] Again, feel free to reject this request if you don't feel it's appropriate, or if you just rather not. It's just I would like her to see our actual appearances, instead of just the picture of us after birth... not going to be my best moment. This is the last thing I ask of you both.

warm [sic] regards,
Helen

Of course Jennifer would know the reasons she was adopted. First of all, we would tell her because it was the right thing to do. Second of all, every piece of information I had read suggested that adoptive children's emotional development is much stronger if they know who their parents were and why adoption was pursued. The more open and honest Helen was with me, the better off Jennifer would be in her life. Nothing was more important than that. During this time, Barnes and Noble and Amazon made a lot of money off of my purchases. I read books on raising an adopted child, taking care of a baby, what was expected in a baby's first year, a no cry sleep solution book, and I had learned baby sign language. I wanted our daughter to have every opportunity that was available. I knew I would make millions of mistakes as a mother, but I refused to allow any to emerge out of my own ignorance. The only issue that bothered me was why on earth Helen and Walter would want copies of Jennifer's ultrasounds. Something seemed unhealthy about it. It was difficult for me to judge since I was on the opposite side of the situation, but it made me uneasy.

Dear Helen,

William found time today to make the feet and bum ultrasound pictures into PDF files. I have attached them to this e-mail; so hopefully, you are able to open them without issue. He is sitting next to me right now and tells me he had to enlarge them so that you could read the captions on them. Let me know if they came through.

As far as the picture you drew for Jennifer, oh yes, please give that to us! I think we were all so overwhelmed at our first meeting, we just spaced it at the end. In addition to hospital pictures, yes, we would love a picture of you and Walter without the hospital setting. You're right to think that Jennifer should see a picture of what you normally look like! Anything and everything you want to give us to help her know where she came from can only benefit her in every way. She needs and deserves to know about her biological family. That said I will include every detail you requested in her adoption story. She will always know how much you and Walter loved her. That is a promise from the bottom of our hearts.

Warmly,
Emma

Hi again!

I really enjoy hearing from you.

What can I say Walter and I are so lucky to have found you both. I can't believe you would allow us to send such personal things with you and Jenifer [sic], and to allow her to know so much about us. From the bottom of my heart, you both are truly a work of God himself. I can't believe he has blessed my child with such earthly angels to parent and take care of her. You are going to be phenominal [sic] Parents [sic]!

If for any reason you need to talk to Walter or I [sic], you know where we are. Anything you need, any information, just ask us. I wish you both well. I hope to here [sic] from you soon! If not, see you in the delivery room.

With much love, and respect,
Helen

Hi Helen!

Please tell Jennifer that I think about her every single day, and so does William. We can't wait to meet her in October!

And speaking of gifts from God, you and Walter are the greatest gift for William and me. You are our angels and we are forever grateful. You are giving us the greatest gift of our lives. You will always be in our thoughts and prayers. Once again, there really are no words.Be well,

Emma

Time simultaneously dragged on and sped forward. One moment it seemed as though our daughter would never arrive, other times it felt like enough time did not exist before we were fully prepared. Then it hit me; no one is ever actually prepared to become a parent. Still, there were many affairs that had to be settled and rooms that had to be prepared. William and I donated half of our closets to Good Will trying to make space for baby paraphernalia. He decided he needed to change all of the doors in the house because the house was built in the 60's. He theorized that lead based paint was located somewhere under all of the layers of paint. Although I doubted that Jennifer would come home and instantly lick the doors, I thought it was adorable that he felt the need to make the constructive changes. Closets were cleared, trips to Home Depot and Lowes abounded.

We bought the paint for our daughter's bedroom, which was my favorite color, lilac. Since Helen and I both loved purple, it felt fitting to paint our baby girl's room that color. We carefully picked out her crib and ordered the furniture to go with it after faithfully researching Consumer Reports. In order to find the number one rated crib, we had to search many places, but it was well worth it to provide the very best in safety. With each purchase that was made, a hint of despair shrouded me with worry that it would all be for nothing. In order to assist this version of shopper's remorse, my best friend, who was over the moon excited for me to finally become a mom, offered up anything and everything related to baby girl paraphernalia. She gave William and me a bathtub, bouncy seat, co-sleeper (for the hotel room), and lots of clothing. Another friend of mine also provided me with clothing and a bassinet. We were officially ready and eager to hear as many updates about how our daughter was doing from Helen. The letters continued frequently.

Dear Emma,

I'm doing great, thank you for asking. How are you? I'm very glad you were able to find the time to write me again, I love hearing from you!

I asked about where you and William will be during my birth. I guess I can only have three support people. Some women have one or two, and some take all three. This means I am able to have you in the room, but William will have to wait in the waiting room. I am assuming you both will end up at the hospital a little later so I will tell the nurses who you are and to let you in, other wise [sic] you will be stuck out in the waiting room as well. There should be no problems, just tell them who you are and when you would like to come in (and please come in when you want, I promise, you're no bother. I actually would like you there). They should let you in no problem. Just in case, they will allow you to contact us through cell phone, so just call Walter's cell phone and I will have them let you in. I know he would be more than happy to give it to you, just ask him if you'd like it.

As for the little girl in my tummy, she's still kicking around in there, as strong as ever now! It actually does feel a bit uncomfortable, because she's gotten so strong. So you're definitely right about the super strong reflexes. It's actually quite amazing! I will definitely tell her that you and William think about her everyday [sic]. I know she feels all of our love, and our impatience to meet her. I can't wait to meet her either! Just a little more than a month, I'm 34 weeks along, so that means 6 more weeks left.

Oh, and Emma, you are absolutely right. There are no words, and I can't wait to bring such joy to you and to the world.

with [sic] warm regards,
Helen

Although I completely understood the hospital's rule, I started to picture what it might be like to be in this woman's room with her boyfriend and mother during one of the most intimate, and let's be honest, disgusting moments of her life. And, I would be there without William. I decided to do something I never do, which was to not obsess over it. If this was the biggest problem, there was no problem. And so it was decided that I would be in there alone. Then I thought back to Helen advising me to just be comfortable. Comfortable, now that was a funny word in this situation.

Speaking of comfort, I thought perhaps it might be comforting for Helen to know what we were doing to prepare for our daughter's arrival. In my response, I thought I should ask her if she would like to hear the details. If it were too painful, I would drop the subject immediately. However, something about our exchanges made me feel that such information would provide her with peace. And so I responded.

Dear Helen,

We completely understand the hospital regulations. We certainly would not want to get in anyone's way during your delivery! William is totally okay with hanging out in the waiting room. So, here is another question. Is it okay with the doctors if I were to bring a camera into the delivery room or should it wait until later? I would not take pictures while you were pushing or anything, I promise. But, is a camera sanitary? I know nothing about this and want to follow all rules carefully. Six more weeks, we can't wait! Do you want to know what we have been doing to get ready? I will not elaborate in case it makes you uncomfortable, but I thought I would let you know that we are in full anticipation mode. Thank you. I feel the need to say that to you and Walter every single day.

Warm regards,
Emma

Dear Emma,

I'm glad you're ok with the hospital regulations, I was hoping, William not being able to stay in the delivery room wouldn't upset you both. If I had it my way, I'd give you both the choice to be in the room. It turns out they're are [sic] really strict with the maturity [sic] ward, and rightfully so! As for the camera in the delivery room, I'm pretty sure you wouldn't take pictures of me in the pushing phase. What a lovely set of pictures to put in the family album, lol! In all seriousness, I'm pretty sure it's ok to take a camera in the delivery room. Two of my friends had just given birth to beautiful baby boy's, [sic] and they both have pictures of them right after birth, so I think it's ok. However, I will double check just in case when I see my doctor this Friday. I will let you know as soon as I know :)

Only five more weeks now, tomorrow I'm 35 weeks. Just so you can follow and count down the days until your daughter arrives, every Tuesday is the start of a new week. I would love to know what you guys are doing to get ready for her, believe me when I say that it gives me peace. Nothing you say to me will make me feel uncomfortable. I have already came [sic] to terms with it, so there is no need to worry. There is a peace when I think about you and William with Jenifer, [sic] so please don't hold back. Oh, and thank you, for just being you. You both are the perfect match in everyway [sic]. There is no one more perfect for Jenifer [sic], and I also feel the need to express this to you every day.

With love and respect,
Helen

Dear Helen,

As far as what we are doing. What aren't we doing? We researched Consumer Reports and found the number one rated crib. The only problem was, we couldn't find it anywhere around here. We called anyone and everyone that sold baby furniture within a 50-mile radius. Last week, we finally found a retailer that sold it and took a 2-hour drive to take a look at it. We loved it and it has now been ordered! It is a crib that turns into a toddler bed, and then a full size bed. Isn't that amazing? We bought the furniture to go with it so that Jennifer will have plenty of storage for her clothes. Being a girl and all, we are just assuming she will want lots of clothes! We also ordered the bedding set. William is replacing all of the doors in the house because he thinks our doors are old and decrepit and thinks Jennifer would want better doors. He also just bought a closet organizer and plans to put that in this weekend. Yes, what can I say; we are already planning for her teenage years. :-) Besides William and me, you and Walter are the only ones who know her name. Everything we do now is, "Well, Jennifer Lila will need this, and Jennifer Lila won't want that." It's like she is already here in a strange way. But it is our little secret, we just keep reminding each other not to slip up and reveal the name to anyone. So far, we've held it in, but it hasn't been easy!

I am definitely doing the countdown right along with you. 35 weeks, so close! We bought the car seat, a stroller, and this weekend, we are going to buy bottles, diapers, clothing, etc. to take with us. We have started a pile. You will probably need your labor/delivery suitcase. We get to have one too! It is SO exciting! I've never looked forward to anything more in my whole life. Have I said thank you yet? :-)

Be well!

Much love,
Emma

Dear Emma,

There are no words to describe how enthralled I am with what you both are doing to get ready for Jenifer. That is just absolutely beautiful. See, that's what I was talking about in the beginning. You are going to give her exactly what she deserves, the best of everything. I can't believe you went through all of that trouble just to get her a top of the line crib. I wounder [sic] how much that coasted [sic] you, never mind everything else that when [sic] with it. I could have never afforded a top of the anything... It's depressing, but the truth. This just makes my decision and my reasons all the more accurate! Thank you for telling me, it puts my heart to rest more and more. I absolutely love everything you're doing, down to the doors. My mother and I thought that was awesome! I could picture William, complaining about how the doors needed to be changed because he's concerned Jenifer [sic] would want better doors. Absolutely adorable!! What a trip that must have been lol. I wish I could have been there for that conversation! Oh, and hey, planning ahead is never a bad thing. Get ready as much as you can for her teen years because those will be the toughest, emotionally that is. My mother reminds me all the time that we were much easier when we were younger. I didn't know her grandparents didn't know the name you picked out. I know they're going to love it! I think it's absolutely beautiful, it must be really hard to contain yourself from telling everyone in site [sic]!

It's Saturday, so now it's almost 34 weeks counting down, when you reply it'll probably be almost 33 weeks. I notice you tend to receive my letters at the end of the week. Makes perfect sense, you are a school teacher. I'm happy that you have everything prepared for when the time comes, because it's just around the corner. Oh, and while on my check up yesterday, she found I was a centimeter dilated! I'm right on time which means she's going to be right on time! Speaking of check up [sic], I asked my doctor about your camera question, and she said it was perfectly fine to bring on [sic] into the delivery room. So you can take lots of pictures. I know my mom will have my camera with her.

Is there anything else you would like me to ask my doctor? I'd be glad to ask! I hope to hear from you soon!

With love,
Helen

Her mother would have her camera with her? Why? Why would they take pictures of this event? First she wants copies of the ultrasound pictures and now she wants copies of the birth experience. How would she ever move on with her life if she had photographic evidence that prevented her from doing that? Again, I was not in her shoes, so it was difficult to judge. Regardless, it made me uneasy.

Dear Helen,

One thing that you said totally confused me. Are you about to reach 36 weeks or am I going mad? The last e-mail you sent me said that you were 35 weeks (last Tuesday), which would put you at 36 weeks this Tuesday. Is that right? Or did your doctors re-evaluate your due date? I hear that happens a lot, but you had mentioned that your doctor thinks you will be going on time, hence, my confusion lingers. Still, I can't believe you are already a cm dilated. That is so amazing!

We went out yesterday and bought diapers, wipes, and blankets. My sister bought us a ton of bottles, and my friends gave us a bathtub, a bouncy seat, a crib for the hotel, and a bunch of outfits. I am putting my "labor and delivery" bags aside because it sounds like Jennifer could arrive at any time. William is actually hanging another door right now. Yes, it was kind of funny for that to be a home improvement that he felt couldn't wait. He makes me laugh. But I have to say; the new doors really spruce up the place! I must admit, I really don't think Jennifer would have a lot of criticism for the old ones, but I guess we'll never know now!

I am so excited I can barely contain myself. Thank you so much for always writing back to me, it has been such an honor to get to know you even better over the last few weeks. I keep pinching myself thinking that this is all some dream. You were clearly sent straight from heaven into our lives.

I just want to remind you again, if for any reason you change your mind about having me in the delivery room, I will completely understand. The last thing I want you to worry about during that time in your life is where the adoptive mom wants to be. Just tell the nurses whatever you decide at that time and that will be that. I just felt the need to say that one more time as I do not want to cause you additional stress while you are experiencing labor.

The laundry bell just buzzed, so I must go fold and sort. If only I could train my dogs to help me with the laundry...Yeah, that wouldn't work to anyone's benefit, even if it were possible. :-)

I wish you a very comfortable day!

With love,
Emma

After I made my little joke about my dogs, sadness overwhelmed me. I looked over at my dogs lying near my feet and my heart sank. We had one yellow Labrador named Daisy and one beagle basset hound mix named Bailey. I loved both of them with all of my heart, but Daisy was very ill. She was mentally ill, not physically ill. For the first three years of her life, she showed very few signs of psychological distress, but there were small pieces of evidence to her underlying issues. We had brought her to obedience training as soon as she was allowed and adopted her at eight weeks of age. The only warning we had received about Daisy was that she had been the runt of the litter and a bit possessive of her food. As a result, we addressed the mealtime issue immediately.

To make sure she was never dangerous, we trained her to allow us to pet her while she was eating. One trainer even helped us figure out how to train her to step away from her food mid munch to ensure that violence was never expressed because of food issues. Although she had never done anything outrageous at the obedience classes, she growled at the other dogs in class and we were asked to keep her away from the other four-legged students. We tried bringing her to dog parks in an attempt to socialize her, but if another dog sniffed her, she would turn around and try to nip at them to make them go away. Not once did she go after another dog, but any dog that approached her was soon running in the other direction. After years of attempting different methods of socialization, we realized that we had to keep her away from all dogs.

As the years moved forward, we visited our veterinarian in search of resolutions. When none worked, we sought out dog acupuncturists, naturopathic medicine, and paid startling sums of money for home trainers to try to help us rehabilitate her. When we were not seeking help from experts in person, we read books and articles in hopes of the magic solution. One article suggested the addition of a second dog might rehabilitate her. Although we initially dismissed such an idea, one Pedigree commercial begging for people to adopt abused animals pulled at our heartstrings and quickly turned that possibility into a certainty. That commercial and petfinder.com was how we ended up with rescuing a four-year-old basset hound/beagle mix, Bailey. Although Daisy learned to tolerate Bailey, the transition was terrible and Bailey had probably wished to return to his shelter life a few times.

Daisy's behavior had been difficult to manage for years, but at the age of four, she nipped one of my friends' children, and we knew it was serious. My friends were not overly concerned since Daisy had not even broken the skin on their little boy, but it was serious to me. In fact, my friend later brought her son to her doctor to make sure that he was alright. One of the reasons we decided on bringing a Labrador into our house in the first place was because the breed was supposedly great with children.

How ironic that the very reason for choosing a particular dog breed resulted in having a dog with violent tendencies.

In addition to nipping my friend's child, Daisy began to act out in other places and towards other people. When we had other friends over, she ended up biting William severely and he probably should have received several stitches to his wound. Several other unprovoked bites followed on multiple occasions, and we had reached the end of our rope. The only consistent factor in the attacks was that someone had touched or petted Daisy before each bite. How tragic for a dog to hate the stroking of her fur, especially since she had adored it for years of her life. Believing that there was a solution to her behavioral issues, we consulted an animal behaviorist.

We forked over $375 for an hour session. Within the hour, the doggie doctor refused to touch Daisy or really approach her at all. Regardless, after asking us a batch of questions, she diagnosed Daisy's issues. She explained that Daisy suffered from fear-induced aggression. "What was she afraid of?" we asked. The doctor told us that there was nothing tangible as it was a psychosis problem. We were hoping since there was a formal diagnosis, it would lead to medication and a solution. Instead, she told us that she believed that anti-anxiety medication would actually result in even worse behavior. Up until this point, she had bitten, and then quickly released. If her mental capabilities were compromised, she might latch on and really, dangerously hurt someone. When we asked if there was anything we could possibly do, she offered two unthinkable options. She said we could continue to live as relatively close to the way we had been living, but were prohibited from ever petting our dog. She also warned us that we needed to make sure that Daisy was never around visitors to our home. When we told her of our hopes of adopting a child someday, she added that we could just keep Daisy separated from the child at all times and make sure she wore a muzzle.

We asked what kind of life that was for a dog and she admitted that it really was not great, but if we were unable to entertain the second option, it was our only choice. We would definitely entertain an option that did not involve a lifetime with a muzzled dog. But then she revealed that the second option was putting her to sleep.

We had been unable to consider this option as long as parenthood remained out of the realm of our reality. For three additional years, we made sure that Daisy was out of sight whenever people visited. As a result, we entertained very infrequently.

Our every move was choreographed to ensure everyone's safety. Everyone included William, Bailey, and me. While William or I fed Daisy, the other one was in another room with the door closed feeding Bailey, to prevent any dog fights. William secured the fenced in yard even more so than it had been to make sure that Daisy never escaped our yard. She earned the phrase Houdini Dog as we had witnessed her slither under ridiculously small gaps to search for the best sticks possible. We exercised her multiple times each day to try to diminish her anxiety, but it never seemed to help. She had been diagnosed with ADHD and OCD on top of the Fear/Anxiety Induced Aggression disorder, which meant that getting a stick or ball out of her mouth, was only on her terms and when she felt ready. Dog trainers paraded through our lives to try to alleviate this problem, but they all admitted that the problem was too much for them to handle.

It was a challenging way to live with a dog, but we had managed. However, with parenthood imminent, we knew we could not keep Daisy. There was no way in the world we would place our baby in harm's way. Although I doubted that Daisy would attack a baby, I had no way of guaranteeing my daughter's safety when I couldn't even guarantee my own safety. William had mentioned that he would be making some phone calls to try to find another solution for Daisy when we had reached the two month waiting period for our daughter. With Helen's last letter, I realized that we had reached that mark. In the meantime, I knew I could not reveal this information to Helen, what would she think of people who were going to possibly relinquish one of their dogs? Yes, it was for the safety of her child, but there was no way I would terrorize her with such a prospect. It might make her change her mind. So the letters continued along as though all was just fine.

Dear Emma,

Yeah, I'm really sorry about the confusion of last weeks [sic] reply... I kind of had a dyslexic moment and went backwards with my numbers instead of forward. I had realized what I said right after I sent the letter, so I couldn't do much about it. Let me clear that up for you. My due date is still the same (Oct.20th) and I am going to be 37 weeks pregnant on this up coming [sic] Tuesday (the 29th of Sept.). Again, really sorry about that... boy do I feel like an idiot, lol.

Wow, It [sic] sounds like you two are just about ready for her to come now! That's so exciting to hear, I'm so excited for you both! You know, you would think It [sic] would be depressing for me to hear about everything that's happening. Knowing that, I would never be able to do anything like this for her, but it's the complete opposite! It makes my heart sing, knowing what you both are doing for Jenifer [sic]. Knowing the love and want behind everything you both are doing. I can sense your excitement and anticipation from here! When you think of it on a much bigger scale, I'm so lucky! I bet the doors that William put in look wonderful, and I know she'll love them!

Thank you, for always writing Me [sic] back! I love hearing from you, I look forward to your responses every week! It makes me so happy and relieved that you enjoy hearing from me too. I was a little worried that I might be bothering you in some way by responding to you all the time. I know your [sic] busy, and I wasn't sure you really enjoyed talking to a 20 year old, even if I am the birth mother of your little girl. I know that we must think on much different scales, seeing as how my brain hasn't even fully developed yet. I would just wonder to myself whether or not you really wanted to hear from Walter or I [sic]. Then again, if you were getting annoyed in anyway, why would you keep writing back? So thank you, I love hearing from you!

Lol, I would love for you to be in the delivery room with me, as I said before, it would bring me great comfort having you there. I chose you as one of my support people for a reason. However, if you didn't want to be in the room because it's making you feel uncomfortable, then I will completely understand. This is something one usually doesn't do unless you are really close to someone... like family close. As for me though, I know it would help me 100% if you were in there with me. I saw the rooms and there are chairs and things to sit on. It's a fairly comfortable room, and the postpartum rooms are even more comfortable. So it's really up to you in the long run, because I know that your presents [sic] will do nothing but help me!

I hope to hear from you again! Talk to you later Emma, and I hope you have another fabulous week at school!

Warm regards,
Helen

And then I received another letter.

Here is hoping that tomorrow's Prenatal [sic] appointment goes like the last! Wish me luck, lol. Last week, I was still only 1 cm dilated, but I might have gone a bit more so don't quote me on that. I'll find out tomorrow if I have dilated anymore. Don't worry, I'll keep you updated. As for a guesstimation of Jenifer's [sic] weight, she said to not quote her, but Jenifer [sic] might be about 6-7 lbs. However, that was 2 weeks ago, so I'll ask her again tomorrow. If there is one thing I do enjoy, it's a good surprise, and this pregnancy has been full of them! It keeps me on my feet. I do hear her heart beat every time I go in, and my lord is it strong! Unfortunately there has [sic] been no more Ultrasounds. I think it has something to do with my insurance only paying for a certain amount. I'll only get more if there is a need for it, so lets [sic] hope we don't get that kind of surprise. Other than that, there really isn't anything new. Just the fact of the days are [sic] counting down. Exciting!

As for me, I'm actually holding up quite good [sic]. I know the end is near, but I don't have any negative emotions. Actually, they are all pretty positive. Even though I'm in for a whirlwind of pain, and I know I am, the thought of Jenifer [sic] having the best crib and the best of everything else overrides any negative emotion that might peak out it's [sic] ugly head. I too like to think in terms of "the glass is half full". When you don't, where does that leave you? Miserable, and who wants to be that?

I have heard many times of women adopting internationally, because to [sic] many times have girls changed there [sic] minds at the last minute. I went into this Adoption process knowing all about how the adoptive parents hold their breaths [sic] until the papers are signed at the very end. I'd like to be very real on this particular subject, mainly because it IS so touchy, if that's ok with you. I wanted nothing more than to maybe attempt to ease yours and William's worries around this matter, even if it was just a little bit. Everyone was telling me different things about what I should be doing around this subject. Some were telling me to leave it because it might scare you even more. Some said to see how close we had gotten before saying anything, and some said it might be ok to bring up. Either way, I was so confused, and didn't want to do any damage, or make anything worse. So, I thought the best thing to do would be to wait it out. I hope you know me enough now to believe me when I say, that there is no chance of that happening...at all. Please don't worry about that, I hope you don't. I love Jenifer [sic] enough to want everything for her, I'm smart enough to know I can't give that to her, and I have grown way to [sic] fond of you to even think about denying you what you have longed and deserved for so much time now. What kind of person would I be? Then I would be selfish. I'm not that person. It was fate that has brought Walter, Jenifer [sic], and I [sic] to you. How could it not be, I saw you in a dream before I knew who you were. I knew it was you before even looking at your portfolio., I saw your picture and said "She's blond, it's her". I am confident enough in my knowledge about this subject to tell you I know this was all meant to happen. Believe me, this is not the first time I have witnessed destiny or a miracle take it's [sic] course.

The more you know about me, the more Jenifer [sic] will make sense to you in the later years. There really isn't much to say about what it's like for me. I've told you every thing [sic] on my mind, and my all of my emotions. I would be lying if I said this wasn't painful, but I have such a peace and a knowing that, I'll be completely fine. That and I have tons of support from everybody around me. My mother, Walter, his family, and all my friends. [sic] Especially my best friend Leslie, who you will meet the day of the delivery. She LOVES you both! I have tons of people on my side, cheering me on, so I'll be fine.

I don't know what to do with myself. To have impacted a complete stranger in such a way, It's [sic] amazing! However, I don't really look at myself as being that

big of a deal. I mean I'm doing the right thing, but shouldn't everyone? To hear
all this makes me feel so good, and it reassures me that I'm doing the right thing.
Thank you, but please, do not forget that you are the wonderful people that are
going to take care of Jenifer [sic], and for that you are my Angels.

Well... off to bed now, it's almost midnight, so I have to attempt to sleep. Getting
up in the morning will be hard for me if I don't. I look forward to hearing from you
soon. Good night Emma :)

With much love,

Helen

I reread the letter over and over again. She basically promised me that she would never
change her mind, ever, no matter what. I wanted to believe her. Even so, I treaded very
carefully in my e-mails. Helen did not even know about my Labrador's mental issues.
Was I a fraud for keeping that information from her? I was willing to be a bit of a fraud
in order to ensure that motherhood was truly in my future. Believe me; I wasn't truly
honest with her in other ways either because only the strongest willpower prevented
me from asking her to promise she would never relent on her decision. I needed reassurance, as despair was always hiding right beneath my optimism, but I hid that from
her as well. For fear of legal ramifications and whatever other ramifications might be
hiding around a corner, my e-mail messages were very carefully crafted.

In the big picture, I decided it hardly mattered. With this last e-mail from Helen,
she was my favorite person in the entire world, although it did bother me that she
continued to spell Jennifer's name with only one n. Regardless of my critique over her
ability to spell my future daughter's name correctly, after all of our misfortune, how
William and I suddenly became so lucky was beyond my comprehension. When did
"Murphy" leave our lives? Well, good riddance! I was more than happy to see him go!
The only thing that bugged me was using the name Jennifer. I love the name; I always
have, but if we were going to call our daughter Jenna, why not just name her Jenna?
Maybe Helen would be able to spell Jenna correctly! I thought about the roster that
teachers receive with student names and believed more and more that we should just

name her what we would call her. When I explained my reasons to William, he agreed wholeheartedly, and so we thought it best to let Helen know that our daughter would be called Jenna Lila, the most perfect name in the universe.

Dear Helen,

I don't know where to begin. I think we just kind of get each other, because everything you said to me was like poetry.

Okay, so we are changing Jennifer's name a little bit. I hope this does not upset you. It's just that there are about 500 Jennifers around here and we wanted her to have a moniker that was a bit more unique. We had debated this from the beginning, but our girl will be Jenna Lila instead of Jennifer Lila. Originally, we planned to make Jennifer the official name and call her Jenna, but as a classroom teacher, I know that the name a teacher receives on a list will prevent little things like nametags, bulletin board labels, mailbox labels, book labels, folder labels, birthday labels, etc. from being written the way we want them to. So, just to bypass the confusion, we realized that we should name her what we plan to call her. Why make things complicated? Does this sit well with you? It's not a dramatic change, but it is a small change that I thought you would want to know about.

William just popped his head over and asked me to ask you if you received the kit from Viacord. If not, let us know and we will call them to follow up.

I can't believe that your doctor estimated Jenna to be between six and seven pounds already. If that is the case, I wonder how big she will be when we meet her! The baby I was holding yesterday was 1 month old and eight or nine pounds. Can you imagine if Jenna comes out at 8 or 9 pounds? William was actually over 10 pounds when he was born, so I know it is possible! Of course, she could come out at just about six pounds, the estimates are only estimates!

I hope you are feeling well and getting a little bit of sleep. I am not sleeping much because I am so excited. I think my body is trying to prepare me for the imminent lack of sleep that will head my way! We got the bassinet yesterday that we will use in the hotel and then in our bedroom until Jenna can use the crib. We are training our dogs for the new addition by carrying around a baby doll and tucking her into the crib, the bouncy seat, etc. They are fascinated already. They can't wait to have a little sister! I know I have thanked you, but my dogs now thank you too. They promise to watch over and protect Jenna in every way that they can.

Have a great day and I can't wait to hear from you again!

Sincerely,
Emma

Clearly, I had reached a new low. I was trying to convince myself that both of my dogs wanted nothing more than a little sister, while the reality was quite different. I stared at Daisy every chance I got. No, I did not pet her often, as I had been warned not to, but I played with her outside for hours each day. If William went through with his pledge, I did not know how many days I had left with her and just wanted her legacy to be of love, even if it had been a bit of a fantasy. Why did I have to make this decision? It felt like our very own Sophie's Choice. Daisy probably would have loved her little sister, she just would not have known how to show it with all of the issues that plagued her.

Hi Emma!

Can I just tell you that I love the name Jenna! I actually like it a little better than Jennifer. I mean, I like the name Jennifer, It's a beautiful name. Though, Jenna you don't hear very often, and it's absolutely adorable. I'm glad you told me, I've been calling her Jennifer for the past few months. Now I have to get used to Jenna, lol !

I did recieve [sic] the ViaCord kit. Walter and I already filled it out and stuff, so you guys don't have to worry about that.

Yup, last appointment she estimated 6-7 lbs. This one that just passed, she estimated 8lbs on my due date. At least this is proof to you that I took good care of myself. I am still one centimeter dilated, and I still should be on time. I mean she said a couple days late is normal, but I won't be going onto labor anytime soon so I should plan to see her for my next weeks [sic] prenatal appointment.

I hope all is well with you and William, and I can see that you're just as ready as ever! Tell your dogs I said thank you for the protection they are going to give their little sister. I hope they have lots of fun with her. Yes, stock up on sleep now, because there isn't going to be much of it your way, well, you have William to help you too! I can't wait to hear from you again hope to hear from you soon! [sic]

Warm regards,
Helen

The due date crept closer and the letters continued. William actively called shelters and rescue groups to try to find a no-kill solution for Daisy. Everyone he spoke with gave him the same message, which was that he should put her down. We called friends asking if they were interested in adopting her, but of course, why would they be interested when they knew the reasons we needed her out of our home? William even called the breeder from where we had adopted Daisy. He remembered that she had told us at the time of the initial adoption that if for any reason we ever needed to "get rid" of our dog, she would help us find a solution.

When he called her, he explained the circumstances, the treatment options we had explored, and our broken hearts and waited for something positive to be returned. Instead, she informed him that she was in no state to help him because her son had suddenly and unexpectedly died over the previous weekend. She suggested that he call shelters and rescue groups. Since he had called over 15 rescue groups and animal rights organizations without luck, this phone call marked the end of options for Daisy. He sadly relayed the story to me and tearfully informed me that one day I would come home, and Daisy would no longer be here. He was determined to put her down with dignity, but knew if I was aware of the day and time, that I might stop him. Each day I drove into the garage after work, I turned off my engine with nerves hoping to hear two dogs barking.

On one morning in particular, I had a bad feeling and spent a little extra time with Daisy. I gave her a spoonful of peanut butter, pledged my deep sorrow and desperate sadness and begged her to forgive us for choosing a baby over allowing her to live out the rest of her life with us, as we had always intended. Although William had not said a word to me, something about his actions in the morning made me fear the worst. As each moment crept by throughout the day, I hoped I was wrong. School could not end soon enough as I wanted to go back home and be proven wrong. How could William really go through with it? Perhaps it would be better to live with a muzzled dog than to put her down. Although I had made that suggestion repeatedly to William, he disagreed vehemently that it would really be crueler to Daisy, as had the behaviorist. When I drove into the garage that day, my fear was confirmed as I only heard one bark. I walked up the stairs hoping for a different explanation, but the spot where Daisy greeted me each day was shockingly empty. Tearfully, I brought Bailey outside alone, and mourned for the loss of Daisy's life, for the loss in our life, and for the fact that no one could find us a way to help her while she was alive.

When William returned home that evening, he replayed the events that transpired. He lovingly stayed home an extra couple of hours to play outside with Daisy, fed her chicken, and reminded her how he loved her very much. He reported that she accompanied him to the Humane Society excited to be in the car and never showed any signs of sadness or fear. The greeter at the office comforted William as they brought Daisy in for her final moments. Her life was over in about 10 seconds and, according to the technicians, she did not suffer. William was crying unabashedly at what had just been done and at his role in doing it, but the staff reminded him over and over again that he did something necessary. There was no question that Daisy was a time bomb waiting to go off unexpectedly. Yes, we had always been careful, but she could have seriously hurt or even killed someone in the wrong situation. Even though the Humane Society helps to rehabilitate dogs, they reminded him that a case like Daisy's lacked solutions. William donated Daisy's cage, food dishes, dog bed, and her leash to the organization and made a monetary donation in her memory as a way to ensure that her life allowed others a chance. It was all he could do.

As he shared the play-by-play events with me, I was amazed at William's bravery, but hurt for the memories he would have to carry around with him for the rest of his life. I hurt for the memories in my own head. Never in my wildest imagination had I ever pictured being the type of person to bring a dog into my home and for it to not be a life-long commitment. What kind of person did that make me? I knew I would always question that decision. Even when I held Jenna in my arms and loved her, even when she was crawling around on our living room floor safely because there was not a vicious dog waiting in the wings, I would still wonder. Did we do the right thing? All I could do was continue on and try to focus all of my attention on the upcoming birth of my child. Keeping the sad news a secret, I continued to reach out to Helen.

Dear Helen,

I am so happy that you like the name Jenna Lila. Jenna has been my favorite name since I was in High School. I can't believe that the doctors have estimated that Jenna will be 8 pounds! I wonder if they are actually right. Only one way to find out! So, now they think you might be a little late? That is pretty normal, at least if I use all my friends as examples. Most of my friends have been at least a few days late, sometimes more. Our phone rang at 6 a.m. yesterday and my heart skipped a beat thinking that it might be time. It is so exciting. I wonder where you will be when it is time. I wonder where Walter will be. Will it be in the morning, in the middle of the night, smack dab in the middle of the day? It is all so unpredictable, which is half the fun! I just wish you a smooth and easy delivery. Okay, perhaps easy is pushing it, but it can happen! My friend had an easy delivery, really! She reported that it was quick and painless. She has sworn that it really was. I know most pregnant women resent her! But, maybe it will happen for you too! Just ask Jenna to be nice; it's never too early to be considerate!

With love,
Emma

Several days passed and I had not heard from Helen. I hoped that all was okay and that she did not suddenly change her mind. Worry and elation were frequently fighting each other for my attention. Emotionally, I was beyond a wreck. I started to cry at the drop of a hat. Of course that was in part, due to the loss of Daisy. Every time I went into my backyard I looked around in vain hoping to see her running around. When it was time to feed my other dog, it was difficult to break the old rituals of closing the door to keep Daisy out. Every part of my life had been choreographed to prevent Daisy from biting me, biting others, breaking free of our fenced in yard, preventing her from eating Bailey's food. Instead of resentment for those rituals, I felt pain over the fact that they were no longer necessary. I actually became angry with people a lot more quickly over silly events, and it normally took an awful lot for me to become angry at all. My psyche had endured enough and I was ready to become a mom and live the next chapter of my life. The waiting was torturous, but sweet relief finally came with another message from Helen.

Dear Emma,

I'm sorry that I'm getting back to you so late. I've been doing quite a bit lately. My appointments are getting heavier and I have more to do now, so I haven't been on as often as I was before. Also, my friend Krista's sister Erika just took me on a huge photo shoot that lasted for three days.

Oh, and I wanted to ask you. Would it be ok if I gave Jenna maybe just a couple more pictures? It's not a lot, only a couple. There are pictures from the shoot that I'm having trouble deciding on. I just wanted to check with you first before just doing something.

On my appointment last Friday, I found out that I was almost two centimeters dilated, and fifty percent effaced. My cervix is thinning out, so she should be right along! Exciting, huh? I can go any day really, I doubt it... but it can still happen. My doctor still suspects that I will be a couple of days late, just because it's normal for first births. However, she did tell me that she wouldn't be surprised if I went a little early. Either way, it's still only less than a week away now! My mother had a similar reaction to a phone call at work. She told me that people play jokes on her and tell her it's time just to see the look on her face. I think it's kind of cute :). I have another appointment tomorrow, so hopefully I can tell you about this one too, there might be something new, who knows?

Well Emma, in case I don't hear from you until I see you in the delivery room, I would just like to say what a pleasure it is and what an important person you have become in my life. In all of our lives [sic]. Both you and William are such truly beautiful and genuine people. You're both a part of us and in our hearts for ever [sic]. I have looked forward [sic] your letters like nothing else before, and I want to thank you for becoming so emotionally and personally involved with me. Not a lot of adopting parents do this. It means everything to me. Thank you.

Well, I hope to hear from you again... and if not then I'll see you in [sic] delivery room! I hope your week is filled with happiness and laughter. Also, I hope you're enjoying the lovely weather, and the changing of the trees. What a beautiful site[sic] it is out there!

Will [sic] much love,
Helen

I was so relieved to finally hear from her again. My heart started to function somewhat normally again. I continued to mourn Daisy, but as each day crept closer, I knew we did what we had to do in order to create a safe house for a newborn. Well, I mostly knew that. Guilt plagued me and I could not stop hoping to get a glimpse of her around the house. The back yard trips were the absolute worst. We had spent endless hours playing out there in all of the extreme weather. Daisy was the reason I learned about fleece lined jeans and L.L. Bean outerwear.

I wondered if Caesar Milan (The Dog Whisperer) would have offered a different opinion or strategy. I had previously searched his website in hopes that he could try to help us, but he did not have an e-mail address or any sort of address for letters. When I located a place on the site that asked for families needing his help, he was only available to help people in the California area. No matter how hard we tried to help Daisy for as many years as we had, I could not help but be filled with regret. My regret increased in intensity by the nature of waiting for Jenna's birth. Everything was really getting to me, but at least now that I had heard from Helen, my faith was restored that this adoption would in fact happen soon.

Dear Helen,

As far as the pictures are concerned, the more the merrier, if you ask me. I do not want it to ever be a secret to Jenna who her birth parents are and where she came from. It is terribly important to her development and to her curiosity! I would like to put a photo album together of you and your family, and hopefully, a few pictures of you, Walter, and Sara holding Jenna, along with her adoption story. In fact, if you had any of your own baby/kid pictures and if Walter did as well, I'd bet that Jenna would LOVE to have those too. Whatever you have, she will love to have, and we will share them with her with absolute pride and joy. I have looked forward to your e-mails as well! I am so happy that we received an opportunity to get to know one another better this way. Words hardly capture what I am feeling in my heart for you, Walter, and this entire process. If someone had told me how much I would love the adoption process, I would never have believed it. I wonder if it is this wonderful for everyone. I highly doubt it. I can't believe how lucky William and I are to have had you and Walter choose us to raise Jenna. I keep pinching myself!

I will jump every time the phone rings until the actual moment is upon us! If you have any updates to send along, I'll be eagerly awaiting. Take care of yourself and try to get some rest before the big delivery date.

With love,
Emma

As ready as we may have felt, the secrecy of the adoption continued to eat us both up, and yet felt completely necessary. Don't get me wrong, plenty of people in our lives now knew, but there were a staggering number of people who loved us and remained in the dark. It was clear that I would have to wait until the actual delivery to really learn Helen's long-term plans. William had zero doubts that we would raise Jenna Lila. I was not as easily convinced. With every move we made, there were two schools of thought arguing with themselves in my head. The first thought was that this was actually going to happen and William and I were going to become parents. This obviously thrilled and terrified me simultaneously.

The second thought was always, "What if she changes her mind?" We are turning our lives upside down in anticipation of this blessed event. If she has a change of heart how will we recover from yet another blow? I tried to banish the second thought from existence, but regardless of how much she ensured me that her plans would not change, and even so far as promising me that she would never change her mind and do such a thing to us, it constantly gnawed at my emotional constitution. One minute I was overjoyed, the next I was terrified. Was I prepared to be a parent? Did it even matter? Were these people as genuine as they seemed?

We were about to find out. It all began on a Sunday. Around 10:30 am, we received the phone call we had been waiting for, the one telling us that Helen's water had broken, she was in labor, and her contractions were 15 minutes apart. In short, we were finally going to meet our daughter. We knew our lives would change forever and could not wait for that change. William and I ran around the house getting every last tiny detail ready in anticipation with our hearts beating wildly. William wanted to secure every piece of the house and load the car perfectly. I ran into the bathroom as he was showering and begged him to move it along because I did not want to miss our daughter's debut.

After I bugged him to hurry up, the phone rang again and Trudy told us that at that point, the doctors were uncertain as to whether or not Helen's water had actually broken. She told us we could still travel to Massachusetts or we could wait an hour and find out what was really going on before getting into a car. We decided to wait it out, and a very long three hours later, we were told that Helen's water really did not break and she was not in labor. What she was experiencing was early labor, which meant that the baby could arrive later that evening, the next day, in four days, or a week. Helen was discharged from the hospital.

William and I waited with crazy anticipation, jumping with each ring of the telephone over the next few days. In the mean time, I had to go back to work with my mind in a million places. William and I agreed that if he received the phone call, he would call the secretaries at my school and ask to be connected with me. I let them in on the details of our plan long ago, as they were trustworthy and wonderful human beings. This of course meant that in addition to jumping with the ring of my home phone, I began to jump with each ring of my classroom telephone. The physical therapist, psychologist, principal, and special education teachers all (unknowingly) teased me with phone calls, but the real event was yet to happen.

JENNA LILA

OUR MOMENT FINALLY arrived on the morning of October 21ˢᵗ. I was in my class-room in the middle of Literature Circles, engrossed in a deep discussion with my students about a Patricia Polacco book, when my students shouted, "Someone on the phone is trying to get your attention." I picked up the phone and the secretary told me that William was on the phone. I knew what that meant! There is a wonderful movie called *Juno*. It is one of our favorite movies in the world, and if anyone has seen it they will understand why that is the case. In the movie, when Juno is about to have a baby she yells to her father, "Thunder cats ago!" That is what William shouted to me, so I knew it was time.

Since the adoption was such a big secret, and only a few people at my school knew, I had to tell my students that a family emergency was going to pull me away from the classroom. It was true, labor was an emergency and it was because my family was expanding! I drove home with my heart beating a million miles per hour and waited for William to come home. Bailey was thrilled to see me, but he knew that something was happening. I told him over and over again that he was about to have a sister! I looked up at the sky and begged Daisy for forgiveness and love once more.

After William arrived, we left pretty quickly, dropped off Bailey with William's parents, and were on our way to finally meet our daughter. We did not know what to expect when we arrived at the hospital, but arrived there around 3 p.m. Helen found out that her water really had started to break on the 18ᵗʰ; she reported to us that her initial belief had been correct. What? How was that even possible? Why have I never seen that scenario on a television show? What happened to the big gush of liquid that has always, in the media world, marked the beginning stages of labor?

My unrealistic fantasies about the childbirth process aside, the reason the doctors did not realize that her water was actually breaking was because it stopped on its own!

At her scheduled appointment on the 21st, the day we received the real phone call, the doctors gave her a test, which proved that her water was breaking. So, they decided to induce her to ensure Jenna's safe arrival. When we entered the hospital, Helen's contractions, according to her, were not yet very difficult, and they were planning on breaking her water sometime soon.

Since when did a woman's water need assistance breaking during labor? Boy, I did not know anything about labor at all. As I stood around the hospital room fidgeting and hoping for everyone to be healthy and happy, I could not get over the realization of my ignorance regarding each stage of the birthing procedure. Of course, my initial picture of the birth of my first child centered on me being the woman giving birth as my husband doted on my every whim and desire. Perhaps I was extra ignorant because I lost out on the privilege of experiencing labor, and I never had to take a birth and delivery class, but seriously, I would have never imagined a team of doctors who disregarded a woman believing that her water was breaking. With the reality of a woman in labor, and that woman not being me, closing in, the toughest shock to get past was the alarming lack of presence of a medical doctor. Hours would go by without Helen's doctor checking in on her or my baby's status. The result of a lack of medical presence was an exorbitant amount of unplanned alone time with Helen, and we felt as though we had to somehow provide her a service.

To try to take Helen's mind off of the task at hand, William and I, and Helen and Walter exchanged anecdotes and stories to keep the mood happy. We chatted about many different topics as we were waiting in that room together, but the light and airy mood came to a halt after the nurse came in and broke the rest of Helen's water. After her water broke, she really started to feel her contractions. As I studied her pained face, I was filled with admiration for this poor woman going through such intense pain for William and me. I wished I could trade places with her and have the baby myself, or at least find a way to take away the look of agony that took over her every move.

The pain was too much for Helen to bear. Although she had initially held every intention of avoiding an epidural, she changed her mind quickly. The doctors and nurses politely kicked everyone out of the room in order to administer the epidural. We were sent to a waiting area where Leslie, Sara, Walter, William, and I collectively sighed, crossed our fingers, and waited with anticipation for baby Jenna.

After about a 20-minute period of awkward glances and forced conversation, Walter, Sara, and I were called back into the room. By 8:00, Helen was seven cm dilated. She went from two cm to seven cm within a matter of a few hours! It was very exciting. Helen's mom, Sara and I screamed together when we heard that she was already seven cm.

Originally, William was not going to be allowed in the delivery room because Helen was only permitted three support people. I already knew from our letter exchanges that the people she had chosen were the birth father, her mother, and me. But, something wonderful happened. After our celebratory scream over the seven cm statistic, Sara declared that she did not belong in the room. She felt overpowered by the thought that William should be in the room instead of her. Sara reasoned that her daughter would have other children, and that William was truly to be Jenna's father. With that, she cleared it with the hospital staff (and Helen) and William was allowed in the delivery room. I could not believe how generous, loving, and sweet this child's biological family behaved during this time. All I could think of was, wow, this child has wonderful genes!

William entered the room, overjoyed at the prospect of watching his daughter entering the world. With a dilation goal of 10 cm, we waited and barely breathed, and by 10:00 pm, Helen reached the 10 cm goal. She started screaming to everyone in the room, "She is coming now, I mean right now, get a nurse!" The thought of Jenna arriving without medical help brought about major panic in my brain, but I hid my emotions from everyone else in the room. Waiting for the delivery nurse to return was excruciating, but she finally returned and verified that Helen was ready to push. The nurse called for a doctor, but our baby's delivery doctor was nowhere to be found. Once again, I was surprised to discover just how infrequently the doctor was expected to be in the room. Instead of waiting for the doctor to arrive, the nurse charged forward and asked me to hold Helen's legs during pushes. She encouraged my involvement and excitedly proclaimed that I would have a birds-eye view of Jenna Lila's debut. I had not planned on actually jumping into the program, for I did not know if I really wanted a birds-eye view of a woman's private area, even if my daughter was about to make her entrance through it. Nonetheless, you follow whatever orders you are given when asked to assist the woman doing you the grandest favor in the world.

Keeping that in mind, I have to comment that the smell was inexplicable. I tried to hide my disdain, as my suffering was miniscule compared with Helen's. But once again, I could not recall any birthing scenario image from my past that alluded to the pungent odors that come from a woman in labor. And yes, I realize that these fictitious images were stories by writers, but they were all I had in my schema. Clearly, realistic circumstances altered longstanding yet ignorant beliefs in a matter of moments.

How did I get here, I wondered? How is it that I am in a woman's delivery room, someone I have only known for about four months, holding her legs, viewing parts of her body that I have never viewed of another woman's in my entire life? This was not how I pictured the birth of my first-born child.

It didn't matter how I felt, because my job was to be there for Helen, and more importantly, I needed to be there for Jenna. My anxieties were meaningless. This self-less woman was giving me my daughter, and that was enough to shut me up. I was a bit nervous about my intimate involvement. Unsure of where to place my hands and how I should press on her legs, I asked Helen what she wanted me to do and she screamed that she did not care. Good point, if I were she, I would not care either.

I tried to tap into my instincts, and felt my nerves evaporate rather quickly. With one push in particular, the nurse said, "You can see her head, look!" I didn't think I could see anything, but sure enough, there was the top of our little girl's head. All I saw was a mop of dark hair and it was the most amazing moment of biology I had ever witnessed. For the next 20 minutes or so, Jenna's head came out a little, and then it went back inside. The doctor, who finally arrived after Helen had been pushing for a solid 25 minutes, suggested that Helen turn over a little bit and push from her left side, and sure enough, when she did that, Jenna's head came out all the way! The pediatric team was standing by to clean her up, so when the doctor gave Helen the okay to make one last push, Jenna's whole body emerged and I could barely believe my eyes. Never had I witnessed anything so magical in my life. William was invited to cut the umbili-cal cord and then our little girl was cleaned up. Immediately after, William started to snap pictures of Jenna Lila with his Blackberry and she was the most beautiful vision of both of our lives. Everyone in the room was crying happy tears.

After Jenna's birth, Helen looked at me and said, "I want you to know that I am still at peace with my decision. You are that little girl's mother, you were meant to be her mom. All of this was worth it just to bring her into the world."

For the next hour we dealt with the Viacord Company. Viacord cryopreserves the umbilical cord and blood in case of any horrible genetic abnormalities or eventual diseases. It was pricey, but we felt it was a worthy investment for our baby girl. After repeating the same information over and over again and securing the packaging, it was clear that Helen needed some alone time with her family. Although we wondered what it would look like if we left immediately, we knew it was the right move for her. It was clear to us that we were on display until Jenna was handed over to begin her life with us. Helen, Walter, their friends, and their family from this point, were watching every move we made and the pressure was indescribably severe.

William and I eventually left the room to let Helen get some rest and to allow us to visit our baby girl in the nursery. I was given a bracelet to visit Jenna, which was quite a big deal. Only two people were permitted bracelets. Helen kept one, but gave the other to me. This meant that I would always be allowed in the maternity wing and in the nursery without anyone else escorting me. William and I scurried in to the nursery room with bleary eyes and remained glued to Jenna's area. We watched as she received I.V. fluids and later as the pediatrician checked her over. Everyone commented on how beautiful Jenna was and how lucky we were. Both statements could not have been any truer.

We had to tear ourselves away from Jenna in the nursery at around 1 in the morning because we had to get the hotel room ready for her. I had very little sleep, although William, as usual, had no problems. My mind was racing with the joys and fears that the next few days would bring. All I wanted to do was fast-forward our lives to the day that Helen and Walter signed the papers that pledged that Jenna was truly our daughter. Until then, I could not fully believe that she would be a part of our family. Regardless, I knew that we would be on display for the birth family's friends and family's eyes for days and was anxious to return to the hospital to remind them that they had made the best decision.

We returned to the hospital the next day by about 10 a.m. Before we entered the hospital room, we stopped at the gift shop to purchase flowers and a stuffed animal puppy. In my research about appropriate gifts in our particular situation, we liked one suggestion, which was that the adoptive parents should buy two identical stuffed animals, giving one to the birth mom, and the other to the child. The stuffed animals would remain a tangible symbol of the lifelong connection between the birth parent and child. It seemed like a fitting gesture, so we took our time finding the most adorable pooch we could. Although anxious about explaining the purchase, we headed over to Helen's hospital room.

We knew that Jenna was staying in Helen's hospital room, which was why we did not stop at the nursery. Being warned that it was very important to our adoptive child to spend time with her birth mother before she was given to us, we tried not to overanalyze this arrangement. Although this made me uneasy, I was assured it was very healthy for both the birth mother and the adoptive child. For the next two days, we spent most of our time with Helen and Walter in Helen's hospital room. We then were introduced to the biological great grandmother on both sides, as well as her biological grandmother on both sides and grandfather on Walter's side. After some pictures were snapped of each family member holding Jenna, Walter's grandmother requested that we send a copy of the pictures, and we figured it was the least we could do. Regardless, alarm bells continued to ring in my head. I could not understand why this family desired these pictures. If I had been in the same situation, I do not think I would want any reminders, but hey, that's me.

In addition to family members, we also met Helen's friend Leslie. Leslie seemed extremely odd to us. She continuously kissed Helen on the mouth and told her how beautiful she was. She asked us inappropriate and private questions that, if a social worker had been present, would have been prohibited. I never knew how to answer her questions. Some of my responses were lies because I did not want her to possess such personal information about us. It appeared as though Leslie were in love with Helen. In fact, while Helen was in labor, Leslie sneaked into the hospital room and competed with Walter for Helen's affection. She even asked Sara, Helen's mother, whether or not she picked up on the vibe that Walter was trying to keep her away from Helen during the delivery process.

When the question was posed, I thought to myself, "Yes, obviously," but I chocked it up to the best friend/boyfriend dynamic. Regardless, this strange friend apparently played with our baby while she was in Helen's belly. She made meow sounds and tried to get her to kick all of the time. Again, I found that extremely odd. Our poor child had to endure this strange girl for however many months during gestation and we wondered if it affected her development somehow. Leslie was a close talker. (The term close talker is a Seinfeld reference, meaning someone who does not provide another person with personal space during a conversation). Whenever she entered the room, William and I were immediately uncomfortable.

Something else that made us uncomfortable was the music that Helen and Walter continually played in the hospital room. It sounded like Yoga or Meditation music and it was creepy. Walter asked us if we wanted copies of the music because they had continuously played it during Jenna's development. Although William and I wanted nothing more than to turn off that music at every moment, we smiled and replied, "That would be wonderful." It was generous that they wanted to share themselves with us to such an extent. We felt lucky, but at the same time, it was trying having to do everything on their terms for all of the hours that we spent in the hospital.

If Helen wanted to hold Jenna, I felt obligated to indulge her with her wish. If their friends came in and requested some bonding time, we also felt the need to oblige. After all, we would soon have Jenna all to ourselves. I repeatedly reminded myself that our lives would be back on our own terms as soon as the papers were signed. In addition, I warned myself how these tiny sacrifices William and I made were minis-cule in comparison with the sacrifice that Helen and Walter were about to make. For every moment of discomfort, we were matched with dreams of hope and happiness. Regardless of how Helen's friends and musical choices made us feel, we knew it was barely a blip on the radar of our future.

One of these blips continued to be Leslie. She spent virtually every moment in the hospital room with Helen and Walter and me. Did she have a job? We found out that she did not have a job, just as Helen and Walter did not hold jobs. All of them were living off their parents without prospects or contributing a dime. What kind of people sponge off others without offering any type of contribution? This thought bothered me, and Leslie really bothered me. At one point, she grabbed my purse and told me that she liked it. I wanted to rip it out of her hands, but controlled myself. She stroked my head and I wanted to recoil, but I did not. After a few hours, she secretly whispered to Helen and then approached us with a bag. She had purchased a beanie baby duck to give to our daughter, as she loved ducks and wanted her best friend's biological child to have one. William and I graciously accepted the gift on Jenna's behalf and were touched, although, put off by this gesture.

Why were all of these people visiting and caring for this child when she was about to be placed with complete strangers? As the questions in my mind swirled, the introductions of friends and relatives continued. We soon met the biological father's brother, Helen's sister, and a few other apparently irresponsible friends of Helen's. Red flags went up everywhere in my mind. Everyone was as sweet as could be and embraced Helen's decision to have William and me adopt Jenna, but to have these people surround us at all times somehow seemed wrong. Regardless, each visitor could not impart us with enough wonderful accolades. Over and over again it was repeated how Jenna was meant to be with us and the room was filled with love for both the little girl and us, the adoptive parents, at every moment. We watched as our daughter was held, kissed, hugged, and videotaped by all the visitors. Jenna paid no attention to who was snapping a picture or holding her in their arms. And although it made us terribly uncomfortable, she did not seem to mind at all.

The only snafu was getting Jenna to eat the first day. The pediatrician switched her to a soy formula, as the regular one seemed to upset her tummy, and suddenly, she loved to eat. Helen fed and burped her, as did Walter, as did William, and of course, as did I. We shared stories with each other about our lives and quickly grew even fonder of each other. My intense guard dropped slightly with each heartfelt conversation and confession we made to one another.

Helen and Walter spoke about their Myspace pages and their love of computer connections. They confessed their hopes and dreams of their futures and hoped we would share all of the information about them with Jenna in the future. Our reciprocity was expected.

Helen and Walter probed deeper into our fertility challenged history in those hours in the hospital room. We shared the details of our miscarriages, artificial reproductive stories, and all of our past heartaches that had somehow, led to our lives intertwining. Although very few people knew about our history, it felt right to share it with them. They declared their happiness for their role in finally bringing us to a happily ever after moment and told us how natural we were with Jenna and how happy they were for us. We were all connected before Jenna came, but with her arrival, our connection felt sealed for life.

Because of our fondness of one another, we did not want to see our relationship end. I wondered how I ever feared these wonderful people and felt as though they were now my family. Even the small annoyances of the past few days evaporated. We discussed how we would continue our relationship in the future. None of us wanted to say goodbye to the other. The simple fact was that Jenna had two sets of parents: biological and adoptive. We would raise her and provide our daughter with everything that Helen and Walter could not, but believed Jenna had every right to get to know them too. We decided to stay connected, even though that had not been the original plan. Of course, who knew what would really happen since life brings people in different directions, but at that moment, in that room, I wanted nothing more than to stay connected for life. I could not believe how wonderful Jenna's biological parents were, and I felt privileged for the time I was given to get to know them.

The last day I had with Helen and Walter in the hospital was the most painful because it was the day that Helen had to finally say goodbye to Jenna. Although she knew that the moment was coming, it was unbelievably emotional for her and for Walter to say their goodbyes. She said over and over again that Jenna Lila was our daughter, and she was the surrogate sent by God to give her to us. Still, she loved Jenna deeply and was devastated to complete God's plan. She wanted to personally hand her to me, from one mother to the next, and there was not a dry eye in the room.

Everyone was crying from a mixture of sadness and elation. Helen repeated over and over again that she was not crying for her daughter because she knew Jenna would have a great life. She asked me to please make sure that Jenna never needed to ask why her birth mother gave her up. The reason for this was simple: she wanted Jenna to live. Those were her words, and they were words that I promised would inspire me to guide my child in the best way I knew how for the rest of my life. Helen finally asked us to leave and begin our life, and it was exceedingly difficult for me to do it.

William and I left Helen's hospital room in tears and waited until our daughter was discharged into our care. We were pulled into a small room while we were waiting for nurses to chat with us and for Helen and Walter to leave. At one point, a nurse walked in and asked if I would be willing to part with my identification bracelet because Helen wanted to keep hers. Only one of us was permitted to keep the bracelet since the other bracelet had to remain on record. It stung, as I had wanted to share the bracelet with Jenna when she was older, but since I felt compelled to soothe Helen's emotions, I agreed. Although it struck me as another odd request, I tried not to over-analyze it. Besides, we did not really need a bracelet memento since we were taking our beautiful baby girl home. Nothing else in the world mattered to us.

Before it was time to leave, the nurse wanted to give us some baby care lessons. She asked me to change Jenna's diaper and outfit in front of her. It was terrifying, and yet simultaneously reassuring to have professional eyes on me as I was maneuvering her around. Petrified I could break her at any moment, the nurse jumped in a couple of times to reassure me that I would do no such harm. She instructed me to place my hand under her neck and head and pointed out how very flexible baby legs were. Helen and Walter had already had these lessons. I wished I had received the lessons on the first day, but I was eternally grateful for the tips at any time.

Before William and I left, the nurses told us that our situation was very unique in the fact that the four of us spent so much time together and loved each other so much. These women also believed that God had planned the entire event in His wisdom. They spoke very highly of Helen and Walter, and let us know that Jenna's birth parents had spoken very highly of us. A nurse named Sylvia told me it was time to relinquish all sadness for Helen and feel the happiness of having a daughter. Sylvia commented how we had clearly been waiting for years for this moment, and it was time to relish the good and shake off the bad memories of the journey.

With a few extra hugs and well wishes from the hospital staff, we took Jenna Lila for her first car ride back to the hotel. Before settling in the car, William took a bag out of the trunk. He smiled and pulled out a stuffed animal puppy. It was identical to the puppy that we had purchased for Helen a few days prior. We waved the puppy in front of Jenna and explained its significance to her. It was never too early to explain our magical situation. The explanation was something we planned to give Jenna thousands of times. We would only stop when she asked us to and when we were sure she was old enough to understand the beauty of adoption and our good fortune in finding each other.

Upon getting Jenna and ourselves settled, we decided it was finally time to make some phone calls. We started to let a few more people in on our wonderful secret for selfish reasons. With my sudden absence from school, I had been bombarded with e-mails and cell phone calls inquiring into my health. Everyone was worried about me and it felt wrong to keep my friends in the dark, especially since Jenna had been released into our custody. Surely if Helen had been able to physically relinquish Jenna into my arms, the worst was over. The phone calls were an indulgence. After feeling cut off from our own lives for the previous four days, it was comforting to speak with our friends and family without worrying about who was listening in on our conversations. Everyone was absolutely thrilled to pieces for us and wanted to start shopping. I asked them to wait until the birth parents signed the papers, and they demanded that I contact them the minute that it happened.

In the meantime, William and I tried to make a hotel room a home, but it was not easy. My aunt had given me an ultraviolet light wand to bring to the hotel to try to make every surface sanitary. Before we picked Jenna up from the hospital, I had spent an hour swiping the wand over every open surface within the hotel room. William and I had secured a two-bedroom suite, and we set up one bedroom as a makeshift baby station. We also set up a bottle station complete with sanitizers, bottle warmers, and several different versions of the soy formula Jenna required. We had ready-made formula, powdered formula, and individual bottles of formula to choose from. Beyond that, we honestly had no idea what we were doing and our ignorance felt magnified in the middle of the night.

The first night was nerve racking, but in a fun way. Seriously, although we were nervous, we were so deliriously happy, it did not matter in the least. The issue was that Jenna had been eating every four hours or so, but on that first night, she decided that she needed to eat every two hours. I think I might have slept an hour! William tried to sleep with his face on Jenna's bassinet because he was so worried about hearing every breath. Of course when he did that, I could only hear his snoring and nothing else.

When I realized that sleep was out of the question, I was ready to begin our first full day as parents with Jenna. I was mildly disappointed that our first day as a family had to be in a hotel room instead of our home, but I still felt incredibly lucky. Jenna officially felt as though she were my baby. I had a daughter. I was a mom. This knowledge probably made our first full day in the hotel room even more nerve racking. William and I were now officially responsible for nurturing another life. This was the most important role we would ever hold. Every little move we made had the potential of everlasting results. We apologized over and over to our little girl for being such amateurs when it came to dressing her, and changing her diaper. She was easily forgiving and we quickly fell head over heels in love with the little life that now blessed our own.

We waited and wondered and hoped for Helen and Walter to officially relinquish their parental rights and make the path clear for William and me to raise Jenna Lila as our own. We had been dreaming of being parents for so many months, for so many years. With each moment, we fell more in love with Jenna, and with each moment, we were more certain it would happen. But, still, it was a scary time for us. It was scary because the thought of not raising her did not seem at all plausible. Helen and Walter had promised us they would never change their minds, and I wanted to believe them, but what if they did? William continuously reminded me that they would not change their minds because as they had pledged time and time again, they loved her enough to sacrifice their own desires of keeping her. While we were waiting, I made sure to send the pictures to Walter's grandmother. This was her response:

Dear Emma and William,

Thank you so much for the pictures. I really felt so good meeting you and I am very comforted knowing the [sic] Jenna will be loved and cherished. I know she is where she should be and I send you all my love and good wishes as a family

William reassured, "See, everyone knows this is what is best for our daughter."

The second and third days with Jenna were very similar to our first day, but we were definitely getting better at the basics. We could not stop staring at Jenna's every move. We studied every part of her face, her hands, her toes, her everything. She emanated love, which made our hearts beat stronger for hers with each passing moment. We experienced some interesting diapers, spit up, the joys of bottle warmers and bottle sanitizers. Her first sponge bath was not something she enjoyed, until I began washing her hair. This blissful look appeared on her face and we were in love with the fact that she loved having her hair washed. It was the most precious expression we had ever seen. William and I established a routine to get her through each part of her day. We had never been this happy in our lives.

As first time parents, we had to bring Jenna to her first pediatrician's appointment. Since we were not permitted to leave the state of Massachusetts, we had to use a clinic. Our insurance would not yet cover Jenna, but we were instructed to present our insurance information to the clinic and straighten everything out when the time came. As we walked in the building I was instantly protective of our little girl. I did not want anyone breathing on her or touching her. When strangers smiled at her beautiful presence, we smiled back while thinking, do not invade her space or we will stop you. The parental instincts that I had always heard about were spontaneously there. She was our daughter; we would lay our life on the line for her.

A woman in the waiting room with a two year old introduced herself and asked how old Jenna was. After we told her, she asked how we were doing without sleep. We were elated, who needed sleep? She laughed and wished us luck right before the nurse called us in to the examination room. The nurse and doctor congratulated us and told us that everyone at the hospital had really great things to say about us, which was why she agreed to see Jenna. We felt honored and extremely appreciative of this fact.

The doctor was very kind and, surprisingly for a doctor who might never see Jenna again, took the time to ask us if we had any questions. Other than a few formula questions, we could not think of anything that the hundreds of books I had read did not answer. It was painful to watch her receive her first inoculation, but Jenna recovered quickly after. When we were speaking, the doctor commented, do you see the way her eyes are moving? She knows you are her mom and dad. Nothing could have meant more to me than that comment. William and I could not wait to bring our little girl home and begin our lives together.

When we returned to the hotel, I decided to do a load of laundry. William had stopped at a grocery store and picked up Dreft laundry detergent, so off I went. As I was waiting for the first load, my cell phone rang. Helen's social worker was on the other line and panic immediately clenched my heart. She assured me that everything was fine; she needed a few pieces of information. In the middle of our conversation, she asked me to hold on because she had received another call. After four or more minutes had passed, she returned, apologizing profusely for keeping me on hold for so long. Coincidentally, Helen had been on the other line and panic returned. I asked the social worker if anything was wrong and she reassured me that everything was totally fine. In fact, Helen and Walter told her that they were ready to come in and sign the papers tomorrow at 4:30. Thank goodness I thought, thank goodness.

When the signing day came, I found myself staring at the clock waiting for the meeting time of 4:30 to begin. A fluttery feeling repeated in my stomach and my heart with each minute that passed. At 2:00, I e-mailed Helen's social worker and my social worker and requested that someone let us know when the papers were signed.

She e-mailed me back and told me not to worry if I did not hear by 5:30 because she planned to meet with them for a while. I had spoken with Helen's social worker the day before and she told me that Helen and Walter were ready to sign the papers, so I felt confident that it would happen.

6:00 passed, as did 7:00 and we were still without word. By 8:00 I had reached full-blown panic mode and sent off another e-mail asking for an update, as we were very concerned. At 8:30, my cell phone rang with a woman named Lina. Lina was covering for our social worker Trudy because Trudy had a family medical emergency. Lina assumed I knew this, but no one had contacted us to share this information with us, so how could we know anything? Regardless, Lina wanted to introduce herself and threw out small talk. When the conversation shifted into my direction, I explained that we were waiting to hear from Helen's social worker and Lina replied, "That is why I have called you."

My heart sank before she even uttered the next sentence, which was; "The birth parents were not ready to sign the papers today."

I asked what that meant and she discouraged me from feeling despair. She tried to convince me that it was very common that birth parents were not ready to sign the first time they were presented with the papers. Although Trudy had warned me of such a possibility, with the exchanges and promises made by Helen and Walter, it did not seem probable. A heavy weight swept over my body and I feared the very worst. Instead of my life changing in every way, the cycle of parenthood being ripped from William's and my grip might continue. She asked me if I had any other questions or wanted to talk, but really, what was there to say? Before hanging up, she let me know that Helen had a second appointment with her social worker the following day at 2:00 and we would all know more then.

That was the line that worried me the most. What was really the difference between today and tomorrow? William and I tried to grasp the straws of hope and convince ourselves that Helen was too emotional to sign and would certainly do so the next day. However, something in my head warned me that this beautiful little girl, the one we had been waiting not only for three and a half months, but also for the last six years of our lives to raise, would be torn from our loving arms.

Although the previous nights had been sleepless due to a child in need of food and diaper changes, this night was sleepless for additional reasons. William and I kept staring at each other with complete despair. We watched the clock tick by all night and the following morning. We barely moved and we did not eat. We tried to memorize every detail of the beautiful baby in front of us fearing the worst, but William assured me that they would never renege on all the promises they made not only to us, but also to Jenna.

"They don't have a pot to piss in," he reassured me. "They don't have jobs, they don't have cars, and they don't have any financial way of providing for her. They want more for her, that is why they pursued adoption in the first place and nothing has changed." As true as that statement was, financial security was not a requirement to parent. Of course, as true as that statement was, anyone pursuing adoption would not be considered without stable financial resources.

This is what angered me. Adoptive parents have to prove that they are capable of raising a child in a million ways, but biological parents never had to prove a thing. Adoptive parents were insignificant and retained no rights. People who are loving and kindhearted and financially stable who for whatever reason cannot procreate are punished multiple times. They are punished with infertility. Perhaps they pursue IVF or other invasive treatments like we did, which punishes an infertile couple's wallet, and in my case, physical health. If that fails, as it did so many times in our case, they must jump through hoops to be approved for adoption. Even when that is over, someone must actually choose them as being worthy to parent their child. And still, when you think you have jumped every hurdle, birth parents have to stick to their word and still follow through and allow you to raise their biological child. Once this occurred, social workers checked up on adoptive parenting ways until the courts and judges deemed that the adoption was final.

I found myself contemplating, what was the magic of genetics? Somehow, being genetically tied to someone gave a person superior parenting rights. For this, I have no explanation. Whatever the reasons are, they seem misguided. Perhaps it is because of the position I sit in, but perhaps, it is because it is also true.

At 3:00 our phone rang and I jumped up with butterflies in places I didn't know butterflies could flutter in a body. Helen's social worker greeted me on the other line as my heart beat wildly and my hands shook with nerves. She empathized, "I know last night must have been one of the most difficult nights of your life." Duh, she was stating the obvious. Then she continued, "Helen and Walter have decided to parent their child."

Although I had feared that this might be the outcome, and make no mistake, this was my worst nightmare coming to fruition, the words stung inexplicably. Somehow, I was still stunned to hear that such a possibility was our new reality. "You have got to be kidding," was all I could muster as a response. To try to explain, she uttered, "As much as you want to parent this little girl, her birth parents want to parent this little girl."

Anger bubbled up with such an insensitive statement and I disgustedly remarked. "Really? So why did they pursue adoption in the first place? These people are clearly all liars."

She argued, "Their relationship they had with you was genuine and they are truly sorry for putting you through this."

Oh please, I thought. If our relationship was one iota genuine, there would not be a possibility of this scenario playing out, of that I was certain. Trying to control my anger I replied, "I am sorry if I have a tough time believing any words that come out of their mouths." I was in no mood to carry on a conversation with this woman or anyone for that matter. So I asked the only question I could, "So what now?"

"You have to bring Jenna to the agency, right now."

I called to William and repeated our worse nightmare coming true. Before he came out of the room with the baby, I heard him weeping. There was no recourse; we had to bring Jenna to the agency and watch her disappear from our lives forever.

We decided to give her one last sponge bath and lovingly change her outfit and diaper before leaving the hotel. We cried and she looked up at us with the most innocent eyes. William and I kept asking one another not only how Helen and Walter could do this to this beautiful little girl, but how could they do this to us? After everything they said and everything they promised, they were personally responsible for breaking our hearts. My heart broke into a million pieces for Helen when it was time to turn Jenna over to me, I wept for her. All I could think about was what a waste of emotions that had been.

We placed Jenna, who would no longer be our little girl, in the car seat and tearfully drove to the agency. It was simultaneously the longest and shortest drive of our lives. When we pulled into the parking lot that once promised us such hope, we slowly unloaded ourselves from the car with heavy hearts. We opened the trunk and removed the photographs, hand drawn pictures, and letters given to us by Helen and Walter. We made sure we found the duck that Leslie had given to Jenna as well. She should have everything that was meant for her, regardless of how angry or hurt we felt. Even though we did not believe Jenna would suffer from a lack of love from her biological family, we could not help but believe that she deserved so much more than she would now ever receive. There was nothing we could do to change her future. Sadly for us, there was even less we could do for ourselves.

Helen's social worker greeted us and gave us a hug. She gave her condolences for our loss and asked if we had any questions. My only question was what circumstances changed for the birth parents that made their plans for their daughter change? We were told that Walter and Helen decided not to go to school. In addition, other family members who had not originally offered any help had now offered financial support to Helen and Walter to raise Jenna, including Sara who all along had promised that she would never renege on their commitment to us and to Jenna.

Immediately, I reflected back on all of the visitors to the hospital room and pondered when all of our fates changed. Was it Helen's grandmother's visit that devastated our lives? Perhaps it was the birth father's parents or an uncle? Whoever offered up help, where were they all these months when we were falling in love with a baby whom we thought was destined to be part of our family? The injustice held no authority, as there was no remedy.

Watching William remove our temporary child from the car seat was the most agonizing moment of my life. Before that moment, I never realized that such a cry could escape my husband's lips. My heart broke for his chance at fatherhood to be snapped away. He was clearly born for the role of dad. I had believed it all along, but for five days and nights, his actions far exceeded my wildest imagination. Now he was heartbroken. I hated Helen and Walter's family for this turn of events, and I hated them for hurting me, but most of all, I hated them for destroying William's shot at fatherhood.

How dare they.

The blame game began. Perhaps I should have never started the e-mail exchanges. Maybe it was bad judgment to spend so much time with Helen, Walter, and their families and friends in the hospital. Why didn't Trudy make it to the hospital and advise us to keep our distance from the birthparents? Clearly, that is what we should have done. If we had kept our distance, maybe they would not have been as relaxed and would not have had an atmosphere conducive to falling in love with our Jenna. Every move we made caused our pain to be greater, and as much as we blamed the biological families, and the social workers, we blamed ourselves as well. We felt like the biggest chumps and like even bigger idiots for buying every line that was fed to us. They stole our hearts, they stole our baby, they stole our dream, and if that were not enough, they stole the baby girl name that we had lovingly created and reserved for our own child. Our belief in inhumanity emerged.

The greatest reminder of inhumanity was driving away from the adoption agency with an empty car seat and even emptier hearts. After we watched our little girl exit our lives, our own lives were supposed to move forward, but how was that humanly possible? We returned to the hotel and William spent hours packing the car with all of the baby paraphernalia that we had tenderly acquired, borrowed, and shopped for in the preceding months. I cursed those purchases; perhaps such preparedness did jinx us. Our hotel room that resembled Babies-R-Us slowly emptied, right along with our hopes and dreams for our family. William went down to the desk to check out as I made the devastating phone calls with the unthinkable news to all of our friends and family members. Not only did Helen and Walter break our hearts, but they also broke the hearts of all of our loved ones. It was clear that such an effect would not impact them in any way and we felt intense resentment with such a realization. All of the pledges they made about how they would never be selfish seemed like a cruel joke.

Helen and Walter were the epitome of selfishness. If they had never handed Jenna to us in the hospital, it would have been extremely heart breaking, but not to this degree. Their actions required us to be Jenna's parents for five days. I had doubts every day in the hospital, but the minute Helen placed Jenna in my arms, I truly believed that the worst was over. After all those months of dreaming, yet keeping my guard up, I exhaled as soon as we exited the hospital. I found myself in complete shock of the situation. Our reality was that we would have to press forward without our baby girl.

During the multitude of phone calls and in each quiet moment I thought about Daisy. Our poor dog died in vain. We put her down to create a safe haven for Jenna. Jenna was not going to live in our house, so Daisy's life was cut short for the wrong reasons. Regret filled my heart and my brain and made me wonder if karma was the reason for the adoption failure.

As I relayed the dreaded details to the people in my life and lamented over our decision to put Daisy down, they all made the same comments. "You did the right thing. You were advised to put her down for years and you kept putting it off. She was a risk to all around her and it was no way for all of you to live." After feeling as though their comments about Daisy appeased me, they asked, "Are you going to continue to pursue adoption?"

How could we answer that question? After this malicious and devastating fate, what could possibly be different the next time? Friends reminded me that a positive outcome would make the adoption process worth any amount of fear and uncertainty, and I did not disagree with that sentiment. Regardless, could William and I emotionally withstand a second or third repeat of an adoption-gone-wrong scenario? Friends offered unsolicited advice such as, "I have read that many people endured three or four situations similar to yours before they finally ended up with a baby. Jenna was just not meant to be your child, but someone else is waiting for you."

I understood where such advice was coming from, but the words did not soothe me, as nothing could. The thought of pursuing an adoption to result in failure again was unfathomable. I truly admired people who were able to withstand such heartbreak over and over again. However, I could not help but wonder if this was how William and I wanted to live the next few years of our lives. What if parenting never became a reality for us? How many more times would we subject ourselves to possible heartbreak for a result of nothing but additional doses of devastation? Had we not suffered enough?

First, we had to get through the next few days of our lives and it was not easy. Everyday life was excruciatingly difficult and for the most inane reasons. Food shopping became a hardship. The reason for this was due to the baby aisle of products located in every grocery store. We tried to avoid them, but sometimes ended up in that aisle because products on the other side of that aisle were on our shopping list. When we were not bombarded with baby images on boxes or formula packages that reminded us of our five days of heaven, babies in strollers and carriages reminded us of what we could not have. When babies were not around, pregnant women abounded, and once again, we mourned for all our losses over the past six years.

Beyond our trips outside our home, our own house served as a constant barrage of baby reminders. Jenna's bedroom was empty, yet it continuously waited for her to no avail. The baby supplies that we borrowed had no place to go, so we housed them in our would-be nursery and in closets wherever there was room. My best friend was moving and could not take the clothes and supplies she lent us back, as she had no where to store them. The extra car seat docket lived in our coat closet, so every time I grabbed a jacket, my heart broke for what we lost. Bottles, sanitizers, formula, diapers, toys, wipes, changing pads, the Diaper Genie, and Dreft laundry detergent were items that no longer served their purpose, but they remained in the nursery and scattered throughout our limited storage spaces.

We closed the door of the would-be nursery and tried to avoid going in there at all costs. Although we contemplated whether or not we should get rid of all evidence that a baby was supposed to join our family, we recognized that we had spent thousands of dollars. Was it smarter for us to donate our purchases to alleviate our pain? Since we were not rolling in money, what if we somehow did become parents and had to make the same purchases again? What if the purchases were made in vain a second time?

The items we purchased were not the only aspect of our home that made it difficult to move forward. Phone calls and e-mails abounded and teased us of what was once a happy time. The umbilical cord banking company, Viacord, initially bombarded us with representatives congratulating us on the birth of our baby. Although we cancelled the umbilical cord and blood cryopreservation the day after Jenna went back to her biological parents, the company continued to haunt us. We spoke with several different representatives, all who offered their sympathies for our ordeal and all pledging to destroy the specimen and remove our charges. Months later, we were still arguing with Viacord and our credit card company over the charges. After several phone calls made by us pleading for them to leave us alone, we were shocked to open our mail and discover certificates congratulating us since they had successfully preserved our newborn's umbilical cord.

The certificate by Viacord was not the only issue we encountered during trips to and from the mailbox. Formula coupons greeted us weekly. Photographers who specialized in baby portraits bombarded us with one image cuter than the next. Toyshops, day care advertisements, and diaper samples peppered our daily pile of mail. My best guess was that our registration with Babies R Us led to all of these unsolicited mailings, which of course, was completely my fault. The formerly mundane chore of retrieving the mail evolved into a tragic Shakespearian experience each day. The universe seemed to rub salt in our wounds at every turn and each grain stung more deeply than the next. If the minutiae of life were this painful, it was clear that moving on was going to be agonizing. We missed our daughter. Yes, she was only our baby girl and in our physical presence for one week, but she was in our lives for four months, a child we had eagerly anticipated for over six years, and our hearts ached with loss.

As the days turned into weeks, the loss had not become easier for either one of us. Lina called and asked us to come in to speak with her the day after Jenna was ripped away from us so heartlessly, but Trudy never checked back in with us. William and I did not feel comfortable pressing forward without Trudy. We were also in no mood to speak to a social worker since we had felt unsupported during the entire process. Although we could have called the agency and possibly requested a meeting or a conversation with Trudy, we did not because we were offended and hurt that she did not attempt to follow up with us. Months went by before Lina finally reached out to us again. In fact, (it seemed to us) the only reason we were contacted was because it was time to renew our paperwork and pay the agency additional fees. William and I have admittedly wallowed a bit over that final insult. Adoption agencies were a business, but we had hoped and previously believed that they were more than that. Without additional phone calls, letters, or e-mails to check in on us, we realized that clearly, they really were just a business. They had already secured thousands of our hard earned money and had been bystanders to the crime of breaking our hearts.

If anyone offered us a baby via adoption, we were unsure if we could travel down that path again. Realistically, we were aware that our chances were not favorable, even in the best of circumstances. To have another healthy birth mother whom did not drink or do drugs choose adoption and then choose us did not seem likely. Even if a miracle occurred and someone out there chose us again, the thought of an open adoption now seemed like the worst idea in the world. Why would we be tempted to invite a birth family into our inner circle ever again?

Although the failed IVF attempts and miscarriages were devastating, at least they had not involved someone consciously deciding to physically take a child away from us. Each process was more heartbreaking than the other. William and I did not know how to move forward, only that we had no choice but to somehow try to do just that. We hoped eventually, as with all of our other losses along the road of parenting, we would find our way. Make no mistake; we would do everything to help each other heal, but truthfully, we knew our wounds would never completely close. There were many holes in William's and my heart from the years of infertility treatments, miscarriages, and now having a child physically removed from our lives. When the small holes added together, it was a wonder that either of our hearts beat at all. However, we still wanted to be parents. If we had learned nothing else, we learned through our experiences that we would never close any doors permanently in our pursuit to build a family.

Several months following the failed adoption, William was cleaning out a closet and came across the stuffed puppy that had been originally meant to serve as a connection between Jenna and her biological mother. Now, it was our only real connection to our lost little girl, and William was desperate for knowledge on how she was developing. He recalled a conversation we had in the hospital where Helen and Walter both spoke about their MySpace pages. Was it cyber stalking if they were the ones who revealed these pages to us? It did not matter, William had to know, but I did not want any reminders. Reminders were not needed in my head. Each morning, I woke up seeing Helen's face, followed by Jenna's face, followed by a deep and unequivocal emptiness. There was no doubt in my mind that Helen was happy with her decision to raise Jenna, which simultaneously brought me comfort and disgust. Why did her happiness have to come at our expense? The last image I wanted to view in my lifetime was a smiling Helen embracing my Jenna.

As he searched the web, I walked away and tried to destroy all mental images that remained a fixture in my head. There was no erasing the memories, and although William did not intend to make them worse, he felt compelled to call me over to take a look at what he discovered. On Helen's page, he stumbled upon a posting that infuriated him and reminded him of the hypocrisy of the situation. Since Helen's webpage was open for public viewing and we were part of the public, he felt it necessary for me to share in his disgust one last time. Although he learned little of Jenna's fate, William came across a posting by Helen that explained her decision to pursue adoption. The following excerpt is, like the previous e-mail messages I shared, directly from Helen. She obviously wrote these feelings down a few months before Jenna's birth.

Why am I going with adoption?

Current mood: infuriated

Category: Life

What do people want from me? Sometimes I don't understand peoples [sic] logic. What is the point of this blog? Is it to get something across, to vent, or even to prove my elf [sic]? I'm not even sure myself. All I know is that I have been deeply hurt and disturbed by something I was told today. I guess I just expect people to look at me for who I am my greater intention... instead of what they think. They're not me, so how could they say these things even after how many times I say it?

Why am I giving up my daughter? Can you tell me? If you know me, truly [sic]. Would you sit there and tell me it's for myself [sic]? Why the HELL would I give up my baby girl for my own benefit. This is wrecking me, destroying me from the inside out, not [sic] helping.

Here is the difference between me and these other idiots having children. I think in the terms of an adult. I do NOT have these DELUSIONS, thinking that just because I'm pregnant I'm going to have things handed to me and have the all American dream with NO work. Does anyone really have any clue just how hard it is to take care of a child, especially now? What makes these disgusting human beings think that they are capable of raising a child? Now when I say this, I don't mean that it would be hard on them... or me. I would work my ass off for this baby. I would do everything I had to for her, I would sacrifice my world. And yes, I would sacrifice college for her as well. Some people have this delusion that just because I talk about college means that I'm giving her up so I can go off and better my life while just dumping her on someone else. 100% wrong! I want to give her the world... yeah, on what an [sic] income? An income that pays minimum wage [sic]? Where the hell does that leave her? I don't want some stranger or daycare raising my child. I don't want my baby to have to move around. Do your research [sic], children need a sturdy foundation to grow. That's why everyone I know is messed up one way or another, it's from parents that shouldn't have been parents. Why would I put my child through that?

What about my mother? Guess what, my mom works over 50 hours a week to keep a roof over my head and get my sister the stuff she needs. She makes at least 17 dollars and [sic] hour and we are still considered POOR. Why would I want that for my baby? My mother already raised her children... why would I put that on her? she [sic] does enough as it is, I cant [sic] be mooching off of her. [sic] And you are calling me selfish? Are you kidding? There is nothing selfish about what I'm doing.

I have tried to think of something.... anything that would allow me to keep my daughter. But NOTHING is good enough for her.... What do [sic] want me to raise her in the slums on welfare like a porch monkey? WHOOOWHOO lets [sic] take advantage of the system like every other looser [sic]. She deserves the world, not sludge.

I'm totally confused as to how someone could actually think this way about what I'm doing. I see all of these horrible disgusting girls who got pregnant to try to trap their boyfriends, Eat [sic] nothing but fast food, drink nothing but soda without countering it with water. Smoke pot, drink and drug [sic] and all they have to say is I don't care. They don't have a definite place to stay, and one doesn't even work or intend to work, and they think this is going to happen. Guess what ladies, WRONG. But what I'm doing isn't completely selfless. Its [sic] actually really selfish when you think about it right? And they aren't because they're keeping their children... and they're going to be one big happy, messed up drug infested family. That [sic] all we need to be raising, more hoods. They want to bring up their children smoking pot. Fucking childish [sic]. What a childish thing to say about me.

Why is it selfish to wish my child everything she deserves? You know what would be selfish?

Selfish would be to keep her. The easy way out would be me keeping her. Saying we'll never have the money to put her through college, get her the things she needs or the things she wants. I can deny her the presence of a mother because I have to work 24/7. Its [sic] ok to let her hear Walter and I fight all the time over fiances [sic], she can tough it out. She doesn't need a safe sturdy HOME (something I NEVER HAD as a child because I moved all over creation with a single working mother) a good and consistent environment with friends and dogs. NO...

because she's with ME.... whats [sic] that ME... that's all I hear from the other girls... me me me... where is their baby in all of this? Did anyone ever think about where the baby would end up? They don't care. All they care about is what they want. How much pain its [sic] going to cause them.

Just denying her a chance [sic]. A simple chance of success [sic]. Did anyone ever think about it that way? What about thinking out side [sic] the box? Just denying her a chance would be the most selfish of all of the reasons.

Lets [sic] go a little further. Who am I to deny these wonderful people the gift of life? I was really picky when I choose [sic] what I thought would be best for her. Where they lived, what type of people they were. I even wanted someone who lived in the country on a coltasack [sic] because I'm hearing about all these kids being hit by idiot drivers... and got it. I made sure everything was perfect for my little angel. I made sure that they no [sic] other children so She [sic] could keep her birth right as the first born, and so she would be looked at with the love of the first born, the excitement and newness of having your first born....Yeah I went that far.

Here are these beautiful people who volunteer and play piano and direct school plays, have abundance with a house and dogs, live exactly where I wanted them two [sic] for HER safety, and they can't have children because the woman is barren. I am a fit healthy 20 year old with non [sic] of that... but I am very capable of having children. She is very capable of taking care of a child, I am not... what a slap in the face to her. I cry myself to sleep because I'm losing my little girl, she'll never even know my name... hear my voice, can you even fathom that type of pain?... but you know what, she's probably crying herself to sleep because she can never experience the gift of life. Feel what it feels to carry a baby inside of her, breast feed, even mother a child. I'm taking my pain and the sacrifice I have to make and I'm giving this woman a gift that I'm watching so many idiots take for granted and destroy.... but Im [sic] selfish because I'm talking about bettering my life afterward.

Denying this family a gift no one else could [sic] understand would be selfish.

Helen defined the meaning of selfish in writing for all of the public to view. Although she had already shared such sentiment with William and with me in person, I found myself shocked, once again, at the irony of her turning into the type of person of whom she once held such a strong disregard. I agreed with her definition of selfish completely because I was confident that Jenna's life would have been blessed with richer opportunity and stability had she remained our daughter. I still could not comprehend how her situation transformed so dramatically in a few days time.

Helen realistically changed her mind in five days. The plans she made for her child that had been sealed for five months were erased in five days. What really happened during those five days that suddenly erased all she had once envisioned for her child's future? In my angered and biased opinion, she was obviously as delusional as the unprepared mothers she targeted in her posting. However, of all the sentiment written in Helen's rant, one word she used to describe me hurt more than any of her gone by the wayside ideologies, pledges, and promises. She described me as barren.

Was barren an adequate description of who I was? Was I barren? I had been pregnant and felt a life growing inside me, albeit for a limited amount of time. Could I still be accurately described as barren? I never attached such an adjective as an explanation. Didn't barren mean completely empty and unable to ever procreate, perhaps somebody without ovaries or a uterus? Dismayed, I reread the word out loud to William. He disagreed with the barren label and reminded me that Helen was uneducated and ignorant. Initially, I denied that such a word belonged in any sentences that described my body or me but I needed evidence. A thesaurus was nearby, so I grabbed it and flipped a few pages until I found the targeted word. The definition in the thesaurus simply read, "Unfruitful, infertile." Defeated, I looked up at William and admitted, "She is right, I am barren." Thanks to Helen and Walter's antics, I never felt more barren than in that moment of realization, and in more places than one.

Since I still possessed Helen's e-mail address, I couldn't help but write the following due to the rage that overpowered me as I read her post.

Dear Helen,

You are a horrible, horrible person. If everyone in your life makes you feel like it was okay to put my husband and me through this emotional devastation, they are absolutely wrong. There is nothing that made your decision to keep Jenna understandable or excusable to us. It is not that you did not originally have the right to keep your baby. You once did, but you gave up that right the minute you chose us to adopt your baby. YOU chose US. We did not seek you out. You and your family called an adoption agency and got the ball rolling. YOU made the decision to give up your baby without any influence from us. We didn't even know you. You turned our world upside down and gave us hope. We believed that your pledge was sincere, and you and your family are solely to blame for that. I always swore that there was no equal gift that you would ever receive to the gift you were giving us. As true as that was, there is no emotional pain that is equal to having your child ripped away from your lives by a bunch of con artists and liars. You and your family did that to us, and you have to live with that. I hope that you think about us every day. Twenty years from now, when you are in a miserable low paying job (unless you milk the system and sit on welfare checks), perhaps you will reflect on the fact that you threw away your chances for a higher education and productive life for Jenna for completely selfish reasons, which sealed your miserable fate. I hope that when you are struggling to keep food on the table and pay your bills, you think about how Jenna could have had a secure and privileged life with my husband and me. If she resents you, I say, "Good." I hope she does. Enjoy your terrible life. You took away her endless opportunities, just like you took away our chances at parenthood. How dare you on both counts. Hopefully Jenna will rise above her deplorably immoral parents and family and find achievement and success on her own. You are a sad excuse for a human being.

I had resisted the temptation for months, but seeing that she referred to me as barren brought up all of my old animosity, so I wrote the letter, and I confess, it made me feel a little superior and loads better. I never sent it, because I scribed it in anger. Even with the intense amount of rage I felt, I was still composed enough to know that such words would do harm and absolutely no good to anybody. I didn't really mean everything

I said anyway. Oh, I meant some of what I said, but I really didn't want Helen to have a terrible life.

During the time I knew her, I liked her, and I know that there was a good person in there. At the end of the day, I understood that Helen and Walter were only 21-year-old kids. They had not lived long enough to understand the sanctity of a promise, or the repercussions their decisions had on my husband or me. They fell in love with their own child and could not let her go. Was that really so terrible?

Logically, I knew their change of heart was not meant to destroy our dreams or hurt us, but emotionally, it was difficult to accept. Even more difficult to accept was the distinct possibility that Jenna might be happier and better adjusted if she were raised by her biological parents. I had to admit that Helen's change of heart might benefit Jenna's development and life, but I did not enjoy entertaining that idea at that moment, so I pushed it aside. Still, I found the letter writing to be therapeutic. The exercise brought me a bit of peace, at least for a second. I often find that ranting and raving can bring someone closer to acceptance and forgiveness, which it kind of did for me. Of course, in the next moment, I thought about the word barren again.

The word barren continues to torture my soul whenever I am asked, "So what are you going to do now? Are you still trying to find a way to have a baby?" Sometimes there are no answers, just questions. On those very rare occasions we have come close to becoming parents, something or someone has thwarted us from fulfilling such a calling. When I think about becoming a mother, the thought is quickly followed by a sad reassurance that it, for whatever reason, might not be meant to be. Fear grips me when I envision continuous additional attempts at motherhood via medicine or adoption. And yet, no matter how I try to distract myself, at any quiet moment in my life all I think about is becoming a mother and making William a father.

And that is my true answer. In my heart of hearts, I am not ready to give up. No doctor has ever told me that I have zero chance of becoming pregnant. In addition, the failed adoption hurt because it failed, but how wonderful would success feel? The point is, as long as there is still a chance for William and me to become parents, I know we need to pursue all options. I recognize that I have to consider the possibility that I may never experience a happily ever after baby story, but I remain unable to do so. Hope, although diminishing, is still alive.

Afterword

WILLIAM AND I made an appointment with our fertility doctor the day after we lost Jenna. Dr. Foster reminded us that all we needed was the perfect embryo and he was absolutely certain that given enough time, he could help us create it.

After a fourth failed in vitro attempt, Dr. Foster put his money where his mouth was. He provided us our treatments at minimal cost. Generously, Dr. Foster covered the fees for the egg extractions and embryo transfers. Unfortunately, the fifth attempt also failed to result in a pregnancy.

Since I had been through so much physically, and William and I together had been through so much mentally, we made a pact that our sixth in vitro fertilization attempt would be our final one. We went in with low expectations and high hopes.

When Dr. Foster spoke with us regarding the quality of our embryos during our sixth attempt, he pledged, "These are by far the best embryos we have ever had." I took a home pregnancy test nine days later and it was positive. Nine and a half months later, our little girl joined our family.

Our daughter has changed our life in every conceivable way. The struggles we had with infertility have made our love and appreciation for being parents that much stronger. Even so, the obstacles in our path have not been forgotten. There has not been one day that has gone by where I have not thanked my doctors out loud and stared at our child with absolute gratitude for joining our family. So many people have commented that if I did not go through all I had, then I would never be a parent to my daughter. Such sentiment is meant to be uplifting, but I find it patronizing. I no longer believe that everything happens for a reason. That mentality makes it sound as if you should just sit idly by and wait for life events to come to you. Instead, I choose to believe that the reactions to the circumstances in your life determine your future. Saying something was meant to be diminishes the journey. We worked tirelessly to build our family with our daughter, but that darn Murphy did not make it easy.

Murphy continued to reside in our home throughout my pregnancy in other ways. Although all turned out well with the birth of a healthy and beautiful girl, my pregnancy and delivery was a story in and of itself. I can look back now, laugh, and admit that my prenatal journey was a fitting follow up to my struggle to conceive. The details of that story, however, will be saved for another day.

Made in the USA
Charleston, SC
25 July 2012